D1208986

I N F I N I T E

Financial Freedom

What to Do Before and After

You Win the Lottery

by Rob Sanford

TitleWaves Publishing, Malibu, California

Infinite Financial Freedom
What To Do Before and After You Win the Lottery
By Rob Sanford

Published by:
TitleWaves Publishing
Post Office Box 943
Malibu, CA 90265
USA

This publication is designed to provide accurate and authoritative information in regard to the subject matter covered. It is sold with the understanding that the publisher is not engaged in rendering legal, accounting, or other professional service. If legal advice or expert assistance is required, the services of a competent professional person should be sought. *From a Declaration of Principles jointly adopted by a Committee of the American Bar Association and a Committee of Publishers.*

Copyright © 1994 by Robert C. Sanford
First Printing, 1994
Printed in the United States of America

Publisher's Cataloging-in-Publication Data
Sanford, Robert C.
Infinite Financial Freedom: What to Do Before and After You Win the Lottery / by Rob Sanford
  p.   cm.
Includes Index
1. Finance, personal—United States.
2. Success—Psychological aspects.
3. Self-actualization (Psychology)
I. Sanford, Rob, II. Title.
LC-class.Sxx   1993   332.x   LC-card
ISBN 1-57077-999-6

Contents

Acknowledgments

Authors always would like to thank more people than space ever allows. I am especially indebted to the many who came before me and on whose shoulders I have been able to stand and see beyond horizons that they could only imagine. Many of these people are cited in quotations sprinkled throughout the book in the hope that their insight will give clearer vision to you as well.

One visionary to thank is Peter Grenader of *Vision* for all his graphics work as well as the cover design. Those making tangible or intangible contributions to this particular project and deserving of many thanks are: Michael Andrade; Mark and Bonnie Ballard; Shelly Beck; John Buck at Bradley; Lisa Campagna; Lara Cartwright at Ten Speed; Keith Chuvala, Ken Miller, and Melody Morris at Gilliland; John and Cathie Courtney; DaMama; Michele Darzi at Penguin; Kathleen Gurney; David and Robin Jensen; Monica Jensen at Nolo; Harvey Kule at LawForms; Eileen Lawrence at Dearborn; Bruce Lyle; the Malibu Library staff; the PMA staff; Marcia Rogers at Prometheus; Carl "CJ" Sanford; Jerry Simmons at Scanline; Mel Srybnik; Mary Valencia; and my clients for their tolerance and understanding of my occasional unavailability while I was buried in this book.

Of course, special thanks go to my bride and pride, Layne and Kendall who are woven into these pages in ways that even I don't know.

1
What To Do First

Here's what to do first:

☐ Go through this book and gut it for good ideas;

☐ Get started today with the very first idea that makes sense to you.

Maybe the very first good idea is this one: Your goal is to *do*—not just read about doing. Acting on good ideas *as you discover them* is your best first move. Then, refine them as you go and grow.

The book that is now pouring words into your mind's eye is here to tell you exactly what to do *Before*, *When*, and *After* you win, so that you can:

☐ Avoid the mistakes of other less fortunate lottery players and winners; and

☐ Achieve your own *Infinite Financial Freedom* with or without the lottery winnings.

Even though the lottery has been here since at least the time of Roman Emperor Nero's rule (54–68 A.D.) when dinner guests would draw "lots" for slave girls and country villas, people still don't know what to do today. Some historians argue that the lottery dates back even earlier to the Ethiopians, Egyptians and Biblical times. But what matters now is that you get the best out of this book so that you don't get burned like the Romans and other winners who lost it all.

Assumptions

So, here are this book's four basic assumptions:

Assumption #1: Amounts of Money

There are two amounts of money:
The *right* amount of money and
The *wrong* amount of money.

Assumption #2: Your Amount of Money

You now have the *wrong* amount of money and you want the *right* amount of money.

Assumption #3: Wealth Acquisition

You want to know what to do with the *wrong* amount of money to turn it into the *right* amount of money as soon as possible.

Assumption #4: Wealth Preservation

You want to know what to do with the *right* amount of money once you get it so that you can keep it from turning into the *wrong* amount of money again.

The *Right* Amount of Money Defined

By now, you may well be asking "What exactly is the *right* amount of money, anyway?". So, let's define it, because *almost* the *right* amount of money is still the *wrong* amount. The definition has two parts:

❑   The *right* amount of money—although varying from person-to-person and from time-to-time with each person—gives you *Infinite Financial Freedom.*

❑   *Infinite Financial Freedom* is the liberty to live-off your assets indefinitely, so that you do not have to work at a job to live the way you want to live.

So, whenever you see terms like "winning the lottery" or "jackpot" or "the big one" in this book, remember that we are talking about winning the *right* amount of money—whatever amount that is for you today—and achieving *Infinite Financial Freedom.*

> *It frees you from doing things you dislike. Since I dislike doing nearly everything, money is handy.*
> Groucho Marx

So, the goal of this book is to help you move from having the *wrong* amount of money to having the *right* amount of money—one way or another. Winning the lottery is one way, but this way alone does not guarantee that you will have the *right* amount of money for very long. One $4.4 Million winner in the *Pennsylvania Lottery* blew through his first check in less than five months. Four and again five months later he was found guilty on six counts of passing bad checks, was placed on over five years of probation, fined over $20,000, and still had to make-good on over $96,000 in bad checks. He didn't have your advantage of having this book.

> *A man is never so on trial as in the moment of excessive good fortune.*
>
> Lew Wallace

Professional casino gamblers will tell you that the lottery is a "sucker bet", because the odds of winning the jackpot are so stacked against you (over 18 million-to-1 in the 6/51 *Lotto* game, for example). So, how do you really win? The way you win is by anticipating losing; that is, by having a contingency plan. Then if you do lose the lottery, you still win in life, because you've bet on the one sure thing: Your own long-term success based upon personal growth and sound, common sense financial principles that will assure your eventual acquisition of wealth—with or without the lottery. This book will give you those principles.

If you *do* win the lottery, then you win "really big" because not only do you have a lot of cash and you get it now, but also you know what to do with it when you get it, so you don't lose it while you're figuring-out what to do with it. Be forewarned that you will have many a happy helper—as you will see in the following chapters—to happily help themselves to a portion of your new-found wealth.

> *You can't hope to be lucky. You have to prepare to be lucky.*
>
> Timothy Dowd

"You've gotta play to win" is a *California Lottery* slogan. "You've gotta *plan* to win" is an *Infinite Financial Freedom* slogan. You *can* do both. Plan to win in life while you play to win in the lottery. Either way, you win. All that winning the lottery jackpot will do for you—and it's a lot—is accelerate your winning in life by collapsing the time frames of wealth acquisition by giving you more chips sooner in the ante of life—cash!

However, you need to be mentally prepared for the opportunity of winning. In fact, you need to become a winner in your mind before you even win a penny in the lottery, if winning is to do you any good. If you can quietly become the winner in your mind that I know each of us is potentially inside, then you can win in life.

> *Luck is what happens when preparation meets opportunity.*
> Elmer G. Leterman

Define your game, make-up your rules for success, commit to your goals for winning, and then play—encounter life. This book will help you collapse the time frames of winning with or without the lottery and accelerate you to whatever winning is for you. Begin now on your inevitable path to *Infinite Financial Freedom* by moving to Chapter 2 and learning the *True Benefits of Winning* the lottery—and you must know by now that it's not just the money.

> *It requires a great deal of boldness and a great deal of caution to make a great fortune; and when you have got it, it requires ten times as much wit to keep it.*
> Meyer Anselm Rothschild

Lottery Trivia

The World's Largest Lottery

By far the World's largest single lottery event is Spain's so-called Navidad (El Gordo).

As you might suspect from its name, this lottery is held a few days prior to Christmas every year in Madrid, Spain.

Over the span of just a few days, Spain awards over $1,000,000,000 (in U.S. dollars) in prizes.

Over 90 individual prizes each totaling over $2,500,000 apiece (again in U.S. dollars) are given away as part of the celebration.

In some cases, the citizens of entire towns pool their funds to buy into the Navidad.

Want to play?
Their telephone number is (1)2625140.

2

True Benefits of Winning

The main, true benefit of winning the lottery jackpot is *not* the money. Most people will already earn over $1 Million in their lifetimes (see Table 2–1). For example, if you earn $25,000 a year for 40 years or $40,000 a year for 25 years or $50,000 a year for 20 years, you're a millionaire, though you may not feel like one. Why?

TABLE 2–1: HOW LONG IT TAKES TO EARN $1 MILLION

You're a Millionaire!	
If you earn this much income/year	For this many years
$25,000	40.0
$30,000	33.3
$35,000	28.6
$40,000	25.0
$45,000	22.2
$50,000	20.0
$60,000	16.7
$75,000	13.3
$100,000	10.0

You don't *feel* like a millionaire, because you don't get your million dollars soon enough. Money is just part of the fortune formula. You will already earn enough money, but not in time enough to make you feel wealthy.

Money itself is nothing—but potential. The true, unadvertised benefit of winning the lottery jackpot is *time*. When you hit the jackpot (the *right* amount of money), you win two kinds of time:

❑   *Your* time; and

❑   *Accelerated* time.

When you "win big", not only do you get the *right* amount of money (see the previous chapter for a definition of *right*), but also you get back all *your time* from the world. Then you can do whatever you truly want with your life. So, you get both—all your money *and* all your time.

Remember that time is money.

Ben Franklin

Plus you get another kind of time: *accelerated* time. Winning the lottery jackpot accelerates your winning in life by collapsing the time frames of wealth acquisition and giving you more cash sooner. So, you get all three when you win the *right* amount of money:

❑   the money;

❑   all your time; and

❑   you get it now (*accelerated* time).

Yes, most people will earn over $1,000,000 in their lifetime, but doing so costs them the *time* of their life. Winning the lottery jackpot gives you back the "time" part of your "life-time", so that you don't have to spend your life's time just to make the money. When you win your jackpot, you can spend your time spending your money—not as an end in itself, of course, but in pursuing something worthwhile.

> *Turn it round about and you get a precious truth—money is time.*
>
> George Robert Gissing

You don't want to spend your time like one *Michigan Lottery* winner of $1 Million. Not long after winning, he was arrested for *selling* eight ounces of cocaine (for $20,000 he shouldn't have needed) to undercover FBI agents. He was then awarded the attendant honor of blowing much of his new-found free time in jail. He was found guilty and sentenced to 3 years in federal prison. You can bet that he doesn't feel like $1 Million in prison. His crime cost him his time and he can't buy back his time, not even with his money.

Or worse, you don't want to lose both your time *and* money, as one $2 Million winner did in the *New York Lottery* who was arrested, tried, and convicted on a sex charge within a year of winning. He has since been serving a 7-to-21 year prison sentence. They also locked-up his cash. His winnings will be waiting for him in a trust account if he ever gets out alive. Fellow inmates are rumored to have a unique dislike for sex offenders, especially multi-million dollar ones.

> *To have money is to have time.*
>
> Albert Camus

CHART 2–1: WAITING FOR PROSPERITY TO COME

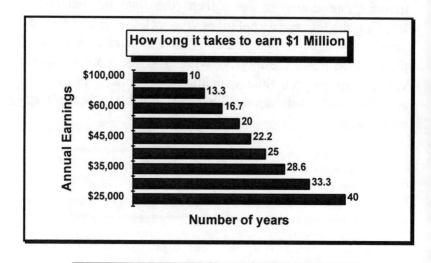

> *The trick is to make sure that you don't die*
> *waiting for prosperity to come.*
>
> Lee Iacocca

So, what you plan to do with your time before and after you win is critical to your long-term success. However, don't bet on winning the jackpot to give you confidence, self-esteem, security, freedom, self-reliance, credibility, peace of mind, or other such vital qualities. You need to develop these valuable and essential aspects of your personality in preparation for winning the lottery and in life. Otherwise, the time that you win in the lottery will do you little good and the money may do you harm.

> *I've got all the money I'll ever need if I die by four*
> *o'clock.*
>
> Henny Youngman

Chapter 4: What To Do Before You Win, gives you advice and a game plan for getting yourself ready to win the "big one". Also included in this chapter is an optional way for you to learn your Money Personality from Dr. Gurney. Knowing your Money Personality will help you to deal effectively with any amount of money in your lifetime, because you will then understand your natural tendencies of relating to money. Many lottery players and winners alike sabotage their success just because they don't know how to relate to money—before *or* after they win. By knowing not only your own Money Personality but also the characteristics of those who deal most successfully with money, you are better able to model the behavior of the best and quicken your pace to *Infinite Financial Freedom.*

Chapter 4: What To Do Before You Win will also help you to begin dealing more effectively with time—the other factor in the fortune formula: Wealth = Time + Money. For more information on time management, see *How To Get Control of Your Time and Your Life* by Alan Lakein (see *Appendix A: Personal Growth Resources* for details).

Winning your jackpot will intensify whatever qualities you do have—positive or negative—as evidenced in the stories of the two lottery "winners" above. To make sure that you stay on the positive side of winning, let's look at the specific *Do's & Don'ts of Smart Lottery Play* in Chapter 3—next.

The way to wealth...depends chiefly on two words, industry and frugality; that is, waste neither time nor money, but make the best use of both. Without industry and frugality, nothing will do; and with them, everything.

Ben Franklin

Lottery Trivia

Fabulous Fortune Foible

March 7, 1992

John Mattinen makes the most brilliant mistake of his life.

John buys one ticket in the Illinois Lottery with two of the same series of numbers that he copies in error.

John Mattinen then becomes the first Illinois Lottery player to win the LOTTO Grand Prize twice on one ticket.

John quickly collects $20,800,000 approximating two-thirds of the total $31,400,000 jackpot in the LOTTO drawing.

3

Do's & Don'ts of Smart Lottery Play

Despite all the good you can do as a result of winning the lottery, there is a lot of not-so-good that can be done to you. This chapter contains 20 such caveats to be aware of and to beware of *before*, *when*, and *after* you win your lottery jackpot. Some of these warnings bear more detailed discussion than given here. In these cases, I have noted where in this book and elsewhere you can find the more thorough treatment.

Now, brace yourself for some very sound advice based on the true-life misfortunes of players and winners who did the wrong things with the *right* amount of money and soon found themselves living with the *wrong* amount of money again. You can avoid their plight by understanding what they did wrong or failed to do right and by not copying them. You will also witness what wrong was done to them and how to prevent the same from happening to you.

1. Don't Bet That $1 Million Jackpot Gets You $1 Million Prize.

First, don't expect $1,000,000 to equal $1,000,000. If you win $1,000,000 in a U.S. Lottery, you do not necessarily *receive* $1,000,000. You are, instead, typically paid $50,000 a year for 20 years. But receiving $50,000 a year over 20 years is *not* the same as receiving $1,000,000 in a lump sum today.

Only your first lottery check is worth $50,000. Then the lottery buys a $950,000 annuity from a life insurance company who then pays you $50,000 a year for the next 19 years. The lottery pays only about $400,000–$450,000 (depending on interest rates, etc.) for the $950,000 annuity.

Why is the insurance company willing to accept about half the dollars that they will eventually pay out? The secret is the *time value of money*. Reportedly, when Einstein was asked what he believed to be the greatest invention of mankind, he quickly responded: "Compound Interest!" The insurance company uses this "greatest invention" to their greatest advantage. You can too.

How do you figure the *time value of money*? You have to determine the present value of each year's future payment. You do this by factoring-in a number variously called an inflation rate or a discount rate or an opportunity cost.

For example, if inflation is averaging 6% a year, then the dollar that you use to buy a lottery ticket today is not worth the same dollar a year from now. That dollar of today is only worth 94¢ a year from now in purchasing power. Due to the 6% inflation rate, your dollar's ability to buy things has dropped by 6¢. Look at the *time value of money* this way: If you were buying M&M's and you could buy 100 M&M's today for one dollar bill, then next year you would get only 94 M&M's for your one dollar bill.

A nickel ain't worth a dime anymore.
                                          Yogi Berra

Assuming a 6% annual inflation rate (a 6% loss of purchasing power), the "$1 Million" jackpot that you win today is truthfully only *worth* about $600,000 in today's dollar value. This jackpot is still a good amount of money and may be even the *right* amount. See Chart 3–1.

CHART 3–1: THE TIME VALUE OF MONEY

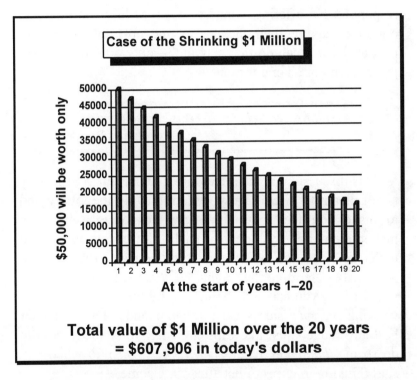

Case of the Shrinking $1 Million

$50,000 will be worth only

At the start of years 1–20

Total value of $1 Million over the 20 years = $607,906 in today's dollars

Why is there a difference in value? Because you receive only 5% of the jackpot each year, you have to wait 20 years to receive all the money. You have to trade your time for the money. And time has a value.

In other words, say that with the first $50,000 check that the lottery gives you today, you can buy 50,000 bags of M&M's. Well, with the $50,000 check they give you in year

20, you are only going to be able to buy about 16,526—not 50,000—bags of M&M's. A diet of 16,526 bags of M&M's a year may still not be peanuts, but if you have grown accustomed to a diet of 50,000 bags of M&M's a year, then in year 20 you are going to be plain hungry (by about 33,474 bags worth).

A few states like Arizona, Ohio and Oregon have responded by offering winners of $1 Million or more an option of taking their jackpot in one up-front, lump-sum payout. How much do they pay out?—only 50% of the total jackpot amount! Time *is* money.

A dollar saved today is 75 cents earned tomorrow.
James Reston

This discussion of the effect that time has on your money is not meant to discourage you from playing the lottery and to make you feel that the lottery jackpot is a lie or a misrepresentation by lottery officials. However, you need to understand and use the *time value of money* so that you can accurately determine the "right" *right* amount of money for you. In fact, you can and should get the *time value of money* working on *your* side by using compound interest to your best advantage—just like Einstein. I tell you exactly how to do so in *Chapter 6: What To Do After You Win* when you start thinking in terms of net after-tax income.

But for now, simply realize that a better deal than getting $50,000 a year for 20 years would be to get all $1,000,000 today in a lump-sum. Even if you paid $400,000 in federal income taxes now, you could invest the remaining $600,000 in a tax-free municipal bond fund. If you averaged an 8% return, you would receive $48,000 a year in tax-free interest income and still have all the $600,000 lump-sum after 20 years and beyond—forever. This technique is a more *Infinite Financial Freedom* type of approach. Whereas with the typical lottery annuity payout, you are out of money after 20 years—unless you invest it wisely (Chapter 6 tells you how).

This extended payment method of your jackpot in annuity form just emphasizes the importance of your establishing a plan and committing to it. Because, over time, the purchasing power of your jackpot shrinks a little every year until it finally disappears forever and, if you're not smart, you find yourself 20 years later where you were 20 years ago. But you *are* smart because you are reading this sentence and now know about another financial secret—the *time value of money*.

---

2. Don't Buy or Buy Into Systems or Schemes.

Don't buy or buy into any systems or schemes of picking winning lottery numbers. Odds are odds. The lottery is random—every time. The numbers 1-2-3-4-5-6 have the same odds of being drawn as any other six numbers in the 6/51 games. See *Appendix D: Lottery Resources* for details on figuring the odds of winning the various lotto games.

He who can predict winning numbers has no need to let off fire-crackers.

Ernest Bramah

Like stock market systems designed to beat the system, don't believe or invest in them. Ask yourself: "If it's such a fantastic money-making system, then why is someone loudly selling it to me or anyone else for so little when they could quietly make so much by just privately using their own system?" Remember that the real people who got rich in the 1849 California Gold Rush were largely *not* the gold-panning prospectors, but the companies that manufactured and sold the shovels and pans (the "system") to the prospectors.

The only possible edge you can have in picking numbers is to pick numbers greater than 31, since so many players use special dates like birthdays and anniversaries. And the only edge that picking numbers over 31 gives you is the less likelihood of having to share a jackpot with multiple winners, since there are no dates over 31. Numbers over 31 have the same chance of being drawn as those 31 and under. However, this trick is losing its edge as more players realize the *date effect* on shared jackpots.

> *One who deceives will always find those who*
> *allow themselves to be deceived.*
>
> Machiavelli

Some of the more unusual ways that multi-million dollar winners have reportedly picked their winning numbers include using these:

❑   a dart board's numbers hit by throwing darts;

❑   a camera's serial number;

❑   the rural route numbers on the commute to buy the winning ticket;

❑   the serial number from a Social Security check;

❑   prayers answered in a prayer garden;

❑   dream visits from a deceased grandfather;

❑   the lot number on a box of doughnuts bought while waiting in line to buy the winning ticket.

3. Promise Nothing.

Don't promise anyone anything. Don't casually promise that you will buy something or do something specific for someone if you ever win. Such promises-in-passing or dreaming-out-loud *before* you win can and will come back to haunt you *after* you win, as it has for other lottery winners. If you want to do something nice for someone, then quietly incorporate the gift or gesture into your plan. Why?

> *Half the promises people say were never kept, were never made.*
>
> Ed Howe

Relationships have been destroyed by such casually made and unfulfilled promises. One case even involves a 60-year-old woman suing a 39-year-old lottery winner for half of the cash while at the same time trying to adopt him! As in all things in life, promise only what you can and know you will deliver. Besides, imagine how much nicer the gift will be for the recipient when received as an unexpected surprise! Follow this rule: It is better to promise nothing and give much than to promise everything and give little.

> *We must not promise what we ought not, lest we be called upon to perform what we cannot.*
>
> Abraham Lincoln

4. Don't Give the Wrong Signals to Your Family and Friends.

Winning the lottery is the luck of the draw. But life's true wealth is way beyond money. Prosperity is much more a state of mind than an amount of money.

Children have more need of models than of critics.

Joubert

So, instill the smart work ethic and *right mind set* in others by what you do *before* and *after* you win your jackpot. Don't give others, whom you may influence, the false impression that acquiring wealth is easy. As you will learn in *Chapter 4: What To Do Before You Win*, the process of achieving prosperity may be *simple* to understand, but wealth is not necessarily *easy* to achieve without focused effort. So, continue to remind others for whom you are an example that "effort focused on results"—not luck—is the vital characteristic of true success.

Be a pattern to others, and then all will go well.

Cicero

5. Stay Humble.

If you win, remember that you won because you were lucky—not smart, talented, etc. You may indeed be smart, talented, etc., but not *because* you won the lottery. Your real brains and talent will serve you in what you do *before* and *after* you win.

> *Those who mistake their good luck for their merit
> are inevitably bound for disaster.*
> J. Christopher Herold

People with new money are often very showy. Conspicuous consumption by new lottery millionaires has led to a number of bankruptcies and divorces. One multi-million dollar winner in the *Pennsylvania Lottery* blew through his first $168,000 lottery check in less than five months. Not to be outdone, a multi-million dollar winner in the *Illinois Lottery* blew through $137,000 of his first $142,000 lottery check within just two months.

Such blatant ostentatiousness makes you an obvious target for *con artists* or other people of questionable repute who have designs on separating you from your money. So, be smart, be humble, and stay in-the-money.

> *Never forget the hard times and the early days.
> Always remember where you came from.*
> David Liederman

6. Beware of the Ex's: Ex-Spouses and Ex-Boyfriends and Ex-Girlfriends...

If you ever win, expect to hear from ex-boy/girl friends and any ex-spouses. Be wary of such people suddenly re-appearing from out of your past. Lottery officials joke that an ex-spouse's attorney is among the first to contact you with congratulations—and a lawsuit for re-negotiating your original divorce settlement.

Be prepared for this probability by having your ex-spouse waive any rights to your future lottery winnings in your initial settlement. Of course, your ex-spouse can still sue you to re-negotiate the original terms even if he/she waived rights to your future winnings in the first settlement. However, you will have a stronger case *after* winning with such a clause placed in the original settlement *before* winning.

> *A fool and her money are soon courted.*
> Helen Rowland

One divorced player, who won $1.4 Million in the *Pennsylvania Lottery*, had no such clause. Within a month, her ex-husband re-romanced her into remarrying him. More notably, she then signed an agreement—drafted and witnessed by an attorney—to split the winnings equally. Sixteen months later she filed for another divorce. She, of course, also tried to rescind the agreement to split the jackpot. The judge felt it was most fair for the pair to share the fare equally and he so ordered. Along with the heart-ache, she spent $700,000 to make her ex-husband go away for the second time—ouch!

7. Don't Bank on Credit.

Banks generally will *not* extend credit based on future lottery income alone, as your winnings are generally not assignable. Further, some states do not allow lenders to attach the future income stream from your winnings as collateral. So, lenders may or may not view you as a better credit risk because of your guaranteed 20-year income.

Most lenders, knowing the unfortunate history of most unprepared lottery winners, may genuinely see you as an *impaired* credit risk. In fact, bankers may consider you a poorer credit risk than before you won the jackpot simply due to the poor financial track record of so many lottery winners. Besides, lenders know, as you now know, that a jackpot of $1 Million (or any other amount) is not $1 Million due to the 20-year payout and the *time value of money*.

> *Time is money and many people pay their debts with it.*
>
> Josh Billings

However, unsecured debt, such as credit cards and unsecured lines of credit may be easier to obtain. Unsolicited offers for unsecured credit will find their way into your mailbox as you begin to have more income and asset visibility in the computer databases of the world. For more information on the best credit cards, see the credit card evaluation services listed in *Appendix B: Financial Growth Resources.*

8. Don't Give-In to Family Pressures.

Family members may pressure you into feeling that you should share all winnings with them equally. It is a common occurrence for distant (and not-so-distant) relatives to phone you and exclaim how happy and relieved they are now that *we* won. One multi-million dollar winner in the *Massachusetts Lottery* was gracious enough to give her son a check for several thousand dollars. He broke her heart when he tossed the check back at her and told her to "try again."

You, of course, will naturally feel a sense of family obligation, especially towards your immediate family. But there is a right and wrong way to help them. The solution is to follow *your* plan, not theirs—there's probably too many of them! Your plan will likely include them, at least to some extent. By committing to and following your plan you will be better able to serve them in the long run. We will cover the details of developing your own long-term *Financial Game Plan* in *Chapter 6: What To Do After You Win.*

> *Always tell your rich relatives how fast you are making money, and always tell the poor ones how fast you are losing it.*
>
> Anon, the Unknown Quoter

9. Expect to Lose Some Friends.

Of course, you will be the same person after you win your jackpot—only with more money. You may not change that much and fundamentally not at all, especially if you prepare for winning as explained in *Chapter 4: What To Do Before You Win.* However, the people around you will change the way that they relate both to you and to what they perceive as your new-found "wealth".

> *Purchase not friends by gifts; when thou ceasest to give, such will cease to love.*
>
> Thomas Fuller

Friends may not understand the mechanics of the lottery jackpot payouts. Often, others will assume that you instantly have huge amounts of disposable income and they may expect you to cover the cost of entire outings—for both you and everyone else. Uninformed friends then may resent or disbelieve you when you do not or cannot pay for everything for everyone.

One benefit of this *friend effect* is that your true friends will become more apparent in this new context. Don't expect to have many true friends. One true friend is a blessing. Part of the cost of winning a jackpot is the loss of those who you *thought* were friends. Expect to lose some such "friends". If you prepare for the loss, you won't be so surprised or hurt when it happens. Human nature is what it is and you, like other winners, will lose some friends. Sorry.

> *It's the friends that you can call up at 4 a.m. that matter.*
>
> Marlene Dietrich

10. Don't Feel Guilty.

Catch yourself if you begin to suffer some guilt for having money without personally having earned it. Trust fund children often experience this sense of guilt when they are born wealthy by coincidence into a rich family and have never had to work for their wealth. This guilt stems largely from a lack of a sense of accomplishment, no direction, and/or poor self-esteem.

> *A guilty conscience is a hidden enemy.*
>
> Indian Proverb

Think of winning your jackpot, instead, as giving you a new opportunity to do something worthwhile and fun with and in your life. Do not let others make you feel guilty. Channel this negative energy into doing something positive for yourself and others. Again, get your life together *before* you win the jackpot, so that you are ready to live the best life *after* you win the jackpot and are able to live the best life even if you *never* win the jackpot.

This whole subject of people's relationships to and with money is a relatively new field of psychology, called *Financial Psychology*, pioneered principally by Dr. Kathleen Gurney. Dr. Gurney has developed a personality profile questionnaire that enables people to identify their financial attitudes, investment preferences and money management styles. She has identified 9 distinct personalities. In *Chapter 4: What To Do Before You Win*, you will find an optional way to learn your own Money Personality based on Dr. Gurney's work. Knowing your tendencies is important because money guilt, manifested by deliberate losing (among other self-damaging behaviors), can torpedo even the best-crafted plans.

> *True guilt is guilt at the obligation one owes to oneself to be oneself.*
>
> R. D. Laing

11. Be Anonymously Generous.

Do not announce that you are going to give your money away to worthy causes and/or all that you want to do is to help others. People who hear you say this *before* you win will come back to collect *after* you win. You may honestly want to be this generous and give away your jackpot and if so, do so. But don't *say* so.

After you win, all kinds of "worthy" people will chase after you for their share of your jackpot. So, be anonymously generous, as far as the media and others are concerned. Otherwise, you might find yourself having to deal with repeated and annoying post-jackpot encounters like one *Maryland Lottery* multi-million dollar winner. After announcing her charitable intents, she had innumerable people approach her explaining that, among others, her brother or sister had sent them to her for help. She had only one problem with this tactic. She's an only child!

They asked Jack Benny if he would do something for the Actor's Orphanage—so he shot both his parents and moved in.

Bob Hope

So, tell those that hound you about worthy causes that you have set-up a "charitable mechanism". Direct them to: "Send your information to our P. O. Box. If your charity has merit and fits our platform, then our people will contact you." This screening device helps you eliminate the inappropriate and illegitimate and to discover the truly worthwhile.

Also, be aware that you can be more generous than you may think, if you invest and plan properly. For details on how, see *Rule #15: Give Smart* in *Chapter 6: What To Do After You Win.*

12. Beware the Double Standard of Divorce!

When the husband wins the jackpot, the courts have consistently ruled that the lottery winnings are marital property. In a divorce proceeding, the courts typically award the ex-wife 50% of the winnings and further order that the ex-husband pay additional alimony out of his remaining half of the jackpot (see, for example, *Bronson v. Bronson*). Moreover, the ex-wife usually gets the house (see *Norby v. Norby*) and, customarily, the custody of the children. This tendency of the courts is, naturally, good news for women.

More good news for women is that when the wife wins the jackpot, the courts typically (if not surprisingly) rule that the lottery winnings are the ex-wife's sole income and that the ex-husband receives zero (see *Holmes v. Holmes*). The bad news for both parties is that whatever each receives is net after paying attorney fees and court costs.

Zsa Zsa Gabor is an expert housekeeper.
Everytime she gets divorced, she keeps the house.
                                        Henny Youngman

Given the above, you should consider having a "family partnership" for serious lottery play, especially if extended family members play together as a group. This pre-planning is best for all parties, with or without a divorce ensuing. For example, if your family partnership stipulates a 50/50 or other split, you can avoid wasting huge portions of your jackpot and time on legal and court costs, should a divorce occur. If you have to go to court to reach a 50/50 split, then you really receive only one-third and your ex-spouse receives only one-third, because the lawyers receive one-third. Unless you enjoy being unnecessarily generous to attorneys, consider drafting a family partnership.

Ideally, there is no need for written family or other partnership agreements because the world and everyone in it is absolutely and continuously perfect. Realistically, though, family partnerships are becoming increasingly popular in these three situations:

1.   For first time newlyweds with significantly disproportionate financial positions (one is wealthy; one is not);

2.   When one or both of the spouses is/are entering their second marriage with children from a previous marriage (in order to protect the children);

3.   In anticipation of a major life-changing event, such as death, an incapacitating disability, or winning a big lottery jackpot.

Lacking such a partnership agreement, one Canadian 16-year-old daughter sued her father for what she felt was her rightful share of his $7.6 Million jackpot (see *Lavigueur v. Lavigueur*). Since the *Canadian Lottery* awards their winners with one lump-sum, tax-free payment, significant and immediate dollars were at stake.

> *Don't marry for money; you can borrow it cheaper.*
> Scottish Proverb

Family Partnerships are a subject of Estate Planning and, as such, are beyond the scope of this book. However, for more information, see *Rule #14: Outsmart Count Taxula* in *Chapter 6: What To Do After You Win* and *Appendix C: Legal Resources*. Also, Forms Man, Inc. and Nolo Press publish a series of user-friendly, self-help legal kits on a variety of topics. Their books contain do-it-yourself, fill-in-the-blanks, tear-out forms typically valid in all 50 states as well as sample documents. See *Appendix C: Legal Resources* for details on these practical books.

13. Budget Your Lottery Play.

Plan in advance how much you can afford to spend and lose on lottery tickets. Pay for your lottery tickets only out of your "discretionary income". Discretionary income is the money that remains after you *first* pay yourself and *then* pay your bills. Always pay yourself first (more on this subject in *Chapter 6: What To Do After You Win*). Use the ratios shown in Chart 3–3 as a guideline for budgeting your lottery play.

CHART 3–3: MONTHLY LOTTERY PLAY BUDGET

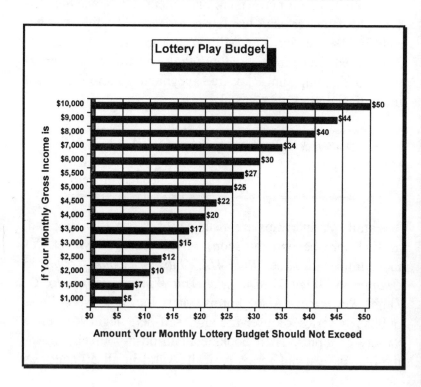

You may want to exceed this budget on special occasions, such as when the jackpot is over a specific amount, say $10 Million or $20 Million. On these occasions, treat yourself to an extra "quick pick" or two. Otherwise, follow your plan. In *Chapter 6: What To Do After You Win*, I give you the *Rulebook* for developing your own plan for achieving what *Infinite Financial Freedom* means to you.

14. Do Not Enter Into Informal Arrangements.

Do not let friends, co-workers, etc., or even family members casually buy tickets for you, even if you give them the money and numbers to do so. You can only safely allow yourself this convenience, if you have a formalized agreement in writing. As unfortunate as it is, legal conflicts over the ownership of the winning ticket consistently ensue when such arrangements are informal. You may well wind up in court to resolve who gets paid how much money (see *Sehnert v. Hildebrand v. Mullen*). Of course, friendships and families can be destroyed in such situations and your lottery winnings severely diluted by the attendant legal and court costs.

> *A verbal contract isn't worth the paper it's written on.*
>
> Samuel Goldwyn

If you must play with others, always stipulate in your written contract, who pays for the lottery ticket and who receives how much of the winnings. The cost of preparing the contract now, especially if you use one of the do-it-yourself legal kits, will be significantly less than an attorney's defense fees later without such an agreement.

State lotteries payout each jackpot to only one individual or entity. Unless under a court order, the lottery officials will not distribute the winnings among group players. The group should, therefore, file with the IRS for its own Federal Employer Identification Number (FEIN). Otherwise, if *you* collect all the money individually, the lottery reports to the IRS that they paid all the money to *your* Social Security Number. Only you will be liable for the federal income taxes. If you then distribute the winnings among the group members, you would be liable for gift taxes on amounts over $10,000 given to each member of your group each year.

Here's how to properly structure group play:

1. Draft a simple group or family partnership agreement using one of the do-it-yourself legal kits listed in *Appendix C: Legal Resources*.

2. Obtain a Federal Employer Identification Number by completing and returning to the IRS Form SS–4, "Application for Employer Identification Number".

3. When your group wins a prize, file your claim with the lottery using your FEIN assigned by the IRS.

4. The lottery will then deduct the federal income tax withholdings using your group's FEIN and pay the balance to your group. The responsibility to distribute the winnings among group members is still yours.

5. If your group wins over $600, report the names and social security numbers of each group member receiving a portion of the winnings by completing and returning to the lottery an IRS Form 5754, "Statement by Person or Persons Receiving Gambling Winnings."

6. The following January, each group member receives a Form W–2G from the lottery showing their portion of the prize and any income tax withheld. Each member then uses this form to prepare their tax return for the year in which they received a payout.

Does all this paperwork plus the potential pitfalls sound like too much of a bother to allow you to safely play in groups? It may be. So, be careful when playing in groups. Unless you properly structure group play, you could see what starts out as a winning group jackpot in the *right* amount of money quickly evaporate into no meaningful money at all. What's worse, winning could even mean losing some friends.

Besides, history tells us that winning tickets, bought and held for you by a friend, have been mysteriously "lost" after the announcement of the winning numbers. You further complicate the situation when you live in a state where lotteries are illegal and you cross state lines to buy tickets. Try taking your "friend" to court to enforce an oral contract for an illegal activity. Don't let anyone do you any such "favors" (see *Kaszuba v. Zientara*). For more information on drafting these contracts, see *Appendix C: Legal Resources.*

15. Don't Try to Cheat the Lottery.

Lottery security officials know all the tricks. They have several high-tech, bar-coding and scanning systems and methods for checking and double-checking the validity of winning tickets. The verification technology is becoming increasingly computerized and sophisticated. So, play it straight—and honestly. Also, make sure that you know and follow the rules of all states involved, if you are playing across state lines or using the mail to buy tickets.

Do not try to counterfeit tickets. Lottery officials are prepared for such attempts. They have and will set-up "sting" operations to make you believe that you have cleverly won, only to nail you for showing-up to collect.

Running a losing ticket through a washing machine and then claiming that the faded and now illegible ticket bears winning numbers seems to be a particularly popular low-tech scam used by the over zealous. Don't bother trying this or other fraud. The lottery officials can tell the difference.

> *There are no new forms of financial fraud; in the last several hundred years, there have only been small variations on a few classic designs.*
> John Kenneth Galbraith

The State of Washington had a wave of incidents in the early 90's involving several unsubstantiated claims of dogs eating winning tickets. The only conclusion that one lottery official could reach was that there was something in the ticket production process that was especially attractive to either the canine palette or the human imagination.

In any case, don't cheat in the lottery or in anything else. Cheating is a no-win game. If you do get caught, you may have to trade some of your time for the offense. If you don't get caught, you will be spending much of your time looking over your shoulder wondering if you will ever get caught. You might call this effect the "time value of fraud".

> *The first and worst of all frauds is to cheat oneself.*
> Gamaliel Bailey

16. Don't Wait to Claim Your Winning Ticket.

Most state lotteries have a 6-month to a 1-year statute of limitations. As amazing as this may sound, certain multi-million dollar jackpots were never claimed in time. See Chart 3–2 for the largest *unclaimed* jackpots exceeding $1 Million.

CHART 3–2: LARGEST UNCLAIMED JACKPOTS

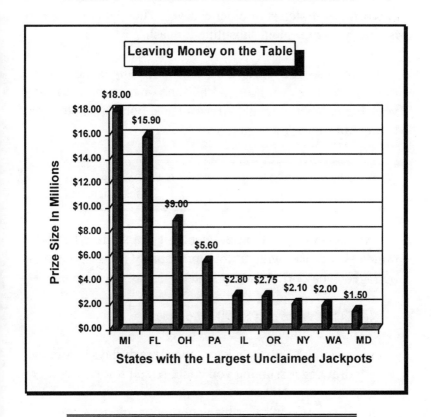

There is, by God's grace, an immeasurable distance between late and too late.

Anne Swetchine

Again, you see another example of the "time is money is time" principle at work. Here, money is lost if not claimed in time and time is lost for not claiming the money.

17. Don't Buy Tickets On Credit.

Don't charge your tickets on your credit card. The only exception to this rule is if you have the rare discipline to pay your credit card balance in full every month without incurring any interest or other charges. Then, your credit card is simply a convenient substitute for cash.

Do not use your credit card to *finance* any consumable. I recommend that you leave all but one or two credit cards in your file cabinet at home. Always leave home without them. Use credit *only* for investments.

> *The only thing to buy on credit is your casket.*
> James Michener

The lottery is *not* an investment—it is a skill-less game of mindless chance with a low probability of a potentially outrageous pay-off. A lottery *ticket* does not appreciate.

Here's the value of a $1.00 lotto ticket:

❑   a stable $1.00 for a very few hours or days before the drawing (assuming you could re-sell it for $1.00); or

❑   if you win, it's worth an annuity which pays you an annual amount in *decreasing* purchasing power over several years (unless you can sell it for a lump-sum worth about 50% of its face value); or

❑   if you lose, it's worth zero.

In the latter case, if you buy your tickets on credit, you are paying an infinite interest rate for the privilege of buying a losing, worthless ticket. So, don't lose twice: once on the ticket and once on the interest rate.

Here are two related, fundamental principles for achieving *Infinite Financial Freedom*:

1. Run your life on cash.
2. Use credit only for opportunity (investments in appreciating assets and/or profitable activities), never consumption.

18. Watch Out: Big Brothers Are Watching You!

Most states cross-check each winner's name(s) against their computer files. If, for example, you have *ever* received welfare payments, you may also receive a bill to reimburse the state for prior welfare payments they made to you. You can also be removed from receiving further state aid, irrespective of circumstance, because of your new "fortune".

Massachusetts is one state requiring reimbursement of prior welfare payments. One winner of a modest (in lottery terms) $25,000 jackpot received a net check of only $6,000 after the state deducted $14,000 off-the-top for previous welfare payments made to the player. Since the Massachusetts Welfare Department considered him to have earned income of the full $25,000, the state removed him from the welfare rolls.

He found himself in a net position *after* he won worse off than *before* he won!

Welfare reimbursement is just the tip of the Big Brother iceberg. The *California Lottery* computer, for example, searches and scans the records of over 100 different federal, state and local agencies. Before giving their first check to you, most states double-check their computers to see at least:

❑   if you're an illegal alien (the INS deports these "winners," though the deportees get to keep the cash);

❑   if you have any outstanding arrest warrants against you (some winners get a check and a handcuff— smile, it will be a media event!);

❑   if you have any outstanding court judgements against you (the judge can garnish your winnings);

❑   if the IRS *says* that you owe any back Federal taxes (Uncle Sam is paid first);

❑   if you owe any back taxes to the state and/or local governments (such as property or income taxes);

❑   if you are delinquent in alimony and/or child support payments (of course, your ex-spouse's attorney will also be among the first to remind you);

❑   if you have received any recoverable unemployment and/or welfare payments (pay-back time);

❑   if you are delinquent on your student loan (shame on you!); and

❑   if you have any outstanding moving violations or unpaid parking tickets.

One winner in the *Oregon Lottery* had the dubious honor of receiving his *net* jackpot check after all deductions. What was the amount? The check was well into seven figures, all right—all zero's: "$0,000,000.00"...not exactly the *right* amount of money.

If we do not discipline ourselves, the world will do it for us.

William Feather

So, get your life in order and keep it in order *before* you win (as detailed in *Chapter 4: What To Do Before You Win*) or you may watch your long-awaited jackpot simply vaporize before your eyes to pay for past "indiscretions". Beware and be certain: your jackpot will pass through many hands before it is placed in your pocket.

19. Watch: Little Brothers Are Watching You, Too!

Your personal demographic and psychographic information is a new world commodity—and it's for sale or rent. Be aware that you will have—probably already have—a digital double of yourself in the binary bowels of several commercial databases. As your notoriety increases, your computerized clone becomes a more valuable trading commodity across many marketing databases. One "jeopardy of the jackpot" is that winning the lottery means losing a lot of privacy just when privacy becomes increasingly important to you.

The U.S. Office of Technology Assessment estimates that the marketplace maintains a total database of over 5 Billion records and churns its data from computer-to-computer at an average rate of 5 times a day! Trust that your binary android is among the bits and bytes boundlessly bouncing between bureaus for bucks. Among the information for sale or rent about you is:

- bank account balances;

- unlisted phone numbers;

- Post Office change of address notices;

- Social Security status, earnings, etc.;

- criminal records;

- litigation history;

- telephone usage statistics;

- work-related injuries;

- medical records;

- insurance files;

- credit card charges;

- driving records;

- employment history;

- educational history;

❏   professional licenses;

❏   club memberships;

❏   bill payment history;

❏   personal data (such as, family composition, buying patterns, and lifestyle); and

❏   names of lottery winners.

So, rest assured (if you can) that many marketers will find you and present their various unsolicited offers to happily separate you from whatever amount of money you may have. Winning the jackpot only makes you a more visible target. Some of their offers may even be good—maybe 1 in 100.

Not only because of the financial wisdom of doing so, but also to protect your privacy, run your life on cash to the greatest extent possible. I outline other ideas for minimizing the invasion of your privacy in *Chapter 5: What To Do When You Win.*

20. Don't Be Compulsive.

Remember *why* you are playing the lottery at all—you're looking for the *right* amount of money. You buy lottery tickets for yourself for the same reason that you should buy life insurance for your heirs: to provide the money you haven't had time to earn yet. Of course, only the life insurance guarantees to pay-off, but, by then, it's too late for you—you're dead.

So, don't bet (and bet and bet and bet...) only on winning the jackpot. You could run out of money or die waiting to win. Always play to win, but live *as if* you will always lose. Arrange your life so that you will be prepared to win, should winning occur. In the meantime, put into motion a plan that will assure that you will achieve you own *Infinite Financial Freedom* with or without the lottery jackpot.

There is but one good throw upon the dice, which is to throw them away.

Paul Chatfield

Make it a game. See which plan—the lottery or yours—bags you the *right* amount of money first. Give the lottery a run for *your* money; but don't let the lottery run away with your money. Keep your wagering in perspective. Don't bet compulsively. Plan your play. Adhere to the Lottery Play Budget guidelines earlier in this chapter. If you think that you or a loved one may have a serious problem with gambling, then see *Appendix D: Lottery Resources* for information on getting help.

So, don't be compulsive—be committed, instead. Be committed to your plan—a plan that you will develop now by establishing what you will do *before*, *when*, and *after* you win. Let's start at the beginning with the *Before You Win* plan in Chapter 4—next.

If you must play, decide upon three things at the start:
>   *1. the rules of the game,*
>   *2. the stakes,*
>   *3. and the quitting time.*

Chinese Proverb

4

What To Do

Before You Win

There are two very critical investments to make *before* you win the lottery—besides making a dollar and buying a ticket. If you want your hopeful jackpot to raise you and not ruin you, financially and otherwise, then you must make these two investments and you must make them in this order:

1.   Invest first in *Personal Growth.*

2.   Invest next in *What You Do Best and Enjoy Most.*

Investment #1: Personal Growth

You must invest in *Personal Growth* first, because all else in your life follows from how you relate to yourself and with the world outside you. *Financial Growth* follows—is a by-product of—*Personal Growth.* This principle is not just self-help pabulum or psycho-babble. The practical truth is that if you do not invest in *Personal Growth* first, then you won't know what to do with your jackpot once you get it.

The first rule of winning: Don't beat yourself.
                                        Football adage

Yes, it's true that there are a few legal ways to get the money you want without an investment in *Personal Growth*. You can, of course, win the lottery or receive an inheritance. However, the only sure way that you will *keep* the lottery or any other money is through developing your *Personal Growth*—not chance.

You do not even have to believe me about the absolute, undeniable pre-requisite of investing first in *Personal Growth*. The history of the lottery is littered with broken dreams of those wishing that they had invested in their own *Personal Growth* ages before they ever thought about buying their first lottery ticket. Heed the words of these "winners":

> *I honestly wish I never won the damn thing. It ruined me.*
> Charles Riddle, $1 Million winner
> Michigan Lottery, 1975

> *I don't think I'd buy that ticket again. I have my regrets.*
> Keith Bergstresser, $1 Million winner
> Pennsylvania Lottery, 1982

> *You win the Megabucks and it's supposed to make your life easier. It's made mine a lot harder.*
> Charles Nelson, $1 Million winner
> Massachusetts Lottery, 1984

> *I wish I could go back to the day Bob brought home that lottery ticket from the grocery—I would just rip it up…in the long run we would have ended-up a whole heck of a lot better…if it wasn't for the money.*
> Betty Bronson, $1 Million co-winner
> Maryland Lottery, 1973

There is no need for you to ever utter such regretful words, if you make your first investment in your own

Personal Growth. All education has a cost. These winners learned their lessons at a dear cost—their jackpots and more.

The typical mistake that such unprepared lottery winners make is that they credit their jackpot for their future fortune *before* they win and then blame their jackpot for their eventual misfortune *after* they win. They fail to realize soon enough that money is only a tool of wealth—not wealth itself. Besides, money doesn't care who has it or where it comes from or where it goes or when or how or why.

> *Draw from other people's dangers the lesson that may profit yourself.*
>
> Terence

Such unprepared winners do not have the *right mind set* (defined in the next section) for winning and dealing with *any* amount of money—lottery jackpots or otherwise. When winning, they find themselves instantly catapulted to prosperity without any understanding of how to properly relate to money. They often panic, manifesting their panic in behavior that turns cash to trash.

> *The winner manages his money. The loser lets the money manage him.*
>
> Nicholas Dandalos

They don't understand and have never seriously considered their relationship with money or their attitude towards it. In short, they don't know their Money Personality. Later in this chapter, you will find an optional way of learning your own Money Personality and how to profit from this knowledge.

Meanwhile, trust that if you have problems *before* you win, they will be magnified and intensified *after* you win the lottery—not solved by it. Winning the lottery does not absolve you from getting your life together—on the contrary, winning demands that you do just that. Fortunately, to eliminate this "problem amplification effect" and to prepare for winning anything in life, all you have to do is climb the *Ladder of Success*.

Ladder of Success

Investing in *Personal Growth* means developing your life up the *Ladder of Success* (see Table 4–1). Take the steps in order, as each step is the foundation for the one following it. We will discuss each step in more detail later, but first here's the framework for the *Ladder*:

TABLE 4–1: STEPS UP THE LADDER OF SUCCESS

LADDER OF SUCCESS
Step 5: Daily Outcomes
Step 4: Life Plan: Statement of Goals
Step 3: Affirmations
Step 2: Guiding Principles
Step 1: Mind Set

Step 1: Mind Set
You must get yourself in the *right mind set*, so that your inner thinking becomes a positive self-fulfilling prophecy and not self-defeating.

Step 2: Guiding Principles

Building upon a positive *Mind Set*, you must develop (write-out) the *Guiding Principles* of your life, those governing fundamentals that align all your outward behavior with your inner belief.

Step 3: Affirmations

Out of your *Guiding Principles* come your empowering *Affirmations* that define and re-inforce the kind of person you wish to become. These *Affirmations* become the outer expression of your inner self-fulfilling prophecy, as dictated by your *Mind Set* and governed by your *Guiding Principles*.

Step 4: Life Plan: Statement of Goals

Following your *Affirmations* is your *Life Plan: Statement of Goals* which today documents all the specifics of your various future achievements.

Step 5: Daily Outcomes

Finally, your *Goals* translate into the *Daily Outcomes* that direct your day-to-day activities in pursuit of your ongoing success. The "Do" of "Do It Now!" should stand for *Daily Outcomes*.

If A = Success,
then the formula is A = X + Y + Z.
X = Work.
Y = Play.
Z = Keep your mouth shut.

Albert Einstein

Your *Mind Set*, *Guiding Principles*, and *Affirmations* are fundamental, universal truths that act as building blocks of your life. As such, the content of these three steps up the *Ladder* will change very little, if at all, and never in essence, once you admit them to yourself and document the details of each in writing.

CHART 4–1: STEPS UP THE LADDER OF SUCCESS

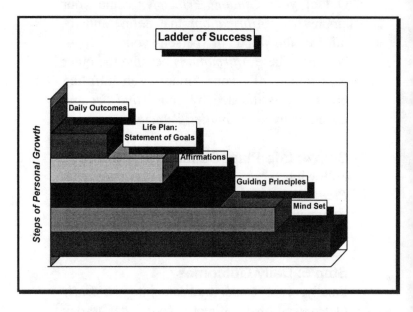

Your *Life Plan: Statement of Goals* and *Daily Outcomes* will, by necessity, change as you achieve certain goals, abandon other goals, and set new ones. Review these goals and outcomes regularly, such as daily upon arising and/or nightly upon retiring. Also, mark your calendar for special monthly, quarterly, and annual check-ups. The week-end before your birthday is an especially good time for your annual review.

If any review date falls on a major holiday, such as Christmas, New Year's Day, etc., then just move your review date up a week-end or two earlier. You do not want the distractions of a holiday to detract from the significance of and the time for your review. Your review is too profound to perform superficially. Your life's path depends upon your critical review and revision of your plan.

Step 1: The Right Mind Set

The losing lottery winners were doomed to lose—even after their numbers won—because they had the *wrong mind set*. Without the *right mind set*, the money may drive you right out of your mind.

Of course, not *all* winners wind up losing. The true winners win and continue to win *after* getting their jackpot because they were winners *before* they got their jackpot. They were already on their path of *Personal Growth*. The lottery winnings simply enhance and quicken the pace for these prepared winners.

Presumably without knowing it (or they would change), losing winners have a *mind set* characterized by:

❑   *Chance thinking*:
    an absence of assignable *design* (no plan);

❑   *Probability thinking*:
    an absence of assignable *cause* (no effort made in any
    specific direction); and a

❑   *Scarcity mentality*:
    a belief in the lack of prosperity (no point in planning
    any effort).

A person with such a *mind set* is not grounded in any particular governing principles, has no notable life plan, and thus takes no definitive action in the pursuit of specific life goals. In other words, such a person is generally reactive, letting events happen *to* them as they may. Only then do they respond, wondering what just happened. Better thinking is pro-active, making things happen according to plan.

Chances rule men and not men chances.

Herodotus

When a person with the *wrong mind set* becomes instantly endowed with a huge sum of money, it's no surprise that they have difficulty dealing with the cash. Such a winner commonly goes through a major life-event tailspin lasting for several months or years while they try to figure out what to do. Thankfully, you can let your thinking evolve much more clearly and effectively, if you prepare for winning in advance. Here's how:

Moving from *Chance* Thinking to *Chase* Thinking

Chance thinking (believing in an absence of assignable *design*), leads to a life without a plan or purpose. Such a thinker believes in pure fate, inescapable destiny, and will typically take uncalculated risks. Life becomes merely a mindless gamble.

Chance is the fool's name for fate.

Fred Astaire

When you invest in your *Personal Growth*, you dare to change from such *chance thinking* to *chase thinking*. You realize that there *can* be an assignable *design* to life and it's called your *plan*. Events do not have to occur haphazardly or just happen to you. You can pro-actively *chase* or *pursue* outcomes. You can effectively plan to make desired results occur repeatedly and so succeed.

Moving from *Probability* Thinking to *Possibility* Thinking

Similarly, *probability thinking* (believing in the absence of an assignable *cause*) leads to a life without effective action. That is, a probability thinker's time is wasted on random activities that are not actively directed toward a specific outcome. Such a thinker believes that life is a blind roll-of-the-dice, that outcomes are a matter of pure luck, that events just happen capriciously. For such a person, life becomes a series of accidental occurrences—some good, some bad. A probability thinker believes that effort does not effect outcome, that history solely determines a future that cannot be altered by one's action today.

> *Destiny: a tyrant's authority for crime, and a fool's excuse for failure.*
> Ambrose Bierce

When you invest in *Personal Growth*, you dare to change from such *probability thinking* to *possibility thinking*. You realize that there *can* be an assignable *cause* in life and it's called *taking action*. With *possibility thinking* anything becomes feasible. Any outcome that you can imagine, you can realize by putting forth the effort to make it happen.

Possibility thinkers look to opportunity, not history, to determine the future.

Whatever the mind of man can conceive and believe, it can achieve.

Napoleon Hill

Moving from a *Scarcity* Mentality to an *Abundance* Mentality

The problem with both *chance thinking* and *probability thinking* is that such thinking produces a *scarcity mentality*. And, if you would believe the dominant media's doom-and-gloom reporting, the world *is* running on empty. Every creature is endangered or in danger of becoming endangered. Every resource is scarce or becoming scarce. Every population is polluted or becoming polluted, ad infinitum, ad nauseam.

Some may even try to tell you that the American Dream itself of life, liberty and the pursuit of happiness is dead. But don't you believe them. The truth is that life itself prospers, that the earth is remarkably regenerative, and that prosperity is yet abundant.

The ultimate proof of this abundance is beyond the scope of this book, but not beyond common observation. Remember this abundance the next time you see a single blade of grass growing through concrete. Life is abundant and will not be denied. For scientific proof, the facts of world abundance are well documented in *The Ultimate Resource* by Julian L. Simon (Princeton University Press). We need to care for the Earth, of course, because it is our life support system. The worst we can do is to stupidly destroy our own ability to live here, but we cannot permanently destroy the Earth or eternally deplete its abundance.

Embrace *chase thinking* and *possibility thinking* and you develop an *abundance mentality*. Then, an amazing phenomenon occurs: An abundance consciousness attracts prosperity. This magnetic effect is the positive power of the self-fulfilling prophecy. And since you presumably control your own thoughts, you can influence your future reality and the prosperity that awaits you by what you allow yourself to think today.

You have, then, two basic ways of viewing and living life:

❑   you can accept a lower quality of life in the finest *scarcity mentality* fashion, believing that there is little point left in pursuing much else, because doing so is futile, so why bother anyway or

❑   you can improve the quality of life with a magnetic *abundance mentality*, knowing that whatever positive reality you choose to pursue, you can experience and that the pursuit will yield the by-product of prosperity for you and those around you.

All successful people share the latter view. If you want to be successful—with money or anything else—then start thinking as successful people do.

Whether you believe you can do a thing or you believe you can't, you are right.
                                             Henry Ford

Self-Talk

The key to developing the *right mind set* is to make a conscious decision about the kind of *self-talk* that you will allow yourself to have inside your mind's ear. The losing lottery winners lost *after* they won their jackpots, because they were already lost *before* they won their jackpots. Winning only accelerated their losing. Most of them learned from their loss, but their education cost them their jackpots and, in some cases, their families and even their freedom.

One divorced winner of $900,000 in the *Massachusetts Lottery* was arrested and imprisoned for failure to pay child support. He was six weeks behind in his $100 per week payment. His ex-wife eventually received 50% of his winnings. He lost his family, half of his $900,000 jackpot, and went to prison all over $600.

Another winner of $1,000,000 in the *New York Lottery* went to jail for stealing $6,000 within 2 years of winning. He had agreed to help manage a convenience store owned by his sister and her husband. He, instead, regularly helped himself to the store's cash register. What were these two winners telling themselves?

> *If you keep saying things are going to be bad, you have a good chance of being a prophet.*
> Isaac Singer

These and other losing winners never literally pronounced: "I live by *chance thinking* and *probability thinking* that creates a *scarcity mentality*"—but their actions said so. They would pervert their prosperity, abolish their abundance, and squelch their wealth, because their *self-talk* told them: "I am not really worthy of this success. I need to get back to where I belong, where I was before I won, what I believe I deserve which is not much." Success was not congruent with their self-image, so they had to revert to their belief of failure to stay aligned with their inner image of themselves. The self-fulfilling prophecy cuts both ways. In an odd twist of logic, their survival demanded their failure.

> *As you dream, so shall you become.*
>
> James Allen

What's important for you to understand is that the *right mind set*, the right attitude, the right mentality is a vital key to your getting your jackpot—with or without the lottery—and to keeping your jackpot after you get it. Remember, there are no wealthy, self-made pessimists. Optimism and prosperity must co-exist.

Self-Talk Test

To learn what kind of self-talk you have, take the Self-Talk Test (see Table 4–2):

1. First, start listening for and to your self-talk.

2. Then freeze-frame a bit of interesting inner dialogue, and see how your internal chatter scores on the Achievement Scale (AS).

The Achievement Scale represents how close you are to getting something done. If you score 100% on the Achievement Scale, then you have achieved the goal in question. If you score 0%, then you have achieved nothing, which—however, seemingly inadvertent—was your inner-stated goal.

TABLE 4–2: SELF-TALK TEST

SELF-TALK TEST		
AS*	SELF-TALK [inner *belief*] [cause]	RESULT [outward *behavior*] [effect]
100%	"I have."	Success ☺
90%	"I will."	Commitment
80%	"I can."	Confidence
70%	"I think I can."	Belief
60%	"I might."	Expectation
50%	"I think I might."	Possibility
40%	"I could think about it."	Indifference ☺
30%	"I wish I could."	Disappointment
20%	"I don't know how."	Frustration
10%	"I can't."	Futility
0%	"I won't."	Failure ☹
*AS = Achievement Scale		

Shallow men believe in luck; wise and strong men in cause and effect.

Ralph Waldo Emerson

The test also shows the results of various forms of self-talk. Your self-talk represents your inner *belief,* the cause that produces the effect manifested by your outward *behavior.* Thinking like the person that you want to become will help you align your *behavior* with your *belief.* Remember, your self-talk—your daily thought—is what makes you live the life you live. Note that with *possibility thinking* ("I think I might"), you are already half way to achieving your goal (50% on the Achievement Scale).

> *No one can make you feel inferior without your consent.*
>
>   Eleanor Roosevelt

Prosperity Insurance

To insure that you get and stay in the *right mind set* follow this rule-of-thumb:

> **Invest at least $2 plus your time into**
> ***Personal Growth***
> **for every $1 you chance on the lottery.**

Commit to this rule and remember it every time you bet a buck on the lottery. By betting heavily on you and lightly on the lottery, you follow a basic tenet of bet management in professional gambling:

❑   Bet lower amounts on hands where you have a better than even chance of losing (like in the lottery); and

❑   Bet higher amounts on hands where you have a better than even chance of winning (like on you).

You can always lose the $1 in the lottery, but you can never lose the $2 plus the time you invest in *Personal Growth*. With each dollar you spend on the lottery, you receive the one-time, either-or, luck-of-the-draw chance to win or lose—and then it's over. With every moment you spend developing your *Personal Growth*, you become that much closer to realizing your goals and assuring prosperity. An investment in *Personal Growth* is cumulative and always pays off. Bet heavily on you.

Step 2: Guiding Principles

A *Guiding Principle* is a universal truth expressed as a directive or a way of being. When you define a *Guiding Principle*, you are essentially admitting to yourself what you believe—what you know in your heart—is true and how you should act based on this belief. A *Guiding Principle* unifies *behavior* with *belief*.

For example, let's take the principle of *learning*. Expressed as a *Guiding Principle*, here is *learning*:

Learning
Systematically acquire and apply the information that improves your performance. Learn by reading, by doing, and by being open to new and improved ideas.

Here, the *belief* is that learning "improves your performance" and the *behavior* is to "systematically acquire and apply information...by reading, by doing, and by being open to new and improved ideas". To help you better understand how to express *Guiding Principles*, here are some more examples:

Generosity
Share your prosperity with others—not to encourage their permanent dependency, but to facilitate their eventual self-sufficiency.

Action
Finish what needs to be done now. Prove your commitment and evaporate procrastination by taking action now.

Success
Succeed by unifying your thought and deed, truth and performance. Strive to align your outward behavior with your inner belief.

Belief
Do what you believe and believe what you do. Believe what your conscience tells you is true.

Productivity
Invest your time only in productive, profitable, and positive deeds of belief.

Go through the exercise, the experience of writing out your *Guiding Principles*. The purpose of admitting to yourself in writing what you say you believe is to allow yourself to begin to live your beliefs, your values. Your goal is to align the things you do (your outward *behavior*) with the things that you say you believe (your inner *belief*).

By developing your own such *Guiding Principles*, you pre-determine what to do before reaching a decision point in your life. When faced with having to make a choice, you will know, almost instinctively, which path is best to take. The result is a oneness, a centeredness with oneself that is amazingly stress-free, liberating, and empowering.

Don't part company with your ideals. They are anchors in a storm.

Arnold Glasgow

For example, if you accept the above *Guiding Principles* of learning and productivity, you can easily decline the offer to go bar-hopping when you have the simultaneous opportunity to go learn about business financing techniques at a seminar. The seminar may well be drier than the bar, but you may learn new information in the class that better enables you to open the restaurant that you want to own one day. You may even make new friends at the meeting in a much more inviting atmosphere than a smoke-filled bar. After the seminar, reward yourself for following your *Guiding Principles* by inviting your new friends out for a late bite to eat and to continue the dialogue.

By having *Guiding Principles*, the correct decisions (for you) will be clear and you will make them quickly and with conviction. These unifying *Guiding Principles* become the foundation upon which you build your *Affirmations* and the goal-achieving actions of your *Life Plan: Statement of Goals*. Armed with your *Guiding Principles*, you know exactly how "to be" because these fundamental truths erase the conflict of self-doubt and opposing peer influence.

> *Chase after truth like hell and you'll free yourself,*
> *even though you never touch its coat-tails.*
>   Clarence Darrow

You can have and should write-out your *Guiding Principles* in at least these areas of your life:

Spiritual
God; inspiration; regeneration, etc.

Moral
Responsibility, respect, integrity, etc.

Sympathetic
Friendship, love, courtesy, etc.

Personal
Self-sufficiency, self-esteem, fun, etc.

Intersocial
Freedom, security, prosperity, etc.

Individual Will
Perseverance, health, effectiveness, etc.

Idea Communication
Honesty, enthusiasm, clarity, etc.

Idea Formation
Curiosity, possibility, creativity, etc.

Causation
Productivity, energy, performance, etc.

Time
Punctuality, timeliness, best use of, etc.

Order
Harmony, congruity, continuity, etc.

Quantity
Abundance, equality, resources, etc.

How do you write your *Guiding Principles*? Ask yourself:

❑ "What is the truth about each of these principles?" —this is your inner *belief*; and

❑ "How will I manifest this truth in my life?" —this is your outward *behavior*.

For a more detailed explanation of the *Guiding Principles of Life* plus a complete listing and written expression of each *Principle*, see the *Self-Centering Manual: How to Align Your Outward Behavior with Your Inner Belief.* This manual also contains an *Alignment Workshop* with exercises to help you discover where you are now relative to the congruity of your behavior with your belief. Refer to *Appendix A: Personal Growth Resources* for more specific information.

Remember, the more centered and grounded you are or become, the less likely it is for someone to come along and shrewdly separate you from your life's jackpot—money or otherwise. Your unified focus will allow your resistance to exceed the persuasion of those who would otherwise profit from your forsaking your plan. They will sense the clarity of your vision and the intensity of your conviction and seek easier prey.

> *If we don't stand for something, we will fall for anything.*
>
> Irene Dunne

Step 3: Affirmations

Out of the *right mind set* and your *Guiding Principles* flow your *Affirmations*. Always write your *Affirmations* as definitive statements drafted in the present tense (that is, in the *now*, as if already existing) and in the first person singular (that is, using the pronoun "I").

For example, an *Affirmation* about *enthusiasm* might be:

Enthusiasm

I start each day with enthusiasm that excites and intensifies my energy and energy that excites and intensifies my enthusiasm.

Note that the tense is the present tense ("start...excites... intensifies") and that the person is the first person singular ("I"). To help you better understand how to express *Affirmations*, here are some other examples:

I keep my commitments and live my beliefs.

I am punctual and prepared to perform.

I am a thoroughly self-sufficient, self-reliant, and responsible individual.

I have vibrant health and am in fantastic physical shape.

I eagerly strive for meaningful self-improvement in all that I do.

I always finish what needs to be done and I finish it now.

I enjoy touring different parts of the warm world regularly.

I feel financially thrilled to be easily able to pay-off my debts with plenty of funds to spare.

As you can see from the above examples, *Affirmations* can be *personal* (about punctuality, self-improvement, etc.) or they can be *material* (about travel, finances, etc.). Such *Affirmations* should also be motivating to you.

To write your *Affirmations*, ask yourself:

❑   "How would I be if I already was the way I would like to be?"—these are your *personal Affirmations;* and

❑   "What would I have if I already had what I would like to have?" —these are your *material Affirmations*.

You can't have everything. Where would you put it?

Steven Wright

The power of *Affirmations* comes from habitual repetition. After writing your *Affirmations*, here's how to make them a good habit:

1.   Beginning on the first day of the month, read and recite your *Affirmations* 3 times daily: once upon arising, once at 12 Noon or before you eat your lunch, and again upon retiring. If possible, also make audio recordings of your *Affirmations* and play them in your car, etc., in addition to your 3 daily recitals.

2.   Repeat the process religiously for 21 consecutive days (there are learning theory reasons for the 21-day repetitive period).

3.   For days 22–26 of the month, take a break and do not read, recite or listen to your *Affirmations*.

4. For the remaining 4–5 days of the month, re-visit your *Guiding Principles* and then revise and refine your *Affirmations*, as you find necessary.

5. Repeat the entire process every month for 3 consecutive months.

After 3 months, the recitations of your *Affirmations* should become habitual. You should catch yourself inadvertently mentally repeating your *Affirmations* in between recitals—which is exactly what you want to have happen. What is occurring is the replacement of all the negative inner self-talk and outside negativity with positive reinforcement of who and what you truly want to be, based upon the fundamental, universal truths of your *Guiding Principles* and the empowering optimism of the *right mind set.*

A man is what he thinks about all day.
James Allen

If you think that this project is too much like work, think again. This drill is your psychological survival training. Face it: humans have self-talk, that inner dialogue we all experience. So, if *you* don't script your own self-talk dialogue, then you are allowing the rest of the world to program your mind for you.

What kind of self-talk will you have then? Will you let the negativity of the news media, dysfunctional family members, twisted peer group people or others arbitrarily write your mind's script and turn you into an apathetic, pessimistic, apprehensive, unmotivated, self-doubting victim with a scarcity mentality? Or will you be pro-active, positive, and deliberate and decide for yourself what kind of mind you will have and person you will be?

If you commit to making this affirmation process a habit, you will become the person you so desire and make the following affirmation simply seem like an understated matter of obvious fact:

> *I am one of the best of the best and I am truly capable of significant accomplishments and meaningful contributions. Every day I am reborn with another opportunity for greatness.*

For more information on *Affirmations*, see the *Self-Centering Manual: How to Align Your Outward Behavior with Your Inner Belief* referenced in *Appendix A: Personal Growth Resources*.

It is a psychological law that we tend to get what we expect.

Dr. Norman Vincent Peale

Step 4: Life Plan: Statement of Goals

The next step up the *Ladder of Success* is the creation of your *Life Plan: Statement of Goals*. Writing and committing to such a plan is impossible without the *right mind set*, which is why your attitude is so important and why *Mind Set* is the very first step on the *Ladder of Success*. Only with *chase thinking, possibility thinking,* and an *abundance mentality* can you successfully design and consistently sustain the pursuit of a winning plan. Your plan should clearly state and define your goals as governed and directed by your *Guiding Principles* and empowered by your *Affirmations*.

How do you have a winning plan? You win, in part, by having a contingency plan against losing. In football and military parlance, the precept is: "The best offense is a good defense". I would extend this maxim to include that the very best offense is both a good defense *and* a good offense.

In other words, plan your life and your success *as if* you will never win the lottery (chances are 18 million-to-one that you will lose the 6/51 *lotto* every time). Also, plan what you would do if you *do* win the lottery. Then, whether you win or lose the lottery, you win in life. If you follow the *Infinite Financial Freedom* ideas in this book, then you will find that these two plans are principally alike. The main difference between them is time.

Do not take this planning process lightly. Your planning effort will make the difference between simply *making a living* and *fashioning a life*. If you are already winning in life and then you hit the lottery jackpot, the new money will merely enhance your already winning life—not change it. Winning the lottery, alone, never guarantees you a winning life. But *you* can guarantee to win in life, if you plan on it.

> *The first great key to success begins with you, a piece of paper, and a pencil.*
>
> Keith DeGreen

Three Phases in Fashioning Your Life Plan

Your *Life Plan* is a compilation of your *Goal Statements* that you prioritize in order of importance to you. You can have goals that fit into at least these 10 basic Goal Categories (listed alphabetically):

1. Artistic	6. Intellectual
2. Career	7. Lifestyle
3. Environmental	8. Physical
4. Family	9. Social
5. Financial	10. Spiritual

You use these categories to fashion your *Life Plan: Statement of Goals* through three fundamental phases of making, prioritizing, and realizing your goals. So, grab a pencil, plenty of scratch paper, and let's get started.

Phase 1: Make Wishlists

Using the Goal Categories above as stimuli, play the ultimate "What-If" game:

1. Make a *Wishlist* sheet for each Goal Category by penciling-in the name of the Goal Category as a heading on the top of a blank piece of paper. Use one piece of paper for each Goal Category.

2. Set a timer for 20 minutes (good time-is-money-is-time training).

3. And pretend:

    ❑   You are free to pursue any wish you want (*chase thinking*);

    ❑   Everything and anything is achievable (*possibility thinking*);

    ❑   Money, time, talent, genius, education, and every other needed resource is plentiful (an *abundance mentality*).

An example of a wish for the Financial Goal Category *Wishlist* might be as broadly stated as: "I would like to be financially free". A wish for the Physical Goal Category *Wishlist* might be: "I'd like to lose 10 pounds". Don't worry about how you are going to make these things happen in this phase. Assume that you can and will. *Phase 1* is the general, big-picture "What" part of your goals. In *Phase 3*, we will bring into focus the details of the "How-to" of each goal.

Imagination is more important than knowledge.
Albert Einstein

So, stretch your thinking. You truly have all the universe about which to dream. Write down these wishes for each Goal Category in any order and, at least, in outline form—but write them down. Again, don't worry about how to make them happen. Just do some wishstorming. And have fun. When the timer signals to stop, stop.

Phase 2: Prioritize Your Wishes

Next, prioritize your wishes in the order of importance to *you*. You prioritize your *Wishlist* by comparing each wish to each of the others using this self-questioning Prioritizing Screen:

Do or Die
"Which one do I want to absolutely make sure that I do before I die?"

Pay-off
"Which one gives me the greatest pay-off (in satisfaction, dollars, self-esteem, etc.)?"

Pain Avoidance
"Which one will cause me the most pain by my *not* doing it?"

For the purposes of illustration, let's say that you have 5 wishes: A, B, C, D, E. See Table 4–3 and the explanation below for the mechanics of how to use this screening process to prioritize.

TABLE 4–3: PRIORITIZING GUIDE

A or B	A or C	A or D	A or E
	B or C	B or D	B or E
		C or D	C or E
			D or E

1. Compare Wish A to B, C, D, and E. Circle the more important of each pair.

2. Compare Wish B to C, D, and E. Circle the more important of each pair.

3. Compare Wish C to D and E. Circle the more important of each pair.

4. Compare Wish D to E. Circle the more important of the pair. By following the above process, you will have compared each wish individually to every other wish in every possible combination.

5. Count the number of times that you circled each wish.
    The wish that you circled the greatest number of times is
    your #1 wish. The wish that you circled the second
    greatest number of times is your #2 wish, and so on.

Use the same process to prioritize any number of wishes
that you may have. Always compare each pair of competing
wishes using the three prioritizing questions given above.
You can also re-use these questions as tie-breakers for those
wishes that score equally on the first round.

By so prioritizing, you will always be doing what you say
you prefer. Instead of the license plate frame of your life
stating that you'd rather be doing something else, the message
becomes: "I am already doing what I'd rather."

---

*Nothing is really work unless you would rather be
doing something else.*
                                              Sir James Barrie

---

Phase 3: Make Your Wishes Come True

To make your wishes come true, you must turn your abstract
wishes into concrete *goals*. Constructing a *Goal Statement* for
each wish transforms your wish from a vague intention into a
definite goal. This transformation from intention to goal occurs
when you give MASS to each intangible wish. To make each
wish come true, make each wish *M*easurable, *A*ction-packed,
*S*pecific, and *S*tretchingly realistic ("MASS"). So, goals must be:

Measurable
You must be able to quantify your goal in
amount, duration, size, etc., so that you will

know by how much and when you achieve your goal.

Action-packed
Your *Goal Statement* must delineate the HOW of achieving your goal. You must determine which actions you must take and in what order to assure that you achieve the goal. Each goal will dictate the level of specificity necessary for step-by-step success. These steps become the *Action Plan* and the basis for your *Daily Outcomes* (discussed below).

Specific
Your *Goal Statement* must specify the WHO-WHAT-WHEN-WHERE-WHY of the goal. The more details that you can provide, the clearer the picture of realization you can have. These specifics help you to visualize your goal with clarity and better enable you to know the outcome for which you are striving.

Stretchingly realistic
Goals should be attainable—"do-able" by anyone within the realm of possibilities and imagination, even if not yet achieved by you.

All our dreams can come true—if we have the courage to pursue them.
                                          Walt Disney

Here is a daydream (an example of what a goal is not):

"We'd sure like to go to Bermuda someday."

To transmute this wishful thought from the abstract world into the material world of a goal, you give it MASS. Here's the same wish transmuted into a goal, incarnate:

> "To reward ourselves for building our *Ladder of Success* and *Financial Game Plan*, we are taking a Bermuda vacation from June 1–14, 2001. On June 1, we're flying to the city of Hamilton, Bermuda aboard Triangle Airlines, Flight #13 departing from Gate #86 out of Los Angeles International Airport at 12:01 p.m. Our seat assignments are 32A and 32B. We will be staying at the Noughtelonjieux Hotel in Room #2B with a southerly ocean view. We are flying coach class and estimate the total trip to cost $2,749.93. We will save money for this trip by following our *Action Plan*."

You know that this wish is now a goal, because this ethereal daydream now has MASS. It is:

Measurable
You have clearly quantified the duration, cost, and other measurable targets of the trip. You have also given the goal a distinct deadline by which you can measure its completion.

Action-packed
You have developed an *Action Plan* for saving enough money for the trip. Your *Action Plan* would detail the HOW of affording the trip: How much money you must save, for how long, at what rate of return, etc. (more on this subject later).

Specific

You have specified all the details of your trip, including WHO (we), WHAT (a Bermuda vacation), WHEN (06/01/01-06/14/01), WHERE (Hamilton's Noughtelonjieux Hotel), and WHY (as a reward).

Stretchingly realistic

Anyone can go to Bermuda. People go every day. Although *you* may have never afforded such a vacation before, you know that you can save enough money to go. This Bermuda vacation may cost, for example, 30% more than any other vacation you have ever taken. However, you were able to save enough money to go on prior trips, so you can realistically stretch to afford this trip, too.

If you don't know where you are going, you will probably wind up somewhere else.

Laurence J. Peter

By the way, I do recommend that you work such a reward goal into your plan exactly as compensation for all the soul-searching you do in building your *Ladder of Success* here and your *Financial Game Plan* in *Chapter 6: What To Do After You Win*. That reward, of course, may take many forms and does not have to include a trip anywhere. Just make the bounty big enough to keep you continuously motivated. The true treasure, of course, is found in the *fashioning of your life*. Since you may not fully realize the value and the power of your planning until after you go through the process and begin to watch your new life evolve, give yourself a goodie to keep you going.

Step 5: Daily Outcomes

When giving the goals of your *Life Plan* MASS, you had to make sure that they were *Action-packed*. That is, you had to develop a logical plan of action that would lead to the achievement of each goal. You can develop this HOW portion of each goal by reducing the challenging outcome to the ridiculously easy to do. Here's how:

Brainstorm
Brainstorm all the imaginable actions leading to your goal's achievement. In any order, list both obstacles and opportunities.

Prioritize
Prioritize the actions into a logical sequence. For example, you would naturally want to select a specific destination city for your reward vacation before checking on airfares, flights, et cetera. Often, by working backwards from the outcome, the best way to order the activities becomes clear.

Divide and Conquer
Divide and conquer these principle actions into logical, manageable sub-actions. You want to develop small, quickly achievable "mini-missions", each requiring very little effort. For example, a principle action may be to review travel books describing your vacation destination. The "mini-mission" could be to schedule a research trip to the library or book store. Or you could split these actions into two separate "mini-missions" and go to each place on separate occasions.

Organize

Organize the activities for each goal in writing to coordinate your actions and track your progress. See Chart 4–2 for an example of a blank *Action Plan* form that you would complete for each goal.

CHART 4–2: ACTION PLAN FORM

ACTION PLAN					
GOAL:			PREPARED ON:		
DAILY OUTCOMES: LISTED BY PRIORITY	GIVEN TO	DATE GIVEN	START DATE	DUE DATE	DONE DATE
☐					
☐					
☐					
☐					
☐					
☐					
☐					
☐					
☐					
☐					
☐					
☐					

Each *Action Plan* form lists the prioritized *Daily Outcomes* that you must produce to achieve your stated goal. You can use this form as your master to-do list for each goal or incorporate each action from the form into your calendar or other daily to-do list—wherever your goals are highly visible.

> *There comes a moment when you have to stop revving up the car and shove it into gear.*
> David Mahoney

Focus on the *outcomes*, the results, of each action more than the process. The means must always be moral, ethical, and legal (to be congruent with your *Guiding Principles*), but the process does not necessarily have to be pretty—it has to be effective. The deeds have to get done. In other words, you can scribble instead of type, as long as you can still read what you wrote well enough to accomplish the tasks.

Wish Reluctance

If you find that you are reluctant to construct a *Goal Statement* and devise an *Action Plan* for a particular wish, then your unwillingness is valuable to you—it does not mean you are lazy. Your reluctance is telling you that your wish is not really very important to you. Maybe you are doing just a little bit of wishful thinking. To achieve your true goals, you must follow all the way through to purposeful doing. For more information on developing a *Life Plan*, see *Life Plan: A Goal Setting Workbook* listed in *Appendix A: Personal Growth Resources*.

> *When a man has not a good reason for doing a thing, he has one good reason for letting it alone.*
> Walter Scott

Simple vs. Easy

If you follow these *Ladder of Success* techniques, you will find over time, that your past is happily littered with wishes comes true and your future is abundant with promises of wishes to be fulfilled. You now have the proven tools for successfully experiencing all those things in life that you feel make your life worth living—this is the *simple* part. However the process is not easy or free, but it *is* worthwhile.

Life demands that you put so much into life to get so much out of life. To get what you want, here is the firm, unnegotiable price you must be willing to pay:

> You must—and only *you* can do this—add that one essential ingredient—that only *you* can add—that will transform your wishes into your reality:

Focused Effort.

Effort is your investment in *Personal Growth*. Effort focused on outcomes produces results. Not even winning the lottery can give you this effort or free you from the necessity of expending your effort. Rather, winning the lottery forces you to redirect your effort into the areas of building and preserving your new-found wealth.

So, if you pour your effort into life, all that you can imagine, you can realize—but only to the extent of the congruity of your inner *belief* with your outward *behavior*. Let your outward actions demonstrate your inner commitment. And always focus on results. Remember this undeniable truth:

People may never believe what you *say*, but they can never deny what you *do*—and neither can you.

Words without actions are the assassins of idealism.

Herbert Hoover

So, positive thinking (having the *right mind set*) by itself is not quite enough. You must move from positive *thinking* all the way up the *Ladder of Success* to positive *doing* (the focused effort of your *Daily Outcomes*). However, as you continue in your pursuit of happiness, you are bound to produce unexpected or undesired outcomes along the way. These are not failures. These are just different results, different outcomes. Learn from each.

Neither fear obstacles—embrace them. Problems are merely disguised solutions—unravel them. There's an old saying that you can find all the people without any problems all in one place: the cemetery. Let problems be invigorating.

In those occasional moments when all this focused effort seems too demanding for you to continue, ask yourself how you would rather be announced at the gates of Heaven:

Attempted great deeds.
Sometimes failed.
Sometimes succeeded.

or

Attempted absolutely nothing.
Succeeded completely.

Attempt great deeds, produce outcomes, and adjust your course accordingly on route to your ultimate success.

> *What would you attempt to do if you knew you could not fail?*
>
> Dr. Robert Schuller

Investment #2: What You Do Best and Enjoy Most

The second critical investment you need to make before winning the lottery is an investment in *What You Do Best and Enjoy Most*. This activity is your true purpose in life because you can perform the feat most effortlessly and with the most pleasure. This ease and joy enables you to succeed more easily, attract greater prosperity, and to give more abundantly.

> *More will be accomplished, and better, and with more ease, if every man does what he is best fitted to do, and nothing else.*
>
> Plato

What is your purpose in life? Follow your passion, your bliss, your heart's desire—something that you enjoy doing and that you can do best of all the things of which you are capable. By so doing, you will make the world at least a little bit better for your having been here. This activity—as long as it's moral, ethical, and legal (remember your *Guiding Principles*)—will also give you a tremendous return on the investment of your life's time: a boundless sense of self-worth.

Frankly, you do not have to wait to win the lottery—and it's better if you don't wait—to find and do this key activity. Ask yourself if you would truly continue tomorrow in your present work (not necessarily present job, but *type* of work) if you won your jackpot today. If the answer is "No!", then begin being honest with yourself and your heart's desire.

The purpose of life is a life of purpose.
Robert Byrne

If you have not yet won your jackpot, you may not—and probably will not—be able to just quit your job today and start your heart's desire tomorrow. However, you can continue in your current job, give-up one TV show (or other low-return activity) and spend 15 focused minutes a day on your heart's desire for one month beginning today. Think of these 15 minutes as part of your preparation for winning your jackpot. Stretch these 15 minutes to 30 minutes in month #2. Stretch the 30 minutes to 1 hour in month #3.

In this way, if you win the jackpot, then you already have a head start on making the transition to doing what you really want to do. And if you never win the jackpot, you still have a head start on making the transition to doing what you really want to do. So, whether or not you win the lottery, you will be pro-actively living the life you have fashioned and you, the people around you, and the world will be better-off for your having been here.

Other winners have lost large amounts of money and time by trying to make their transition while simultaneously being catapulted through the changes that automatically come with winning the lottery jackpot. You have an advantage: the opportunity to get a running start on your heart's desire now, so that you can hit the ground running to your true happiness, when the jackpot hits—and even if it never does.

Besides, winners often feel empty and lost and don't know what to do with themselves after they win, quit their jobs, and have hollow days to fill. Design your *Game Plan* in advance, so that you will have direction in your life after you win. Even if you never win the money, you still have something more valuable than the jackpot has been able to provide for any winner: *direction* to following your passion in the life that you have fashioned.

> *There is only one success—to be able to spend your life in your own way.*
> Christopher Morley

Financial Growth

Once you are on the path of *Personal Growth* and doing *What You Do Best and Enjoy Most*, you can begin to apply your evolving skills to anything you want to see grow—money, for example. Once you are on the path to *Infinite Financial Freedom*, you have effectively already won your jackpot (or anything else for that matter). The question now becomes not *if* you will win your jackpot, but *when* you will win your jackpot.

As we discussed earlier, winning by winning the lottery collapses time frames and enables you to win your jackpot sooner than by winning through *Personal Growth* alone. But only by developing your *Personal Growth* will you know what to do with any amount of money that you may amass. You can assure that you will win and keep your jackpot by first becoming a winner yourself. Once you are a winner, you can turn whatever you choose into a winning outcome—and this ability is *truly* winning. Remember, if you win your jackpot from the lottery and are not a winner personally, then you may just become a bigger potential loser: one who has more money to lose without knowing how to win. You win by being the best you can be at what you do best.

> *The roots of true achievement lie in the will to*
> *become the best that you can become.*
>
> Harold Taylor

In *Chapter 6: What To Do After You Win*, you will find the vital step that you must take to assure that you keep your winnings and keep them growing: Developing a *Financial Game Plan*. When you read the *Financial Game Plan Rulebook*, use numbers to reflect where you are today, financially, and where you want to go and grow. The principles presented in the *Rulebook* work with any amount of money. However, you will need to revise specific strategies based on whether you are in the Wealth Acquisition mode (*before* you win and seeking the *right* amount of money) or in the Wealth Preservation mode (*after* you win and keeping and growing the *right* amount of money).

Your Money Personality

Unlike any other aspect of human experience, there exists a special relationship between your personality and your use of money. How you think and feel about money (your inner *belief*) determines what you will do with money (your outward *behavior*). This unique interplay between your money belief and your money behavior is known as your Money Personality. Your Money Personality represents the convergence of *Personal Growth* with *Financial Growth*.

As mentioned earlier, Dr. Kathleen Gurney pioneered the Money Personality concept in the emerging field of Financial Psychology. After nearly 10 years of development, she has identified 9 distinct money personalities. Each personality type holds certain attitudes towards money and finances as manifested in the way each pursues financial goals and objectives. Knowing your Money Personality provides you with a short-cut method to developing the *Personal Growth* traits that help you achieve your goals effectively.

To help people determine their Money Personality, Dr. Gurney developed the *MoneyMax® Profile*. This profile is the product of extensive national research and testing on tens of thousands of individuals. This confidential profile begins with a self-administered one-page response questionnaire that measures your existing financial personality traits in 13 different areas. The results of your profile enable you to understand how you relate to money now and what you can do to improve the way you deal with money in the future.

I've never been poor, only broke. Being poor is a frame of mind. Being broke is only a temporary situation.

Mike Todd

If you are interested in receiving your own Dr. Gurney *MoneyMax® Profile* so that you can learn your Money Personality, complete and return a copy of the Questionnaire Request Form (Form 4–1 shown below) to Benefits Resource Group (follow the instructions on the form). You will then receive your confidential *MoneyMax® Profile* Questionnaire to complete and return for your personalized results. The process is enlightening *and* useful, because you learn your tendencies and can redirect your thinking, as necessary, for taking the most effective and profitable action.

FORM 4–1

DR. GURNEY'S *MONEYMAX®* PROFILE QUESTIONNAIRE REQUEST FORM

Please send my Dr. Gurney's *MoneyMax®* Profile Questionnaire to:

Name

Address

City   State   ZIP

Phone Number:

I understand that, after completing and returning my confidential questionnaire, I will receive my personalized Dr. Gurney *MoneyMax®* Profile that includes these 4 reports:
1. Trait Evaluation Report
2. Trait Description Report
3. Profile Overview Report
4. Money Action Plan Report

☐ For each *MoneyMax®* Profile, I have enclosed my $49.00 check with a completed copy of this form to:
Benefits Resource Group
P. O. Box 943, Malibu, CA 90265.

Please make your check(s) payable to:
"Benefits Resource Group"

Note: *MoneyMax®* Profile is a registered trademark of Kathleen Gurney, Ph.D. and Financial Psychology Corporation.

After returning your completed questionnaire, you will receive these Dr. Gurney reports:

Trait Evaluation Report
This Dr. Gurney summary report shows your individual score in 13 different areas of your personality. The report also portrays how your

score compares with national scores in each of the 13 personal financial traits surveyed. Dr. Gurney presents the information in both tabular and graphic formats.

Trait Description Report
This report is Dr. Gurney's narrative interpretation of your score in each of the 13 personality traits evaluated in the first report. Here, Dr. Gurney explains in words the results depicted in your Trait Evaluation Report.

Profile Overview Report
In this synopsis, Dr. Gurney provides a summary of the key distinguishing characteristics of the national profile group into which you currently fall. This report helps you to understand your distinct money management style and financial traits.

Money Action Plan Report
In this report, Dr. Gurney provides guidance for improving your money management skills and achieving financial congruity. Here, you will find the historical investment preferences of those with your personality style, so that you are better able to make investment choices (outward *behavior*) consistent with your Money Personality (inner *belief*).

Learning is Active Reading

Remember that the secret to financial success dwells up the path of *Personal Growth*. So, whatever your current financial figures are, take them with you up the path of

Personal Growth and they, too, will grow. One of the best methods of developing both *Personal Growth* and greater expertise in *What You Do Best and Enjoy Most* begins with reading—*active reading.*

Active reading is reading that you do to acquire information and knowledge that you can apply today. Do not confuse *active reading* with the reading that you may do purely for its passive or escapist entertainment value. *Active reading* is learning.

> *The great end of life is not knowledge, but action.*
> Thomas Huxley

Read the writings of others who are farther along the path than you are. Note that there will always be those in front of and behind each of us along the way, but do not compare yourself to them. Compare yourself only to your own relative position along your own path of personal development. And remember that different paths can reach the same mountain peak. For recommended *active reading* lists, see *Appendix A: Personal Growth Resources* and *Appendix B: Financial Growth Resources.*

> *All that mankind has done, thought, gained or been…is lying as in magic preservation in the pages of books.*
> Thomas Carlyle

Armed with the foundation of the *right mind set*, your *Guiding Principles*, *Affirmations*, *Life Plan: Statement of Goals*, and *Daily Outcomes*, you cannot lose—whether or not you ever hit the lottery jackpot. But, just in case you do "hit the big one", you don't want to fly into a major life-event tailspin. So, move on to *Chapter 5: What To Do When You Win* to find out exactly what to do and *not* to do if and when your big lottery jackpot day finally comes.

If only God would give me a clear sign! Like making a large deposit in my name at a Swiss bank.

Woody Allen

5

What To Do
When You Win

You've won! Now what? Based on other winners' miscues, here are the mechanics of exactly what to do *as* you are going through the winning process. Here, also, is what to expect as you are instantly elevated from having the *wrong* amount of money to having the *right* amount of money and how to insure that you ultimately receive from the lottery what you have apparently won.

Certain securities and protections are essential if you are to avoid the losses of other winners. Failing to heed these caveats are the 13 Big Mistakes lottery winners make. So, here's what to say, what not to say, where to go, where to tell your job to go, and how much money to blow.

1. Secure Your Winning Ticket.

Immediately upon learning that you have won, but before you get the money, secure your winning ticket. Most lotteries require that you sign the ticket to indicate ownership. In any case, photocopy both the front and back of the winning ticket and keep all the documents in a safe deposit box.

Decide *before* you win on a safe place where you will keep all your tickets or other lottery information and records. You do not want to be scrambling around your house searching for a safe place to stash your winning ticket *after* you win a big jackpot. Certain winners who picked a too-clever hiding place after they won temporarily forgot where they put their winning tickets. You will be under enough stress after you win without having to add this unnecessary pressure. Decide now where the winning ticket goes and then put it there.

2. Temper Your Enthusiasm.

Don't be overly-enthusiastic or elated. First of all, you don't know how many other winners will be splitting the jackpot with you. After sharing the prize, you may have won much less that you initially thought. Don't set yourself up for this disappointment. Stay cool. You will know all the details soon enough.

> *Remember that there is nothing stable in human affairs; therefore avoid undue elation in prosperity, or undue depression in adversity.*
>
> Socrates

Also, as you will see below, there are other reasons why your winning ticket may not be a winner at all. The fact that the numbers on your ticket match the numbers drawn is just the first step in determining if you have officially won the jackpot. There are other hurdles to clear before you can be sure that you will receive even a penny.

The best time to be enthusiastic is when the first lottery check clears your bank. Then, and only then, can you be reasonably sure that you have won. In the meantime, channel your excitement into determination of doing all that's necessary to guarantee that you will finally get your money.

3. Beware of Defective Tickets.

The possibility of having a defective ticket is another reason not to become overly-excited. Some apparent "winners" upon notifying the lottery of their good fortune are deeply disappointed to learn that they have a defective ticket. Lottery officials explain to them that the most such winners can receive in return for their defective lottery ticket is the return of their dollar or the option of another lottery ticket.

The courts have supported the lottery in cases that become litigated. What starts out as a celebration for the hopeful winner can turn into a bitter and costly legal experience. Instead of winning cash, you will only waste cash on legal fees and, of course, time. Don't pursue suing the lottery over a defective ticket. Lottery rules explicitly state in writing that the lottery is *not* responsible for defective tickets and that you agree to all the rules just by playing. Read the fine print. The judge will.

The plainest print cannot be read through a gold eagle.

Abraham Lincoln

4. Claim Your Prize Correctly.

As we saw in *Chapter 3: The Do's and Don'ts of Smart Lottery Play*, millions of jackpot dollars have gone unclaimed. For whatever reasons, unknown players holding winning tickets let the statute of limitations expire without ever notifying the lottery officials.

In addition, even if you notify the lottery within the specified number of days of the winning draw date, you have to do so properly. If you do not follow their rules specifically, you could invalidate your ability to collect your prize.

It is not enough merely to be holding a winning ticket. You must have your winning ticket "validated". Most states have detailed procedures for you to follow to validate your winning ticket. The validation process typically involves you, your ticket, the retailer who sold you the ticket, the winning draw date, a claim form, and sometimes a postmark. So, keep your wits about you as you take care of the business of finally collecting your jackpot prize—another reason not to be blinded by undue enthusiasm.

We can lick gravity, but sometimes the paperwork is overwhelming.

Wernher von Braun

Lottery officials do not impose these validation procedures to make your life miserable or to discourage players from collecting. However, since the dollars involved are sometimes so massive, officials must impose certain security measures to catch those who might try cheating the lottery. Lottery security procedures ultimately protect all players, winners, and the social programs that are funded by the games. So, be patient, but pay attention to the details, so that they can pay you your winnings.

5. Do Nothing!

OK—you followed all the rules and now you have the cash in hand. Now what? The first and foremost thing that you do with the money is: *Nothing!* Do absolutely nothing. From a spending and investment standpoint, sit still. Do nothing for at least 90 days. Why?

> *The only question with wealth is what you do with it.*
>
> John D. Rockefeller

If you are like most winners, you will probably not be accustomed to having a new, large sum of money all at once. So, give yourself some time to get comfortable with the cash. Giving yourself time allows you not to over-react to having the new amount of money. Over-reacting can turn the *right* amount of money into the *wrong* amount of money overnight—one trip to Las Vegas or Atlantic City can do the trick. One $1 Million dollar winner of the *Michigan Lottery* immediately started to play the commodities market about which he knew little and he quickly lost over $100,000. The commodities traders did quite well, however.

Then what do you do with the cash? Don't go to the track. If you cannot trust yourself to leave it alone, then lock-up the money in a 90-day CD (Certificate of Deposit) at a bank. If you *can* honestly trust yourself to not touch it for 90 days, then I prefer that you park the cash in a double tax-free money market mutual fund. Unlike the CD, earnings from the double tax-free money market mutual fund are free of both state and federal income taxes.

If you choose the CD, do not invest more than $100,000 at each bank. (Don't let the bigger numbers scare you; you'll get use to them—that's why you're doing nothing for 90 days.) New FDIC (Federal Deposit Insurance Corporation) regulations may not necessarily guarantee deposits in excess of $100,000 at any one institution. So, spread the risk over several banks, if you are lucky enough to receive a lump-sum over $100,000.

Cash and securities invested in mutual funds are generally insured up to $100,000 and $400,000 per account, respectively, but these guarantees can vary. Some mutual funds even buy additional protection to insure larger account balances. Always ask the fund about the guarantees, both through the SIPC (Securities Investor Protection Corporation) and the fund's own in-house supplemental insurance, if any. Since different guarantees can apply to cash and to securities, ask for clarification of the insured limits on each. As with banks, allocate your jackpot over as many funds or accounts as necessary to keep your balances within the insured limits.

> *When prosperity comes, do not use all of it.*
> Confucius

So what do you do while you do nothing? One of the main reasons for doing nothing, financially, for 90 days is that you will be very busy taking care of the housekeeping items outlined in the rest of this section. You do not want to have to deal with money decisions while you are going through this life-event transition. Even the most grounded of winners have said that they never want to have to go through another six months like those immediately following their winning the lottery jackpot.

6. Shut Up!

Again, I have to stress: Do not tell anyone that you have won anything. This recommended silence is not intended to encourage or guarantee selfishness—exactly just the opposite is true. Silence will help you to achieve your planned goals and, in the long run, do the most good for the most people. Remain quietly anonymous or you can bet on suffering the painful consequences of social and psychological isolation like many other winners.

Besides, you don't want to broadcast your investments now or in the future. People of different means should not necessarily invest in the same investment vehicles as you. You may be able to afford to sustain a loss or temporary downturn in an investment that could destroy others. You don't want the responsibility of inadvertently recommending unsuitable investments to others. Be deliberately vague regarding the use of your funds.

Any such public investment proclamation by you while you are in the limelight could cause enough of a buying or selling frenzy to ruin an otherwise viable investment. You, other investors, and those depending on the investment (such as a manufacturer's employees and their families) could all be hurt by such an announcement. So, be quiet. Be smart.

A fool uttereth all his mind.

Proverbs 29:11

Besides, you will be busy enough dodging reporters, curiosity-seekers, charities and others wondering what you are doing with your money. How do they find you? In most states, the list of winners is public information. Also, most lotteries have some fine print in their rules regarding your privacy like this fine example from the *California Lottery*:

"California Lottery winners agree to participate in publicity upon winning, and to the use of their name

and/or likeness for advertising and publicity purposes
thereafter without compensation."

Unfortunately, the larger your prize, the greater the notoriety
and publicity you can expect to receive—and the longer
"thereafter without compensation" will last. When badgered by
"jackpot chasers" demanding to know what you are doing with
your cash, tell them no more than that you are following the
principles outlined in *Infinite Financial Freedom*. The focus can
then shift off you and onto the book. If they continue to pry (and
they will), buy some time by telling them to read the book and
get back to you. By then, they shouldn't be able to find you very
easily, if you follow the other recommendations in the rest of
this chapter. After all, you should be too busy *doing* to be just
talking about doing.

> *Better to remain silent and be thought a fool than
> to speak out and remove all doubt.*
>
> Abraham Lincoln

7. Get an Unlisted Phone Number.

Get an unlisted phone number at once. Winners are
historically flooded with phone calls, especially in the early
months. You may even have to change your unlisted number
regularly after the number "slips out" (is rented) to the
commercial databases that market such information. Still, be
very judicious about releasing your phone number. Preserving
your privacy is a pre-requisite to enjoying your time.

Also, of course, buy an answering machine, a voice mail
board for your computer, call-screener services from the
phone company or hire an answering service. The hardware

represents a one-time higher cash outlay than the service providers who charge smaller, ongoing fees that ultimately cost more. Either way, you will still want to screen your calls, even though your number is supposedly "unlisted". Unlisted does not mean unknown.

I must cultivate privacy. It is very dissipating to be with people too much.

Henry David Thoreau

---

8. Get a Post Office Box.

Rent a Post Office Box right away. Other winners have been barraged with mounds of unsolicited mail. Countless people write to you with their "tales of woe". Suddenly, everybody wants you to be the savior of their unique cause. Like other winners, you will be inundated with heart-wrenching, tear-jerking, and donation-seeking letters. Ignore them all.

Know that you will do your best work by not squandering time and money on these unknown claims. There are too many *con artists* trying to get to your money for you to ever know which stories are the true ones. Don't be swayed by the endless pleas. Even though some such requests may be legitimate, you will do ultimately much more good by pre-planning your charitable giving and following your plan. See *Rule #15: Give Smart* in *Chapter 6: What To Do After You Win* for details on the best ways to give.

Like other winners, expect also to receive your share of:

❑ propositions for business schemes;

❑ media deals;

❑ requests to buy tickets for others (since you now possess some magical winning "touch");

❑ perverted religious messages ("give me your money or lose your soul for all eternity, etc."); and even

❑ marriage proposals (from all three sexes).

Again, ignore the tug of all these communications and firmly follow your plan.

> *There are three kicks in every dollar: one, when you make it...two, when you have it...third, when you give it away—and it is the biggest kick of all.*
> William A. White

Note that a U. S. Postal Service Post Office Box (at the Post Office) is less expensive than a commercial Post Office Box, but you often have to wait several months for a USPS Post Office Box to become available (depending on where you live). You can usually rent a commercial P. O. Box immediately. Also, a commercial Post Office Box *may* provide some greater degree of privacy, as most providers do not rent their customer lists to other marketers. Call a commercial P. O. Box provider and ask them if they rent their customer list for mail order projects. If they are willing to rent information about their box holders, then pick another P. O. Box provider.

If a USPS Post Office Box is not available immediately, then ask the Post Office to place you on their waiting list. In the meantime, rent a commercial Post Office Box from a privacy-sensitive provider—and get a big one!

Caution: If you ever move, do *not* file a change of address notice with the U. S. Postal Service. The USPS rents your change of address notice information to over 22 different computer database companies who in turn rent the data to any number of direct marketers, investigators, and whoever else is willing to pay for the information. Send personal change of address notices directly only to those people and companies that you want to keep posted of your whereabouts.

9. Buy a Security System.

Personal security is another sound reason for remaining quietly anonymous about winning. As bizarre as this may seem, several lottery winners have had their homes burglarized immediately upon just the announcement of their winning—even before receiving any cash or having had the time or inclination to buy "high price ticket" items. Part of the responsibility of winning the lottery jackpot today is protecting not merely your winnings, but also your family and your life.

> *The more things you have, the more things have you.*
> David E. Jensen

Your home security system should include, at least, these hardware protections:

❑   perimeter contacts on all doors;

❑   perimeter contacts on all windows;

❑   interior infrared motion detectors;

❑   motion-sensitive lighting; and

❑   an audible, on-site alarm.

Along with the above equipment, you should buy the 24-hour monitoring service, so that any breach also signals the security company's central station alarm. The security company, in turn, notifies the police of the security breach and requests a response. Also buy the drive-by armed guard service, even if you have to hire a separate company to provide it. Explain to the security company that you are a new lottery jackpot winner and that you want high-level armed guard visibility at your residence for the first 6-to-9 months. Be willing to pay for the extra vigilance of their security team.

Do not view these precautions as overkill. You are sending a signal to those who may be casing your home and family. Such criminals will naturally take the path of least resistance. If you make them realize how hard they will have to work to successfully hit you, then they will seek other victims with fewer and less sophisticated levels of security to overcome.

Who is to guard the guards themselves?
D. J. Juvenal

If you decide to arm yourself, a short-barrel shotgun is often the gun of choice for home protection purposes for these chief reasons:

1.   The sound of a shotgun being cocked is well-known to and feared by would-be intruders;

2.   Your aim does not have to be too accurate, especially if you use a scatter-load type of shell;

3.   The shorter barrel enables greater movement
     flexibility in hallways and other cramped quarters;

4.   The short range is less likely to put bullet holes into
     your neighbor's house or your neighbor.

Of course, you must comply with all gun registration and other laws in your locale regarding firearms. Use common sense precautions and, if you are unfamiliar with guns, take a firearms training course.

10. Buy a Kidnap & Ransom Insurance Policy

Don't laugh. Instead, quietly arrange for the purchase of a "Kidnap & Ransom" insurance policy. Annual premiums typically run between $800–$1,000 for a policy with a $1,000,000 limit. Such a policy provides the money to pay the ransom in a kidnapping, extortion or hostage case.

Make sure that you receive a "numbered" policy, that is, a policy without your name appearing on it anywhere. Then, do not tell anyone that you are buying or own such a policy. The knowledge of the existence of the insurance coverage can lead others to kidnap you or your loved ones, since the nappers would know that the policy could provide the ransom funds.

The agent who sold you your homeowner's policy may or may not be able to help you acquire this coverage, but start with him or her. If you can communicate directly with the underwriter at the insurance company without the agent involved, then do so. The fewer people—no matter how trustworthy—that know about the policy, the less likely the word of its existence will slip out to the untrustworthy. This coverage is extremely confidential and sensitive, so the agent should not mind stepping aside from the underwriting process out of respect for your privacy. Explain to the agent that he or she will still receive the commission, so the agent has nothing to lose by letting you work directly with the underwriter at the carrier.

One of the best insurance companies offering this type of coverage is the Chubb Group. They even provide security training for you and your family from their group of former FBI and CIA agents who manage Chubb's risk control program for this coverage. Once insured, if you are ever threatened, go to these experts before you go to the police. These security professionals will know when to involve the police, the FBI, and other authorities. Their primary goal in a kidnap case is to get your loved ones back home safely. Their secondary goal is to recover any ransom money they may have paid to the kidnappers. They will not jeopardize the first two goals just to catch the kidnappers. The FBI's priorities may be somewhat different.

> *Don't think there are no crocodiles because the water is calm.*
>
> Malayan Proverb

Although you may be thinking that buying such coverage is a paranoid extravagance, know that some lottery winners (who choose to remain anonymous) have suffered terribly from attempts at extortion and kidnapping. The "Kidnap & Ransom" insurance policy provides not only the money to fund such events, but also the more meaningful security expertise and guidance to prevent such crimes from occurring. When you are certain that you are truly receiving the money that you have apparently won, then quietly buy the policy and follow the advice of the insurance company's security specialists.

11. Quit Your Job!

If you work for others, immediately take a leave of absence. Expect not to return. If you already love what you do, then consider starting a consulting business. Know that you will not long be able to work as an employee for an owner, supervisor or manager who makes significantly less money than you do.

This job loss phenomenon occurs in lottery winner after lottery winner not because of the winner's attitude towards their employer and co-workers, but because of the employer's and co-workers' attitudes towards the winner. You won't have to quit your job. Your pre-jackpot job will, instead, quit you. Why?

Supervisors and fellow employees may try to make you feel guilty for taking or keeping your job or position from some other person perceived as more needy. Co-workers become jealous and resentful. Bosses assume that you will eventually quit anyway, so your promotion is unlikely and your responsibilities may become increasingly limited. Also, many "jackpot chasers" will phone you at work (especially since your home phone number is now unlisted) causing even further disruption of the workplace.

Work is a high human function...the most dignified thing in the life of man.
David Ben-Gurion

Quitting your *job* does not mean quitting your *work*. Read that sentence again twice. You should continue to work. Work has a special intrinsic value and helps to embellish your sense of self-worth.

"Work at what?" you ask. Finding the answer to this question is a process of self-discovery—a journey that the jackpot can help you accelerate. However, you should already be on this journey because you have done the smart preparation as recommended and explained in *Chapter 4: What To Do Before You Win*. So, expect a job change, whether or not such a change is your original intention. Your new "job" becomes working on you.

> *It is the first of all problems for a man to find out what kind of work he is to do in this universe.*
>
> Thomas Carlyle

12. Blow 10%!

That's right—blow it! Take up to 10% off-the-top of your first lottery check—and *only* the first lottery check—and blow it. Enjoy yourself.

Spend the money mindlessly. Light a $5.00 cigar with a $100 bill. Get the squandering out of your system. Be self-indulgent, even decadent. Break Waterford crystal champagne glasses in a fireplace. Watch *Brewster's Millions* (the movie).

> *Money, it turned out, was exactly like sex; you thought of nothing else if you didn't have it and thought of other things if you did.*
>
> James Balwin

Once you have the crass, indiscriminate consumption out of your system, then *plan* your future spending and investing of the subsequent jackpot checks. Mindless, conspicuous consumption will leave you as empty as sex without love—it may be fun for a night or two, but it will never satisfy your soul and sustain your feelings in the long run.

So, blow your 10%. Experience your momentary financial irresponsibility and decadence. Then, get back to achieving your *Infinite Financial Freedom.*

> *After the first million, it doesn't matter. You can only eat 3 meals a day—I tried eating four and I got sick.*
>
> Joseph Hirshhorn, multi-millionaire

13. Get Out of Town!

Take an *inexpensive, working* trip. This is not your reward vacation as discussed in *Chapter 4: What To Do Before You Win.* Leave town quietly. Notify only key people like the police, the Post Office, your home security company, and the like, that you will be gone. Even consider going to another country. Why?

> *The gratification of wealth is not found in mere possession or in lavish expenditure, but in its wise application.*
>
> Cervantes

You need the quiet and solitude for a very critical purpose: to plan. Do not confuse this trip with blowing 10% of your first lottery check—that was fun. This trip is work—very special work. You are planning your *Infinite Financial Freedom*.

Think of planning as writing. Don't be scared by the word "writing". This writing is not literary or grammatical writing—it's more important than that. Think of this writing as reducing your thoughts down onto paper. Your writing/planning can be simple scribble and in outline form. The point of this planning/writing is to help you organize your thoughts and game plan from this juncture forward.

> *Before everything else, getting ready is the secret of success.*
>
> Henry Ford

Map out the journey of your life as if you are the Head Coach of a multi-championship football team sketching on a game chalkboard the plays that you've designed to get you over the goal line and win. Remember from *Chapter 4: What To Do Before You Win* that you have moved from simply *making a living* to *fashioning a life*. Use this out-of-town working trip first to revise your *Life Plan: Statement of Goals* and *Daily Outcomes* in light of your winning the jackpot. Secondly, use this time to develop your new *Financial Game Plan* based on the *Rulebook* in *Chapter 6: What To Do After You Win*—next.

> *To acquire wealth is difficult, to preserve it more difficult, but to spend it wisely most difficult of all.*
>
> Edward Parsons Day

6

What To Do
After You Win

Finally, you've won. It happened. It's real. And you were ready for it. You heeded all the warnings and followed all the suggestions in Chapters 3, 4, and 5.

For now, your tempered thrill of the winning moment is over. You've blown your 10% and you're finally getting used to the idea of having the money. Now, you're ready for the next step. What do you do *after* you win and reality sets in?

The Secret to Keeping What You Win and Winning What You Keep.

After you win, how do you avoid losing it all as some other lottery winners have? Winning a big lottery jackpot is a single event (unless you're *extremely* lucky), but *keeping* the cash is a life-long, continuous challenge. With so many potential pitfalls, what happens if you mess-up and you inadvertently do something wrong or you fail to do something right? Won't winning just become yet another misfortune of life? Won't you end-up spending all your waking moments burdened with the fear of doing or not doing something that just junks your jackpot?

Unless you take *one very important step*, you may be continuously tormented by the fear of losing it all. This *one very important step* is the terminator of your torment and the secret of keeping what you win and winning what you keep. With this *one very important step* you can relax and enjoy your jackpot for life. This *one very important step* will assure your *Infinite Financial Freedom*. What is it?

You can call this *one very important step* by various names. But whatever you call it, *it* is your sure bet, financial ace in the hole. Without *it*, you will never win in the long run and you may as well fold, because the only way you stand a chance of ever doubling your money is by folding it in half. With *it*, you can never lose. *It* is very simple to understand, but not necessarily easy to get done. Why?

Because it *is* so simple, *it* is often overlooked, assumed or simply missed. People get sidetracked or overwhelmed by the over-abundance of investment choices. Too many choices lead to inaction through confusion or wrong action through desperation or greed. You must step back from *choices* and think about *principles*. Just as the *Guiding Principles* of your personal life provide you with pre-decision proficiency, so too do financial principles guide you in making the best investment judgments.

Order is the first requisite of liberty.

Hegel

So, the key to simplifying and guaranteeing your *Infinite Financial Freedom* is a pro-active, well conceived, proven plan for success and one that is fun to follow—like a game. The secret to your future financial life of liberty is your:

FINANCIAL GAME PLAN RULEBOOK

Use whatever favorite name you like to label your plan. Why not just name it after you, since it will be yours alone? Call it: [*My name's*] *Financial Game Plan Rulebook*. The words are not nearly as important as the *action*. Whatever you call *it*, you need to devise one (a game plan), commit to *it* without wavering, and then follow *it* without fail. How?

Here are the 18 key principles of the *Financial Game Plan Rulebook* for achieving *Infinite Financial Freedom*. Make them your own and prosper.

> *The toughest thing about success is that you've got to keep on being a success.*
> Irving Berlin

Rule #1: Set Goals.

"Again?" you say. "Still," say I. Even though you already set goals *before* you won the jackpot (see *Chapter 4: What To Do Before You Win*), you must review and reset your goals now—and regularly. Financial goal review is part of the annual reality check-up of all your goals. However, any major life-changing event, like a major lottery win, requires that you take time to re-evaluate all aspects of your life, including the financial ones.

Typical post-jackpot investment-related goal topics might now include:

❑   buying or starting a business of your own;

❑ traveling;

❑ buying a new home or vacation home;

❑ funding college for your children;

❑ funding new learning experiences (education) for yourself;

❑ meeting charitable or social objectives;

❑ planning your retirement. Remember, someday the lottery checks will stop coming and you will still want to eat.

Your new or revised financial goals will suggest various objectives that your choice of investments should match (see Figure 6–1). We will discuss the importance and how-to's of matching your *personal* goals and objectives with your *investment* goals and objectives in greater detail throughout your *Rulebook*.

FIGURE 6–1: INVESTMENT OBJECTIVES & YOUR GOALS

WHAT INVESTMENT SEEKS	WHAT YOU WANT
Current Income	Cash Now
Some Current Income and Some Future Growth	Some Cash Now and More Cash Later
Conservative Growth	Sure Cash Later
Aggressive Growth	A Shot at Lots of Cash Later

For now, reset your goals. For a refresher, refer to *Life Plan: Statement of Goals* in *Chapter 4: What To Do Before You Win* and tactic #13: Get Out of Town in *Chapter 5: What To Do When You Win*. For more specific and step-by-step guidance on setting goals, goal categories, goal setting techniques, etc., read *LifePlan: A Goal Setting Workbook* (see *Appendix A: Personal Growth Resources* for details on this book and others).

Rule #2: Cover Your Assets.

You have two major protections to consider:

1. an adequate *Emergency Fund*; and

2. sufficient insurance.

These protections cover the back door of your financial life, so that you can safely move forward without losing your gains to date.

Emergency Fund

First, your *Emergency Fund* should equal 9–12 months of your living expenses. That is, you should have an *Emergency Fund* with enough money to fully support you and your lifestyle for at least 9–12 months in case you have no income from any other source (lottery included). You can put together this size fund with cash, a line of credit or a combination of both.

After you win your jackpot (and even *before* to a lesser extent), unsolicited credit card and line of credit offers will pour into your mailbox. So, you should be able to amass the credit you need for your *Emergency Fund*. Be selective. Only pick credit cards with no annual fees and *never* use the cards for consumption. Store each card in its own folder under "Emergency Fund" in your file cabinet—not in your wallet. For information on finding the best credit cards, see the card evaluation services listed in *Appendix B: Financial Growth Resources*.

Whenever dealing with credit, always let these two *Infinite Financial Freedom* principles (introduced in Chapter 3) guide your decisions:

1.   Run your life on cash; and

2.   Use credit only for opportunity, never consumption.

Principle #1 refers to using cash for the consumables of life: food, clothing, furniture, energy, entertainment, travel, toiletries, toys (adult's and children's), and the like. Consumables are simply goods or services that you use up or that depreciate in value. If you are in doubt about what constitutes a consumable, just review the offers that your current credit card companies send to you with your statement. They always tease you with offers for tempting consumables. Just treat these offers for consumables as an extra educational service being provided for free by the charge card companies to teach you how *not* to use credit.

I am indeed rich since my income is superior to my expense, and my expense is equal to my wishes.

Edward Gibbon

Principle #2 refers to using credit only to fund investments in appreciating assets and/or profit-generating activities, like real estate (including your home, rental property, etc.), stocks and bonds (including mutual funds), a business opportunity in *What You Do Best & Enjoy Most*, and so on. If the activity does not involve appreciating assets or producing profits, then the venture is not creditworthy. In this case, refer to Principle #1 for instructions.

Insurance

In tandem with an *Emergency Fund*, you also need sufficient insurance coverage. Your *Emergency Fund* represents the risks of life that you have decided to retain on your own. Insurance represents those more catastrophic risks that you transfer over to the insurance company in return for the premium that you pay to them. Here are the essential coverages that you should have:

❑   Medical Insurance (for both hospital and doctor bills);

❑   Dental Insurance;

❑   Homeowner's (or renter's) Insurance;

❑   Life Insurance;

❑   Disability Insurance;

❑   Automobile Insurance;

❑   Personal Umbrella Liability Insurance;

❑   Kidnap & Ransom Insurance; and

❑   Business Insurance coverages.

Medical & Dental Insurance

The cheapest form of Medical and Dental insurance is to simply stay healthy. After all, what good is all the money in the world if you're too sick to enjoy it? Don't foolishly get into excesses just because you can better afford them now.

> *The poorest man would not part with health for money, but the richest would gladly part with all their money for health.*
>
> C. C. Colton

You stay healthy through prevention: good eating habits, regular exercise, and a positive attitude. Don't believe that a fad diet will somehow trick your body into health while allowing you to continue practicing bad habits. Permanent, preventive and positive lifestyle habits are the only techniques that yield true health. Short cuts to health can lead to long cuts on the operating table.

> *No diet will remove all the fat from your body, because the brain is entirely fat. Without a brain you might look good, but all you could do is run for public office.*
>
> Covert Bailey

So, get and stay in the *right mind set*, include health directives in your *Guiding Principles*, health assertions in your *Affirmations*, and health goals under the Physical category in your *Life Plan: Statement of Goals* that will translate into the routines of your *Daily Outcomes*. See

Chapter 4: What To Do Before You Win for a review of these ideas and techniques.

Homeowner's & Auto Insurance

Your Homeowner's policy and Auto policy insurance limits change, of course, as you add and delete properties and vehicles. Most importantly, however, increase your liability limits on these and all policies. Carry limits of at least $300,000 to $1,000,000 on all your basic, underlying liability policies. Further, always verify that your liability policies are "occurrence" contracts (the broadest available) and not "claims-made" (which can be much more limiting, if potential claims are not reported within specified time periods).

Umbrella Liability Insurance

Absolutely purchase an Umbrella Liability Policy with limits in amounts sufficient to cover you for all that you can lose. Remember that your net worth is now a target for the unscrupulous who play the "litigation lottery". If you win a $10,000,000 lottery jackpot, then buy $10,000,000 in liability limits on your Umbrella policy plus enough additional limit to cover the net value of other assets that you own.

What good is a $500,000 annual lottery check for 20 years, if you just have to give it to somebody else because you once dented their fender and the courts decide that you gave the "victim" a whiplash-induced permanent partial disability? Transfer this risk of loss to an insurance company by trading a few of your dollars for a policy. A $1,000,000 personal Umbrella policy typically costs between $800–$1,200 a year. Each additional $1,000,000 in limit is less expensive after you buy the first $1,000,000.

Buy high enough liability limits and make sure that there are no "gaps" in coverage or limits between your underlying and Umbrella policies. The Umbrella policy limit should start where each underlying policy limit ends.

Disability Insurance

Disability insurance to cover your jackpot income is not necessary since the lottery pays you whether or not you are disabled or even alive. However, if you start a business or have other earnings that you wish to protect, then you should buy disability insurance to cover the potential loss of that other income. Fully disclose your lottery winnings and explain to the insurance company underwriters exactly which income you are protecting. If necessary, have them manuscript an endorsement to specify that the covered income is from a source other than your lottery winnings. Confirm this agreement in a letter to the insurance company *underwriter* and send a copy to the insurance agent or broker.

Eventually, once you have achieved *Infinite Financial Freedom*, you will no longer need such disability insurance and can drop the coverage. You will, in essence, be self-insured: your income won't stop or be reduced due to a possible physical or mental impairment that you may suffer.

Kidnap & Ransom Insurance

We already discussed the quiet need for a numbered (not named) Kidnap & Ransom Policy in tactic #10 in *Chapter 5: What To Do When You Win*. Review that tactic remembering that now not only are your assets the target of the litigation lottery players, but also you and your family are now personal targets of the crime-does-pay sect. If it's any consolation, winning at *anything* makes you such a target. All successful people are targets. You are, at least, in good company.

Business Insurance

If you start a business, you will need to insure your company's exposure to various losses. Do incorporate immediately to help protect you and your personal assets from liability. The discussion of the many and distinct forms of business insurance is beyond the scope of this book, but you must have such protection, especially liability and business interruption coverages. Also, if you hire employees, be sure to buy Employment Practices Liability insurance for the new wave of "victim claims" that have arisen in the latter 20th Century: Wrongful Termination, Discrimination, and Sexual Harassment. Coverage for such claims is excluded under other business insurance policies to the unhappy surprise of many a regretful business owner.

For detailed explanations, recommendations, and translations from *insurance-ese* into English, see *The Insurance Survival Kit Series*. There is a series for both personal and business insurance. See *Appendix B: Financial Growth Resources* for specifics on the books in this series.

Life Insurance

Your life insurance needs typically change after any major life-event, including winning the lottery. The main function of life insurance for most people is to create for relatively little premium an "instant fortune" in case you die before you amass one. If you die too soon (before you amass your fortune), your heirs use this insurance fortune to pay-off your debts, protect and support themselves as you intended, and to pay your estate taxes. So, you should carry enough life insurance to fund these needs.

The Deadly Truth About Life Insurance

Just as there is the *right* amount of money and the *wrong* amount of money, there is the right kind and wrong kind of life insurance. This product shouldn't even be called *life* insurance, but the industry uses the misnomer for marketing reasons. This financial instrument is and should be called *death* insurance, since the policy only pays on the death of the person insured. This policy is the only insurance contract that you buy to cover a guaranteed event: death.

Never go to a doctor whose office plants have died.

Erma Bombeck

People *inside* the life insurance industry consistently sing the "savings" praises and preach the "permanent" gospel of *cash value* life insurance policies. They call such policies by such inventive names as:

Whole life   Flexible life
Universal life   Flexible Adjustable life
Variable life   Endowment life
Universal Variable life   Modified life
Permanent life   This life-That life
                All kinds of life.

These *cash value* life insurance policies (or their latest euphemism) combine and commingle straight *term* insurance (like the kind you have on your car or house) with some supposed "savings" or "investment" component *inside* the policy. Due to an inherent design flaw (from a consumer's standpoint), *cash value* life insurance policies have these four principal problems:

1. *Cash value* policies typically cost 8 times or more than *term* policies providing the same amount of life insurance coverage;

2. Whatever you do with the insurance coverage (the death benefit) adversely effects the so-called "savings" or "investment" component (the living benefit) inside the policy contract;

3. Whatever you do with the "savings" or "investment" component (the living benefit) adversely effects the life insurance coverage (the death benefit); and

4. The rate of return on the "savings" or "investment" portion of the contract is poor.

Their high cost, their commingling of "savings" or "investment" funds with the death benefit proceeds, and their poor rates of return make *cash value* policies ineffective and unacceptable for those seeking *Infinite Financial Freedom.* Interestingly enough, advisors *outside* the life insurance industry uniformly recommend that most people should buy only *term* insurance. Why? They give the same reasons as given above: *Cash value* life insurance premiums are too high, the returns are too low, and there are too many policy restrictions due to the commingling of the living benefits with the death benefits.

So, buy only inexpensive *term* insurance and make your investments *outside* and independently of any insurance contract. If still in doubt, remember this life insurance salesperson's dictum: "If you sell *cash value* life insurance, you can't sleep (due to guilt because the product is overpriced, restrictive, and underperforms), but if you sell *term* insurance, you can't eat (because the commission dollars are too low)." Suffice it to say that most life agents eat much better than they sleep. Forgive them, as they are merely hungry, mis-indoctrinated souls trying to make a living. Of course, there are notable, individual exceptions. Still, they don't need to feed on you.

> *As a well-spent day brings happy sleep, so a life well spent brings happy death.*
>
> Leonardo Da Vinci

The analysis, derivation, and proof of the financial wisdom of buying *term* over *cash value* insurance is beyond the scope of this book, but not beyond the scope of your understanding. Any consumer-oriented publication from *Consumer Reports* and *Money* magazine to books by Venita Van Caspel, Andrew Tobias, Arthur Milton, and many, many, other advisors provide broad and repeated endorsement of the recommendation to purchase *term* insurance.

The Right Amount of Life Insurance

How much life insurance do you really need? An oversimplified, but workable rule-of-life is to buy an amount equal to 8-to-10 times your annual income. To find the *exact* amount of coverage that you need, financial planners can perform a so-called "Needs Analysis" assessment that considers: certain present value and future value calculations; assumptions regarding life expectancies, future inflation rates, and future investment rates of return; estimates of survivor Social Security benefits; allowances for other sources of funds; and so on. In either case, the main purpose of such insurance coverage is to provide *Infinite Financial Freedom* for your heirs if you die before you have enough time to create sufficient wealth for yourself and them.

The Insurance Exchange™

As a *free*, no obligation service to *Infinite Financial Freedom* readers, *The Insurance Exchange*™ will search their database for the most competitive quotes from the best-rated and most aggressively priced *term* life insurance companies in the country and mail the results to you. If you choose to buy the coverage, they hope, of course, that you consider buying your policy through them, but you have no obligation to do so and they will respect your privacy (translation: "They won't bug you."). For *free* life insurance quotations and/or for information about obtaining a formal life insurance "Needs Analysis", just copy, complete, and return their *Life Insurance Reality Check Request* (Form 6–1 below) to *The Insurance Exchange*™ as instructed on the form.

An as example, *The Insurance Exchange*™ tells me that, as of this writing, a 35-year-old male non-smoker with a reasonably good health history can buy $500,000 of *term* life insurance for a flat annual premium of $825 that is guaranteed not to change for 20 years. Many other pricing structures are also available, even one that starts at a premium of only $335 in the first year for the $500,000 in coverage.

So, whatever type or amount of life insurance you may now have, you should check its pricing as part of your regular review to assure that your policy is still competitive. Different insurance companies base their rates on different mortality tables (life expectancy statistics). Since people now live longer, you want rates from the company that uses the latest mortality table showing the longest life spans. Some insurance companies use tables that are over 20 years old and the shorter life spans listed in those tables produce higher rates.

FORM 6—1: LIFE INSURANCE REALITY CHECK REQUEST

LIFE INSURANCE REALITY CHECK REQUEST FORM
Name
Address
City   State   ZIP
Phone Number:
Date of Birth (month/day/year):
Gender (circle one):   Male   Female
Are you a smoker or tobacco user? Yes   No
Amount of Insurance you want: $
□ Please send my *free*, no obligation, personalized report showing the best Term Life Insurance quotes from the most competitive companies in America.
I am also interested in: □ Health Insurance   □ Disability Income Replacement   □ Life Insurance Needs Analysis
Mail your completed form with an S.A.S.E. to: *The Insurance Exchange*™   **Benefits Resource Group**   **P. O. Box 943, Malibu, CA 90265.**
Note: Please copy, complete & return one form with a Self-Addressed Stamped Envelope (S.A.S.E.) for each person that wants a quotation.

You need not "shop" your policy every year, but as long as you remain in reasonably good health, you should review your policy's pricing today and then every five years.

Remember, the more money that you save on life (death) insurance, the more money that you can invest in creating *Infinite Financial Freedom* for yourself and your heirs.

After all, the *right* amount of money is *inside* a life insurance policy only if you are a life insurance company. Once you have the *right* amount of money yourself, your need for personal life insurance disappears. Estate tax-avoidance strategies and meeting charitable goals are two special situations in which life insurance can still be a very useful tool—even after you have achieved *Infinite Financial Freedom*. We will discuss these two special situations later in Rules #14 and #15 of your *Rulebook*.

Rule #3: Run On Automatic Pilot.

How do you keep your finances organized to help you keep your plan on track while expending the least amount of your time and energy? Automate it.

By automating your program, you can build-in painless discipline and achieve convenience. However, do not confuse running your finances on automatic pilot with "flying blind". You must still pay attention and oversee your plan. How do you automate?

Use a so-called "asset management account" or "cash management account" to automate as much of your plan as possible. Such accounts, available through stock brokerage houses, typically summarize all your monthly transactions into a single consolidated statement that gives you an ongoing overview of your financial position. Use such an account to establish your *Operating Fund* for living expenses. At the beginning of the year, you will place a sufficient portion of your cash winnings into your *Operating Fund*. You can then easily run your life on the cash in this fund for one year.

The best such accounts have the following features:

❑ Double tax-free Money Market Mutual Fund with check writing privileges

Use this fund for your *Operating Fund*. It replaces your standard checking account at your local bank. Earnings on this fund should be free of both state and federal income taxes. If you live in a state for which such a fund is not offered because there is no state income tax (such as Florida or Nevada), then you need only use a Money Market Fund that is free of federal income taxes. The brokerage should have Money Market Funds that are state-specific for the major states in the country.

❑ Free, unlimited check writing privileges

Although you will be writing fewer checks with this account, you still want the freedom and flexibility of unlimited check writing without a per check charge. You don't want the annoyance of counting checks and being "nickeled & dimed" for writing them.

❑ "Sweep" Provision

This feature automatically "sweeps" or invests interest, dividends or other cash in amounts that you pre-specify into a selection of other investments. This provision guarantees that you will automatically "pay yourself first" to fund specific goals and objectives.

❑ Deposit Insurance

Insurance should cover deposits of $500,000 or more. Check to see how much insurance coverage applies to cash (usually $100,000) and how much applies to securities (usually $400,000). Check also to see if this insurance limit applies per investor or per each account held by the investor. Coverage per account, rather than per investor, is preferable, because this option gives you more total insurance. How the brokerage applies the limit is not important as long as you have sufficient coverage for your invested funds. There should, of course, be no charge for this insurance benefit.

❑ Toll-free 800 Numbers for free access to all services

The account should provide 24-hour, free access to all services. You should be able to speak with either a "live" representative or use the automated options at any time.

❑ Complete stock brokerage services

Make sure that the broker provides a full range of mutual funds from many different no-load or low-load families, stocks, bonds, and other investments. Also, verify that you can use a margin account for borrowing against your investments at the low broker margin rates.

❑ Consolidated Statements

You should receive monthly and year-end summary statements showing all transactions including automated bill card activity, deposits, ATM cash withdrawals, and the like. The statements should be well-organized, easy to read, and simple to understand.

❑ Credit or Debit Card

You should receive either a credit or debit card (at your choice) to access your account at national ATM (Automated Teller Machine) networks for quick, easy and wide access to your cash. You can also use the card as a cash alternative for the convenience of making purchases without having to carry much cash. The wealthier the individual, the less cash they carry until the wealthiest carry no cash at all.

Charges for purchases are automatically paid for you from your *Operating Fund*, giving you one less check to write. However, you cannot yet use expense codes with your credit/debit card transactions as you can with your checks.

❑ Automated Bill Payment Services

Make sure that you have this feature, so that you can stop writing checks, stuffing envelopes, licking stamps, and going to the post office as often. For *fixed* payments, such as fixed-amount mortgages, leases, car payments, etc., you can arrange for payments to be made every month automatically out of your *Operating Fund* on the day of the month that you pre-specify. Put as many of your bills as possible on this "automatic payment pilot" to simplify your life.

For recurring *variable* payments, such as utilities, telephone, dry cleaning, etc., you can either pay these over the phone (using a toll-free number) by punching-in the dates and amounts on the phone keypad or by talking to a bill-payment representative "live" anytime from any phone.

These payments (both *fixed* and *variable*) will also be expense-coded along with checks that you write. Note that although there is typically a flat monthly fee for using a bill payment service, the money that you save on postage alone is usually greater than the fee. More importantly, you save something much more valuable—your time. A bill payment service handles the mechanics of paying your bills, so that you can go do something else more valuable with your time.

❑ Expense Coding

The ability to place an expense code on all checks and bill payments is a tremendous organizational and time-saving tool. Here's how it works: First, you write-out a check just as you normally would. Then, in a designated box on the check, you also write a two-digit expense code number from 01 to 99. Only you know what the coded expense numbers mean. You use these expense codes not only with the checks that you write, but also with all your pre-specified, automated *fixed* and *variable* bill payments. The more payments that you can code, the easier your financial life will be.

The brokerage firm should provide you with a running total of year-to-date expenses by code number every month plus an annual year-end summary statement. The year-end summary is especially helpful for preparing your income tax returns and for formulating a less fettered future.

The following listing is an example of how you might classify and organize your expense codes into a personal "Chart of Accounts". Use this chart as a model to modify for your own situation.

EXPENSE CODE CHART OF ACCOUNTS

HOME EXPENSES	
Code#	Expense Category
01	Water: Utility
02	Water: Drinking
03	Home Maintenance
04	Home Repairs
05	Appliances
06	Appliance Repairs
07	Improvements
08	Garbage Collection
09	Mortgage: Property #1
10	Mortgage: Property #2
11	Mortgage: Property #3
12	H.O. Dues: Property #2
13	H.O. Dues: Property #3
14	Other Home Financing
15	Furnishings
16	Electricity
17	Gas: Natural
18	Telephone
19	Miscellaneous Home

AUTO EXPENSES	
Code#	Expense Category
20	Lease/Pmt.: Auto #1
21	Lease/Pmt.: Auto #2
22	Gasoline: Auto #1
23	Gasoline: Auto #2
24	Dept.Mtr.Veh.: Auto #1
25	Dept.Mtr.Veh.: Auto #2
26	Maintenance: Auto #1
27	Maintenance: Auto #2
28	Parking
29	Miscellaneous Auto

INSURANCE EXPENSES	
Code#	Expense Category
30	Auto
31	Home
32	Life
33	Long Term Disability
34	Personal Umbrella
35	Medical
36	Dental
37	Rental Property #1
38	Rental Property #2
39	Miscellaneous Insurance

TAXES	
Code#	Expense Category
40	Federal Income
41	State Income
42	Property #1
43	Property #2
44	Property #3
45	Medicare
46	State Disability
47	Social Security
48	Other Tax
49	Miscellaneous Taxes

INVESTMENT & CHARITABLE EXPENSES	
Code#	Expense Category
50	Active Investments
51	Passive Investments
52	Commissions Paid
53	Investment Interest Paid
54	Service Charges
55	Misc. Investments
56	Charity #1
57	Charity #2
58	Lottery
59	Miscellaneous Charity

PERSONAL EXPENSES	
Code#	Expense Category
60	Clothing
61	Education
62	Groceries
63	Laundry/Dry Cleaning
64	Medical
65	Dental
66	Travel
67	Entertainment
68	Recreation
69	Photography
70	Firearms
71	Toiletries
72	Music
73	Dining Out
74	Haircuts
75	Cable TV
76	Exercise
77	Child Care
78	Toys
79	Miscellaneous Personal

The above categories are of, course, just examples of those you might use. If Photography is not a hobby of yours, then use expense code #69 for another hobby or other recurring Personal Expense. Just customize the categories for your specific situation using the above framework as your guide.

You may currently need fewer than the 79 expense codes listed here. Still, you should use the main categories of Home, Auto, Insurance, Taxes, Investment & Charitable, and Personal and leave room for expansion and changes. If, for example, you have only one car, you won't use all ten expense codes under the Auto category. Nevertheless, you should set-up the Auto category as shown in case you buy a second car. By allowing for growth, you eliminate the inconvenience of related expense codes having non-consecutive numbers or of redoing your entire chart of accounts just to keep the code numbers organized. Keeping the same code numbers over time allows you to more easily review your spending and investment patterns and make the appropriate adjustments.

If you have or start a business, you could either use the remaining 20 expense codes for the business or start a new asset/cash management account and have 99 new codes to use for the business. You might start the business using the remaining 20 expense codes in your personal account and then move to a second account for business when needed. If you use the remaining 20 expense codes for a business, here is the Chart of Accounts to use as your model:

BUSINESS EXPENSES	
Code#	Expense Category
80	Business Publications
81	Conventions
82	Dues: Professional
83	Licenses: Professional
84	Legal
85	Office Supplies
86	Postage
87	Professional Service
88	Gifts
89	Advertising/Promotion
90	Rent
91	Safe Deposit Box
92	Travel
93	Entertainment
94	Business Meals
95	Furniture & Equipment
96	Bank Service Fees
97	Electric Utility
98	Telephone
99	Miscellaneous Business

Despite all the advantages to using an asset/cash management account, there are a few special caveats:

1. Such consolidated broker accounts cannot yet accept actual cash (dollar bills), so you may still need to maintain a small savings account at your local bank for your own convenience. Keep a minimum balance to avoid any local bank service charges. You may occasionally need your local bank to handle some cash transactions involving money orders, cashier's checks, traveler's checks, and the like.

2. Privacy is, of course, a special concern. Your account information may be rented to marketers who intend to solicit you for various reasons. In this case, you are faced with a trade-off between convenience and privacy. If you insulate yourself sufficiently as described in *Chapter 5: What To Do When You Win*, then your privacy should be protected to the point where you can reasonably opt for the convenience of the asset/cash management account.

Most so-called "full service" (meaning full commission) as well as discount stock brokerages offer asset/cash management accounts. As of this writing, these are the principal firms offering such accounts:

Fidelity Investments	Merrill Lynch
Kidder Peabody	Dean Witter
Charles Schwab	Smith Barney
Shearson Lehman	Kemper
Paine Webber	Prudential

A. G. Edwards

Of these, I can only recommend Fidelity and Schwab. Why? Currently, all the others share your master account information with their in-house stockbrokers/salespeople. These brokers will search through your account data to find available money to help you "invest" so as to generate commissions and fees for themselves, so that they can eat this week. Forgive them; it's their job. Their investment recommendations may even be good on occasion. However, since you are now pro-active, you do not need them badgering you with such additional investment choices.

If an automated bill payment service is important to you (and it should be, if you want the most freedom), then I can only recommend the *Ultra Service Account* from Fidelity Investments. Their service is excellent and their people are well informed. They will do what you ask of them very effectively and then respect your privacy. Plus they do have over 73 walk-in Investment Centers located in most major cities across the country.

Be aware that all brokerages change their asset/cash management account offerings and terms over time. Do a double-check survey of the principal existing brokerage firms when you are ready to open such an account. Use the above list of features as a checklist for selecting the best account for your needs.

Evolving Technology

As technology is harnessed to meet our evolving needs, look for more on-line banking and brokerage services to become available. A number of such alternatives are already offered on the *Prodigy* on-line computer service. Several banks offer various levels of on-line bill payment capabilities and several brokers offer trading capabilities through your personal computer modem on the *Prodigy* service.

Most discount brokerages like Fidelity, Schwab, and Quick & Reilly already offer on-line computerized brokerage services that link your computer directly with theirs. You can even place your own buy and sell trades in the market using your personal computer. *CompuServe* on-line computer service also has similar brokerage services available as well as significant research capabilities.

These services evolve quickly, so check with the providers mentioned for their most current offerings and prices. Survey the field before you make your purchase decision. Ask for a "demo" program so that you can see a demonstration of each service before buying.

Keep in mind that you are reviewing such programs to automate your financial management and thereby simplify your life so that you can do the non-financial things that are most important to you. If, however, computers are a hobby for you, then you will find no lack of available financial and other services and choices to keep you mesmerized by the monitor screen for many moments on end. If you are not computer-ready or inclined, then the asset/cash management account alone will effectively achieve the goal of "simplification through automation" that you seek.

Rule #4: Keep All Your Eggs in Enough Baskets.

This rule refers to your properly using *diversification* to your best advantage. Diversification is the technique of reducing risk in your total portfolio by spreading the risk over a number of different investment vehicles. If one or more investments fail to perform as expected, then the remaining investments that do perform well yield an acceptable total return, so that you don't get hurt, financially.

Diversification is somewhat like playing two hands at a time at a blackjack table—you're spreading the risk of loss over both hands. Even better diversification, if it were possible, would be to simultaneously play one hand at the blackjack table while placing a bet on a spin of the roulette wheel and a roll of the dice at the craps table. In gambling, however, diversification may just quicken the rate of loss and allow you to lose more money in various ways all at once. With investing, you have much better odds, because you won't be playing the house—you will be *designing* the house.

As with all the ways of achieving *Infinite Financial Freedom*, there is a right and a wrong way to diversify. You want to diversify enough to spread or reduce the risk, but not so much as to dilute your return. There is a point after which diversification does no further good and serves only to complicate investing due to the excessive number of investment vehicles that you must track. Your *Rulebook* will assure that you remain sufficiently, but not overly, diversified.

There are two levels of diversification: your investment portfolio's and your portfolio manager's. We will discuss your portfolio manager's diversification in Rule #5. Your *portfolio manager* is simply the guy who manages your investment portfolio. Here, we want to discuss the diversification of your investment portfolio itself. Your *investment portfolio* is simply the money or assets that you have to invest after establishing an adequate *Emergency Fund* and obtaining sufficient insurance protections (see Rule #2) and starting an *Operating Fund* for living expenses (see Rule #3). Given the above, use these basic percentages for diversifying or allocating your investment portfolio into these three funds that you create:

| Infinite Financial Freedom Fund |

| Balanced Fund |

| Possibility Fund |

INVESTMENT PORTFOLIO
ALLOCATION & DIVERSIFICATION TARGETS

Percent of Portfolio	Fund Name	Investment Vehicle
25%	*Infinite Financial Freedom Fund*	Tax-Free municipal bond mutual fund
25%	*Infinite Financial Freedom Fund*	Tax-Deferred Annuity
25%	*Balanced Fund*	Growth and Income mutual fund
25%	*Possibility Fund*	Direct Equity Investments

Use these diversification targets as your starting points for the allocation of investments within your portfolio (see Chart 6–1). Your particular goals, your *Rulebook*, and time will dictate how you might amend the percentages of this basic model. We will discuss the specifics of the investment vehicles listed above as we move through your *Rulebook*, so don't let their financial names confuse you for the moment.

CHART 6–1: INVESTMENT PORTFOLIO
ALLOCATION & DIVERSIFICATION TARGETS

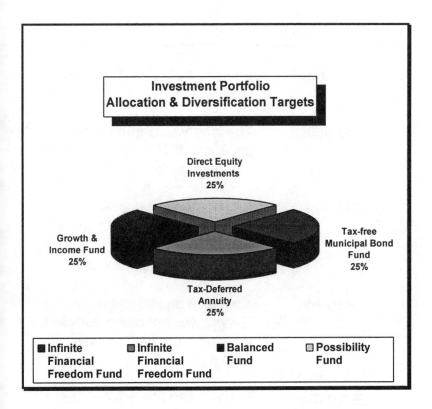

Note that the above model is not necessarily appropriate if you have the *wrong* amount of money. For example, if you are temporarily in a low income tax bracket, then a tax-free investment is not necessary. Additionally, a direct equity investment may have more risk or be less liquid than is appropriate for you in your current situation. The suitability of investments will become clearer after we introduce the *Ladder of Investments* in Rule #5 and how to determine your tolerance for risk in Rule #6 of your *Rulebook*.

Let's look at an example of how to use the basic allocation/diversification model. Let's use these assumptions:

Dollar Amount	Assumption
$5,000,000	You win a $5,000,000 lottery jackpot!
$250,000/yr.	The lottery/insurance annuity pays you $250,000 a year over 20 years (before taxes)
$200,000/yr.	You really receive only $200,000 a year for 20 years after 20% or $50,000 in federal taxes are withheld annually.
Variable	You have an adequate *Emergency Fund* and sufficient insurance protections (see Rule #2).
$50,000/yr.	You put $50,000 a year into your *Operating Fund* for living expenses (see Rule #3)
$150,000/yr.	You have $150,000 a year for 20 years to invest after taxes and living expenses.

Notice that the above assumptions show that you discipline yourself to live on $50,000 a year. You could, of course, live a more flashy and flamboyant lifestyle consuming all $200,000 a year and more by using credit. If you follow the extravagant lifestyle course, then you bankrupt your future and sentence yourself to eventual financial slavery. When the lottery checks stop coming, the bills you owe won't and it's back to work you go. Only now you will be 20 years older and deeper in debt. If you want to make the lifestyle of the rich and foolish successful, you need to plan on winning the lottery at age 5 (which is illegal), so that somebody will still be willing to hire you at minimum wage at age 25 when your checks stop.

On the other hand, by following our basic allocation and diversification model you know exactly how to divide this $150,000 in available annual assets to assure your future *Infinite Financial Freedom* while you live on $50,000 a year with all your time to enjoy. Here's how to divide that $150,000 using our model:

INVESTMENT PORTFOLIO ALLOCATION & DIVERSIFICATION OF $150,000		
Amount Invested	Fund Name	Investment Vehicle
$37,500	*Infinite Financial Freedom Fund*	Tax-Free municipal bond mutual fund
$37,500	*Infinite Financial Freedom Fund*	Tax-Deferred Annuity
$37,500	*Balanced Fund*	Growth and Income mutual fund
$37,500	*Possibility Fund*	Direct Equity Investments

Infinite Financial Freedom Fund

This fund is so named to remind you of its very special purpose and meaning in your life: *Infinite Financial Freedom*. Perpetuating your economic independence into infinity requires that you keep this *Infinite Financial Freedom* investment commandment:

PAY YOURSELF FIRST.

After all, someday the lottery checks will stop coming and all you will have left *is* yourself. So, you had better pay yourself first because you are the only one that will last.

Note that your *Infinite Financial Freedom Fund* consists of two investments of $37,500 each for a total of $75,000 or one half of your "investable" assets. Here is the power of paying these funds to yourself first:

❑   If you invest $75,000 a year for 20 years with an average 4% after-tax return, you will have a fund worth over $2.2 Million on the day that your jackpot checks stop coming.

❑   If this fund then continues to earn an average 4% after-tax return per year and you *never* add even a penny to it, you can withdraw $75,000 a year (in today's dollars) *forever* and still have all the $2.2 Million in the fund! You can even allow for an average inflation rate of 3% and maintain your accustomed standard of living—indefinitely. This is *Infinite Financial Freedom*.

So, your reward for the discipline of paying yourself first the $75,000 a year for 20 years is to continue to receive

$75,000 a year endlessly—not a bad trade-off of dollars for discipline. Discipline does have its rewards: You will never outlive your resources. Unfortunately, many people today are living longer only to find that their reward is to outlive their resources. You do not have to be one of them—no one does.

Infinite Financial Freedom alone is not a bad return on your investment in effective discipline. However, this lifetime security also gives you the additional liberty and peace of mind to be more aggressive with the remaining half of investable funds. Further, you are being a socially responsible investor by contributing to the improvement of your municipalities by buying bonds that fund projects that benefit not only you, but also your neighbors and visitors alike.

Tax-Free Municipal Bond Mutual Fund

To make sure that we are all talking the same language, let me quickly define a few terms. First, a *mutual fund* is simply a group of people who pool their money and give it to a company that hires a bright investment guy to manage it for everybody. The Investment Company Institute (a mutual fund trade group) defines a mutual fund more formally this way:

> An investment company that pools money from shareholders and invests in a variety of securities, including stocks, bonds, and money market securities. A mutual fund stands ready to buy back (redeem) its shares at their current net asset value. The value of the shares depends on the market value of the fund's portfolio securities at the time. Most mutual funds offer new shares continuously.

A Tax-Free Municipal Bond mutual fund invests in bonds issued to states and municipalities to finance public projects such as schools, highways, hospitals, airports, bridges, water and sewer works, and the like. In other words, they invest principally in the creation, maintenance and repair of the infrastructure of our country. The federal government does not tax the income you earn from these bonds to encourage (and effectively subsidize) investments into these projects. If you invest in such a fund that contains the bonds of your state only, then the income you earn is free from both state and federal income taxes. (Technical note: Some of the income of certain taxpayers in special situations *may* be subject to the federal so-called alternative minimum tax.)

Note that although lottery winnings are often state income tax free, the *earnings* on those winnings *are* subject to both state and federal income tax. So, if you live in a state that imposes income taxes, pick a double tax-free Municipal Bond mutual fund; that is, one that is free of both state and federal income taxes. In Rule #5, you will learn exactly how to pick the best mutual funds.

Tax-Deferred Annuity

We first met the concept of an annuity in *Chapter 3: The Do's and Don'ts of Smart Lottery Play* when we discussed how a $1 Million jackpot is not a $1 Million prize. Instead of giving you a $1 Million prize, the lottery gives you $50,000 and then buys an annuity for about $450,000 from an insurance company who then guarantees to pay you $50,000 a year for 19 more years.

There is another method of using an annuity, instead of giving the insurance company a one-time lump sum and then having them immediately begin guaranteed payments to you over a specified time. You can, instead, make fixed or flexible investments *into* an annuity and then let the account grow until you need the money someday in the future. This second method is the way you use the annuity for your *Infinite Financial Freedom Fund.*

With a Tax-Deferred Annuity, you do not have to pay federal income taxes on the earnings until you withdraw the cash. So, your earnings and the earnings on those earnings can compound without taking a tax hit every year (Einstein would love it!). Annuities can have either fixed or variable returns. For your *Infinite Financial Freedom Fund,* you should use a guaranteed annuity with a fixed return. These annuities have current rates that are fixed and guaranteed not to change for at least a year as well as an overall minimum guaranteed rate under which they will never fall.

The return on variable annuities can change continuously, subject to the investment performance of their underlying portfolio, like mutual funds. Such annuities have greater potential reward, but also bear greater inherent risk. Variable annuities certainly have a place in the investment spectrum, but not in your *Infinite Financial Freedom Fund.*

The Annuity Exchange™ tells me that, as of this writing, the best tax-deferred, guaranteed annuity available today pays a current rate of 5.25% with an additional 8% "signing bonus" for a total first year yield of 13.67%. The 8% bonus, which is added to the current rate every year, applies to all new money that you invest over the first 5 years. Beginning in years 6 and after the insurance company adds a 5% bonus to the then current rate on all new money invested. As an alternative to a CD (Certificate of Deposit), such an annuity can't be beat. The details of this annuity are shown in Table 6–1, courtesy of *The Annuity Exchange*™.

TABLE 6–1: TAX-DEFERRED ANNUITY WITH BONUSES

TAX-DEFERRED ANNUITY WITH BONUSES	
Sales Charges	None
Minimum Investment	$25 per month for IRA's; $100 per month for non-IRA's; $1,000 single payment
Current Guaranteed Interest Rate	5.25% for first year; then a new Current Rate is set every year
Annuity Bonus for first 5 years	8% bonus added to Current Rate on initial & new money
Annuity Bonus for years 6 and after	5% bonus added to Current Rate on all new money
Guaranteed Rate	4% minimum, years 2 and after
Surrender Charges	None
Front-End Loads	None, if annuitized after year one and over at least 5 years; otherwise 5% net on deposits made during the first 5 years
Withdrawal Privilege	May withdraw at any time, but reduces Annuity Value
Loans	Available on non-IRA's at 2% net interest rate; may borrow up to ½ of the cash surrender value to a maximum of $50,000

Why Not CD's?

Many people buy Certificate of Deposits thinking that CD's are one of the safest investments that they can make. However, if your CD does not outpace inflation, then you are just "safely" losing the purchasing power of your money. As we saw in our discussion of the *time value of money* in Chapter 3, you need a rate of return that outperforms inflation just to stay even; that is, to insure that your dollar of tomorrow will buy at least what your dollar of today will buy. Further, for your *Infinite Financial Freedom Fund*, you want the benefit of tax-advantaged growth working for you. Otherwise, you have to give-up a portion of your earnings every year to Uncle Sam (see Chart 6–2 & Table 6–2 below).

CHART 6–2: THE POWER OF TAX-ADVANTAGED GROWTH

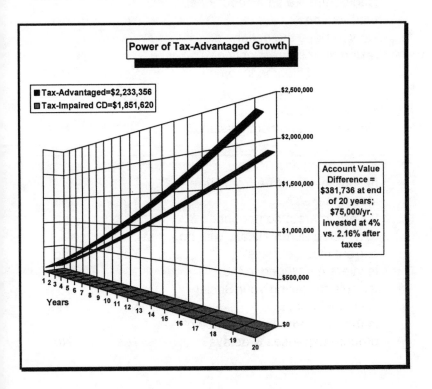

TABLE 6–2: ANNUITY VS. CERTIFICATE OF DEPOSIT

TAX-DEFERRED ANNUITY VS. CERTIFICATE OF DEPOSIT		
	TDA	CD
SAFETY		
Is principal 100% guaranteed?	Yes	Yes
Is your money free from market risk and price fluctuations?	Yes	Yes
LIQUIDITY		
Can you make early cash withdrawals without penalties?	Yes	No
Is there a guaranteed lifetime income provision?	Yes	No
FLEXIBILITY		
Can you make small additional contributions?	Yes	No
Do you have the options of taking your interest only or a guaranteed lifetime income?	Yes	No
SALES CHARGES		
Do you pay any commissions?	No	No
FAVORABLE TAXATION		
Is your interest free from current income taxes?	Yes	No
Is your interest compounded & reinvested automatically with no current income taxes?	Yes	No
Is interest included in the formula for taxing your Social Security benefits?	No	Yes
Is there automatic avoidance of probate expenses & delays?	Yes	No

As you can see from the above, a Tax-Deferred Annuity has several advantages over a Certificate of Deposit. Note that the difference in dollars returned on a Tax-Advantaged versus a Tax-Impaired investment grows, in geometric fashion, greater and greater over time (see Table 6–3). This continuously increasing cumulative effect is the true power of Tax-Advantaged growth.

TABLE 6–3: INCREASING DOLLAR DIFFERENCE OVER TIME

CONTINUOUSLY INCREASING CUMULATIVE RETURN: TAX-ADVANTAGED VS. TAX-IMPAIRED INVESTMENT		
Each 5-Year Period	Per Period Difference	Cumulative Difference
Years 1–5	$14,670	$14,670
Years 6–10	$58,526	$73,196
Years 11–15	$116,469	$189,665
Years 16–20	$192,071	$381,736

A further advantage of an annuity becomes apparent when used as a vehicle for funding a child's college education. As long as the student does not own the annuity, the annuity's value does not count as an asset when qualifying the student for financial aid. If funding a child's college education is a goal of yours, then keep an annuity in mind when allocating money to your *Possibility Fund* (which we discuss later). If the hopeful student elects not to attend college, then you still have the annuity in your name and can use the funds freely.

The Annuity Exchange™

As a no obligation service to *Infinite Financial Freedom* readers, *The Annuity Exchange*™ will search their database for the best annuity with the most aggressive rates in the country and mail the results to you. If you choose to invest in the annuity, you can do so through *The Annuity Exchange*™. For a *free*, no obligation annuity quotation, just copy, complete, and return the *Annuity Quotation Request* (Form 6–2) to *The Annuity Exchange*™ as instructed on the form.

FORM 6–2: ANNUITY QUOTATION REQUEST

ANNUITY QUOTATION REQUEST FORM
Name
Address
City   State   ZIP
Phone Number:
Date of Birth (month/day/year):
Gender (circle one):   Male   Female
I anticipate making a single initial investment, a monthly investment or both as shown below: ☐ Anticipated initial investment: $
☐ Anticipated monthly investment: $
☐ My Federal Income Tax Bracket:
☐ Please send my *free*, no obligation, personalized report showing the best Annuity for me from the most competitive companies in America.
I am also interested in: ☐ Health Insurance ☐ Disability Income Replacement ☐ Life Insurance
Mail your completed form with an S.A.S.E. to: *The Annuity Exchange*™ Benefits Resource Group P. O. Box 943, Malibu, CA 90265.
Note: Please copy, complete & return one form with a Self-Addressed Stamped Envelope (S.A.S.E.) for each person that wants a quotation.

Balanced Fund

Using our allocation/diversification model, you should invest 25% of available dollars (or $37,500 in our example) into your *Balanced Fund*. Investments into your *Balanced Fund* will be more aggressive than investments into your *Infinite Financial Freedom Fund*, but the investment vehicles that you use should still be somewhat conservative.

You should use an "appropriate" growth and income stock mutual fund for your *Balanced Fund*. This investment will give you some conservative growth through the mutual fund's so-called "blue chip" stock holdings (stocks of major, established companies) as well as some dividend income. Use the dividends to reinvest into additional shares of the mutual fund, since you are living-off the money in your *Operating Fund* and won't need this other cash. The fund company gives you the option to automatically reinvest the dividends in additional mutual fund shares, so you can do so very easily.

Reinvesting the dividends into additional fund shares rather than consuming all the income on extravagances is another example of "paying yourself first". If there could be an Eleventh Commandment, it should be this: "Pay Yourself First!". If more people followed this would-be Eleventh Commandment, then they probably wouldn't be as "broke" as the other Ten.

Which "appropriate" mutual fund should you use? In Rule #5 of your *Rulebook* we discuss mutual funds in detail and develop a profile of the ideal mutual fund. By using this profile, you will know exactly how to pick the best of the best of the over 3,800 mutual funds available to meet your particular objectives.

Possibility Fund

Following our allocation/diversification model, you should invest 25% of available dollars (or $37,500 in our example) into your *Possibility Fund*. This fund is so named because anything is possible, investment-wise, with the money earmarked for this part of your portfolio. However, you should still make wise investments, not wild speculations, and never gamble with these dollars.

You should use more direct or aggressive investments in this fund than in either of your other two funds. That is, invest directly into the activity's product or service itself, such as:

❑   individual business opportunities in enterprises that you know best and enjoy most;

❑   rental properties;

❑   stocks and bonds of individual companies;

❑   certain "sector" mutual funds concentrating in single industry-specific securities;

❑   precious metals (gold, silver, platinum, etc.); and

❑   collectibles (rare coins, stamps, fine art, antique furniture or cars, baseball cards, etc.).

Such direct investments are more challenging and potentially more rewarding, and therefore have more risk, than those in your other two investment funds. Consequently, you must use more of your time to sufficiently "investigate before you invest". Since this investing requires more of your time, pick an activity (product or service) that you do or know best and enjoy most. Then, investigation becomes discovery and is fun.

For example, if you love antique furniture and fine art, then you could spend these *Possibility Fund* dollars on furnishing and decorating your house with your investments and not feel as if you are wasting money on depreciating consumables. (Technical note: If you buy fine art, make sure to buy a "Fine Arts Floater" from your insurance company to cover your inventory. Standard homeowner policies have very low, if any, limits for fine art.) Or you could own rental property in a resort area and rightfully have to make tax-deductible visits there often to properly manage the investment. You see, there *is* a smart way to spend money while simultaneously enjoying and profiting from the expenditure. But be honest with yourself and use common sense. Wallpapering a bathroom with collectible baseball cards or classic comic books would be crossing the line of wisdom into the land of absurdity.

You can afford the greater risk for the greater reward potential of these investments, because your *Infinite Financial Freedom Fund* assures your eventual *Infinite Financial Freedom* and liberates you to be more "gutsy" with your *Possibility Fund* dollars. You can afford more fluctuation in value and less liquidity and lower marketability with these investments, because time is on your side. You can wait until it's a seller's market before you sell. For more ideas on other investment vehicle candidates for your *Possibility Fund*, let's look now at Rule #5 that includes the *Ladder of Investments* and information on picking the best mutual funds.

Almost any man knows how to earn money, but not one in a million knows how to spend it.
Henry David Thoreau

Rule #5: Know the Odds Before You Place Your Bets.

"Know the odds before you place your bets" is the gambler's way of saying "investigate before you invest". To make your investigation easier, you need to shrink the universe of possible investments. You reduce the number of prospective investments by using your *Financial Game Plan Rulebook* screen to shake-out the investment *contenders* from the investment *pretenders*.

Your *Rulebook* will dictate and reduce the amount of homework that you will need to do. Without such a *Rulebook*, you will spend countless hours chasing innumerable investments many of which, although possibly good in themselves, may do little or nothing to help you comfortably achieve *your* goals. The Investment Company Institute (a mutual fund trade group), for example, itemizes 21 different potential goal categories pursued by over 3,800 various mutual funds. Now, just pick the right fund for you. You cannot—and fortunately do not need to—investigate all these funds, as you will see in a moment.

First, you investigate mutual funds through a document called the *prospectus* (published by the fund itself) and through other independent rating services (see *Appendix B: Financial Growth Resources* for such rating services). For an explanation of how to read a mutual fund prospectus, see the Investment Company Institute's *Directory of Mutual Funds* (currently available for $5.00 from the ICI, POB 66140, Washington, D.C. 20035). Their book helps you to translate the prospectus into a language that you can understand, so that you can determine how and if a particular mutual fund complies with your *Rulebook*.

The same approach applies to considering any investment (stocks, bonds, real estate, gold, etc.). You should investigate any investment's:

❑ Goals: *What* it hopes to achieve.

❑ Policies: *How* it hopes to achieve it.

❑ Risk: How *risky* it is.

❑ Cost: How much it *costs* to buy, hold, and sell it.

❑ Results: What its *performance history* tells you.

Using the above guidelines, you can develop the pertinent criteria for effectively selecting the best mutual funds for your *Infinite Financial Freedom Fund*, *Balanced Fund*, and *Possibility Fund*.

Picking the Best Mutual Funds: The Nine Mutual Fund Profile Standards

With mutual funds, like all investments, performance alone is not sufficient information. A *contender* fund should, to the extent possible, have a profile based on the following 9 standards for picking the best mutual funds:

① Consistency

Look for consistency of both the mutual fund's return *and* the tenure of the fund manager. When you buy a mutual fund, you are essentially buying the Wall Street smarts of the fund's portfolio manager. Make sure that the fund manager with the investment acumen to create the historically good performance track record is still running the show today.

However, the prospectus usually does *not* reveal the fund manager's name. Further, the fund "manager" is sometimes not an individual, but instead a committee of several advisors stirring the stew of stocks. Some independent rating services reveal the name of the fund manager. The *Forbes* magazine "Honor Roll of Mutual Funds" (published every Fall) includes the fund manager's name and the number of years that the fund manager has been directing the fund.

You should verify the fund manager's name at least every year—every quarter is even better. Despite printed sources, your best bet is to simply call the *contender* fund and ask these three questions:

1. "Who is the fund manager?"

2. "How long has he/she been the fund manager?"

3. "Will he/she continue as the fund manager?"

You buy the manager as well as the fund because history shows that both manager and track record are intimately related. The manager cannot keep his thumbprint off of the fund's performance. Here are two truths to remember about mutual funds and their managers:

1. As a fund manager's tenure increases, so does the success of the fund (*Morningstar Data Fund Study*, January 1993).

2. Following a fund manager change, the best performing funds typically do worse and the worst performing

funds typically do better (*CDA/Wiesenberger Study*, December 1992).

So, the more stable and consistent the fund manager, the more faith you can have that the past performance data is a viable indicator, though not a guarantee, of future results.

② Diversification

The fund should hold no less than 20 and no more than 50 different companies' securities in its portfolio. This type of diversification is the second level of diversification we mentioned in Rule #4 when we discussed *your* diversification or allocation of available dollars into your three investment funds. Now, we are looking at the *fund's* level of diversification by reviewing the number of different securities in its portfolio.

Unfortunately, a mutual fund prospectus no longer includes the portfolio listing of all the securities that the fund holds, but you can get this information easily enough. To review the fund's portfolio of specific holdings, always ask for the fund's "Statement of Additional Information" for those funds that become your investment *contenders*. Thankfully, funds do not charge for either the prospectus or the Statement of Additional Information.

③ Fund Size

As funds grow to over $1 Billion in total assets, the fund manager becomes increasingly challenged to make any trades that produce significant positive impact on return. For example, let's say that each fund in a group of differently sized funds can each sell a block of stock and each make $1 Million in profit.

Each fund experiences the result of this profit differently. Refer to Table 6–4 for details.

TABLE 6–4: HOW FUND SIZE EFFECTS
RETURN ON $1 MILLION PROFIT

	HOW FUND SIZE EFFECTS RETURN ON $1 MILLION PROFIT	
Fund	Fund Size (Asset Value)	Profit as a % of Fund's Asset Value
A	$1 Billion	.1%
B	$500 Million	.2%
C	$100 Million	1%
D	$50 Million	2%
E	$10 Million	10%

Since Fund A's asset value is $1 Billion, the $1 Million profit is only .1% of the fund's total value, so this profit is too small to make much of an impact on the fund's overall return. However, since Fund E's asset value is only $10 Million, the $1 Million profit represents 10% of the fund's total value and this profit is large enough to noticeably impact the fund's overall return.

Of course, if Fund A and Fund E spent the same dollar amount on the initial investment (say $500,000), then Fund A was risking much less of its value than Fund E on the initial purchase. So, there are risk-reward trade-off's, as an equal dollar loss would also negatively impact Fund E more than it would Fund A.

Although there are some notable historic exceptions (such as Fidelity's Magellan Fund), pick funds:

❑   smaller than $1.5 Billion in total assets so as to not dilute returns; and

❑   greater than $10 Million in total assets so as to not expose your investment to too much risk.

④ Portfolio Turnover Rate

Portfolio turnover refers to the percentage of the fund's holdings that the fund sells each year. Pick a fund with a portfolio turnover rate of under 50% per year. Why? The best performing funds have historically been those with portfolio turnover rates of under 50%. That is, these funds have sold ("turned over") under half of their assets per year.

High portfolio turnover generates more brokerage transaction fees that only serve to dilute your return. The lower the turnover, the less of your investment evaporates into buy and sell commissions.

Further, a very high turnover rate could signal poor initial stock picks by the fund manager (who is unloading his losers out of desperation instead of expertise), high risk trading techniques (trading on margin, aggressive use of options, etc.), high redemption rates by other shareholders (what do they know that you don't?), or a combination of these and other factors. So, stick with a fund with a portfolio turnover rate of under 50%.

⑤ True No-Loads

Just what is a "load"? A so-called "load" is a sales charge that the fund pays to a salesperson. These up-front charges most typically range from 2% to 8.5% of your investment.

For example, if you invest $100,000 in a mutual fund with an 8.5% up-front load, then the sales commission equals $8,500 and your net investment into the fund is only $91,500. The $8,500 load is split between the individual stockbroker ("Registered Representative") and the brokerage house.

Loaded-fund salespeople will argue that the overall return—and not the load—is what matters and that you should not focus on the little load (although *they* do). As long as the fund's performance is good, they say, you will make your load and more back over time and you will do just as well in a load versus a no-load fund. And in some cases, this performance argument may indeed hold true, especially if you can hold the fund long enough.

However, this load versus no-load controversy always focuses on the fund's ultimate future performance and misses the hidden loss in a load fund. That hidden loss is the potential earnings on the load itself. In our example of a $100,000 investment in an 8.5% loaded fund, the commission is $8,500. If you were to invest that $8,500 at 10% per year over the next 10 years, that $8,500 would grow to over $23,000! Just ask yourself: "If the loaded fund's performance is good enough to make back the $8,500 sales load, will it also be good enough to make back another $14,500 in earnings on that $8,500 over the next 10 years?"

Loaded-fund salespeople are trained to tell you that the fund's past performance may suggest, but does not guarantee, that the fund will more than make-up for this loss of earnings on the sales charge, too. And, if you feel that the overall investment guidance that you may be receiving from the stockbroker/salesperson is truly worth the sales load *plus* the earnings on the load, then by all means buy the load fund without hesitation (assuming the fund otherwise matches your goals, objectives, desired fund profile, etc.).

If, however, you are not so enamored with such advice or service, then pass on the load fund. If you need professional help in picking a fund, then you are better served by paying a non-commissioned advisor or newsletter a flat-fee for fund recommendations. The fee-for-advice approach eliminates the conflict of interest unfortunately inherent in a fund recommendation from a salesperson who then receives a commission on the mutual fund recommended.

Also, be especially aware that loaded mutual fund companies are becoming extremely creative in finding new ways to load funds. Remember a load by any other name, still stings. Fortunately, the prospectus must disclose all loads, fees, charges, and the like.

My stockbroker friends will hate me for this, but load funds are loaded with too many potential pitfalls for me to recommend load funds. So, pick mutual funds with no "loads" of any kind:

❑   No front-end loads;

❑   No back-end loads;

❑   No "12b–1" fees;

❑   No redemption fees;

❑   No wrap fees;

❑   No deferred sales charges;

❑   No deferred contingent sales charges;

❑   No loads on various classes of shares;

❑   No combination of loads;

❑   No "loads of the week" loads;

❑   No any loads.

No matter how creative the euphemism, a load is a load is a load. So, take a load off your mind and money, simplify your life, and invest only in total and complete no-load funds.

⑥ Low Annual Expense Ratio

Don't confuse a fund's annual expense charge with "loads". All funds—loads and no-loads alike—have annual operating expenses. These costs result from paying the fund's investment advisory firm for managing the fund's portfolio, the printing and mailing of prospectuses, the production of client statements, and other administrative, marketing and operating expenses.

This expense is expressed as a percentage of the fund's total annual asset value. Invest only in funds with annual expense ratios under 2% and preferably 1.5% or lower. The expense ratio is prominently disclosed in the fund's prospectus and Statement of Additional Information.

⑦ Investment Objectives

The fund's investment objective should match your own goal for the investment. Although funds can be categorized even more specifically, stock and bond (non money market) mutual funds generally pursue the principal objectives shown in Table 6–5.

TABLE 6–5: MUTUAL FUND OBJECTIVES

FUND NAME	OBJECTIVE	PORTFOLIO MIX
Aggressive Growth	Maximum Capital Appreciation	Equities of small, new, fledgling companies, etc. Includes Sector Funds w/ single industry securities like computer, health care, biotechnology, etc.
Balanced	Income & Growth	Bonds, preferred stocks & common stocks
Growth	Long-term Conservative Growth	Common stocks of well-established companies
Growth & Income	Long-term Growth & Income	Common stocks with solid growth & dividend history. Includes Utilities Funds.
International	Primarily Growth w/some Income	Non-USA Securities. Includes pure International Funds with 2/3 of assets in equities outside USA & Global Funds with equities both in & outside USA
Municipal Bond	Tax-Exempt Income	Tax-exempt issues of state & local municipalities
Precious Metals	Growth & Inflation Hedge	2/3 of assets in precious & strategic metals stocks (gold/silver/platinum/etc.)
Taxable Bonds	High level of Current Income	Government & corporate debt or preferred stock. Includes Corporate Bond Funds w/assets in corporate bonds & High-Yield ("junk") Bond Funds with 2/3 of assets in lower-rated corporate bonds w/ higher yields

In addition to the above stock and bond funds, there are money market mutual funds. Do not confuse a money market *account* at a bank with a money market *fund*. The former is a bank account essentially based on the return of a money market mutual fund. Funds usually pay a slightly higher rate, have lower expenses, and more flexibility than money market accounts at banks. For example, you can quickly transfer dollars from a money market mutual fund to a stock or bond fund (or back) in the same family with just a toll-free phone call. This two-way transfer feature alone makes the money market *fund* preferable to the money market *account*.

There are two basic types of money market mutual funds, tax-free and taxable:

FUND NAME	OBJECTIVE	PORTFOLIO MIX
Tax-free	Tax-free income with minimum risk	Municipal securities with short maturities
Taxable	Taxable income with minimum risk	High-grade money market securities with maturities averaging 90 days or less

The tax-free money market mutual fund is the investment vehicle to use for you *Operating Fund*.

Each mutual fund must list its specific goals and objectives in its prospectus. By reviewing the prospectuses of *contender* funds, you can eliminate those funds that do not match your own goals and objectives for the money you are investing. There are short-cuts to reading through a pile of prospectuses and we will discuss these quicker methods after completing the profile. However, you should still absolutely read through the prospectus and Statement of Additional Information of each "finalist" fund *before* you send them your money. If you follow the *Infinite Financial Freedom* principles of reducing the universe of funds, you will be reading just a very few fund prospectuses and Statements of Additional Information.

⑧ Performance

Many a fund's performance can be a one-calendar-quarter-marvel on *Barron's* charts, just like a 60's one-hit-wonder rock band that disappears after producing one Top Ten record on the *Billboard* charts. So, look at the fund's 10-year annualized return. You want to see how well the fund has fared over several up and down markets, not just the most recent three months.

Any fund manager can get lucky over one calendar quarter and report a stunning three-month performance. Although this information may give you some sense of the fund's current trend in comparison to other funds and to the market as a whole, always focus on the long-term return data when viewing funds through your profile screen. Consider the fund's long-term performance track-record in light of your own required rate of return (which we will discuss in Rule #18 of your *Rulebook*).

⑨ Volatility

A fund's riskiness relative to the market as a whole is measured by a volatility factor known as its *beta co-efficient* or simply *beta*. Despite its technical sounding name, here is all that you need to know about a fund's *beta*:

❑   If its *beta* = 0.75, then the fund is 75% as volatile as the market (the fund swings up and down less deeply than the market);

❑   If its *beta* = 1.00, then the fund is 100% as volatile as
     the market (the fund swings with the market);

❑   If its *beta* = 1.50, then the fund is 150% as volatile as
     the market (the fund swings up and down more
     deeply than the market).

Beta reflects the fund's risk-reward relationship relative to
the entire market. The greater the fund's volatility (the higher
its *beta*), the greater the potential reward you should expect
and the greater risk you should be willing to accept. So, when
looking at a fund's *beta*, see if the fund's return is paying-off
for the greater volatility risk it takes. We will discuss this
risk-reward relationship in more detail when we raise the
Ladder of Investments subject later in this Rule.

You can use *beta* as a tie-breaker to decide between
otherwise comparable funds. For example, if you discover
two funds with comparable profiles including equal 10-year
annualized return figures, pick the fund with the lower *beta*.
The fund with the lower *beta* has produced the same return
with less volatility risk.

Don't let a high *beta* scare you, if the fund's return justifies
the high volatility and the fund otherwise matches your
profile. You can telephone the fund toll-free for *beta*
information. Rating services, such as *CDA/Wiesenberger* and
Morningstar, also publish this and other fund information for
a fee (see *Appendix B: Financial Growth Resources*).

Shrinking the Universe of Mutual Funds
Using Your Fund Profile Screen

Given the above fund profile Standards, you can sift
through the universe of over 3,800 mutual funds using your

profile screen to eliminate all but a few funds. Fortunately, there are computer on-line, subscription, and service bureau firms available to help accelerate your process of fund elimination. Otherwise, you could spend what might seem like eons sifting through mounds of data manually.

CompuServe and *Prodigy* are two of the most prominent on-line computer services that offer such services as part of their broader news and information retrieval databases. However, these and other on-line services charge a monthly subscription fee, connect time charges and communication surcharges. If all that you want is the mutual fund information, then these services can be cost prohibitive. If you want to subscribe to one of their levels of service anyway and you gain access to the mutual fund information as well, then these on-line services can make sense.

Of course, you must have the computer and modem hardware and software to access these on-line services. The connect software is nominal (about $25), because the services make their money from your ongoing subscription and connect time charges. However, the hardware including a printer could cost you $2,500 to $5,000 for an adequate to excellent system, respectively. If you must have real-time, on-demand data continuously at your fingertips, then the on-line computer-based services are your best choice.

Morningstar and *CDA/Wiesenberger* are two companies that offer their data in either hard copy or CD-ROM computer disk format. These services, too, charge subscription fees for the initial information and the ongoing updates. If you buy their services (they're not cheap), then you should enroll in the updating program to stay current.

The simplest alternative is to just have a service bureau do the search for you for a nominal fee on an as-needed basis.

You provide the profile; they do the search and send you the results. This alternative is the most cost-effective if you are just interested in picking your initial funds and then reviewing them quarterly or annually (more on this alternative below).

To illustrate the principle of using your mutual fund profile to shrink the universe of funds to just a few *contenders* within seconds, we recently asked *The Fund Exchange*™ to do a computer search for us. We asked them to find the best fund from the universe of over 3,800 mutual funds based on our profile. Unless you can read at the speed of light, it will take you longer to read about the results of the search than it took *The Fund Exchange*™ to do the search. Notice how the number of *contender* funds shrinks as we apply each criterion of our mutual fund profile screen. See Table 6–6.

TABLE 6–6: SHRINKING THE UNIVERSE OF MUTUAL FUNDS

SHRINKING THE UNIVERSE OF MUTUAL FUNDS		
Profile Screen Criteria	Our Choice	# of Funds Remaining
Fund Type	Aggressive Growth	193
Load Fee	No-load	90
Redemption Fee	None	65
12b-1 Fees	None	51
Annual Expense	Less than 1.5%	34
Performance	High-to-Very High	4
Asset Size	$500,000 & over	2

Keeping in mind that these results are for a snapshot in time, here are highlights of the differences between the two *contender* funds:

	Twentieth Century Ultra	Janus Fund Twenty
Current Return	13.9%	2.6%
1 Year	39.2%	16.7%
3 Year	28.4%	16.4%
5 year	24.5%	23.8%
10 Year	13.6%	N/A
Annual Expenses	1.00%	1.08%

As you can tell from the above results, the longer that you hold on to the funds, the closer the returns resemble each other. In addition, the annual expense ratios are nearly the same. Still, Twentieth Century Ultra looks like the better investment candidate. We can use *beta* versus performance as a tie-breaker and confirmation of our choice between the two *contender* funds:

	Twentieth Century Ultra	Janus Fund Twenty
Beta Co-efficient	1.52	1.27

Since *beta* is a performance factor relative to the market, *The Fund Exchange*™ also reports relative performance in the most recent Bull (up cycle) and Bear (down cycle) markets:

	20th Century Ultra	Janus Fund 20	Ultra minus Janus	S&P 500 Index	Ultra minus S&P
Bull 10/90–6/93	159.5%	95.8%	+63.7 points	60.9%	+98.6 points
Bear 5/90–10/90	-17.1%	-16.7%	-0.4 points	-14.5%	-2.6 points

These relative returns are as you might expect. During the Bull up-market cycle, Twentieth Century Ultra with the higher *beta*, significantly outperformed Janus by 63.7 percentage points. Both funds outperformed the market as measured by the return on the S&P 500 Index (Standard & Poor's Index of 500 stocks).

However, during the Bear down-market cycle, Twentieth Century Ultra underperformed Janus by only 0.4 percentage points and underperformed the market (S&P 500) by only 2.6 percentage points. Given the above results, you should pick the 20th Century Ultra Fund over the Janus Fund 20. Why?

Twentieth Century Ultra consistently and significantly outperforms Janus over time, even though Twentieth Century Ultra is more volatile (has a higher *beta*). In a down market, the downside potential for Twentieth Century Ultra compared to Janus is almost non-existent (a 0.4 percentage point difference) and compared to the market is small (only 2.6 percentage points). However, in an up market, the upside potential for Twentieth Century Ultra compared to either Janus or the market is quite significant (+63.7 and +98.6 percentage points, respectively).

In other words, when Twentieth Century Ultra drops, the fund drops about the same as Janus and not much more than the market. However, when Twentieth Ultra goes up, the fund goes way up, well beyond either Janus or the market.

Given the above performance, Twentieth Century Ultra is the better choice (assuming history repeats itself and the fund otherwise matches your profile). Remember that the figures are historical and represent a snapshot in time. You will need to keep snapping these shots of history as part of your regular ongoing review.

Also, keep in mind that, in the above example, we were comparing two of the best Aggressive Growth funds possible. You might want to order the prospectus and Statement of Additional Information for each fund for further review before making a final decision. You don't have to ultimately pick one or the other fund. If you find two funds that are both stellar, then you can always split your investable dollars between the two funds for additional diversification.

The Fund Exchange™

Reducing the universe of over 3,800 mutual funds down to one takes time and, therefore, money. You can do the analysis manually, but your time is probably worth more than the time that manual analysis requires. Earlier, we discussed a number of ways to collapse the analysis time frames for picking a mutual fund.

As a service to *Infinite Financial Freedom* readers, *The Fund Exchange*™ will perform computer searches at a reduced charge. *The Fund Exchange*™ normally charges $50 per search and $20 per additional search requested at the same time. However, for *Infinite Financial Freedom* readers, they will charge only $25 for the first search and only $10 for each additional search requested at the same time. Results can be mailed or faxed back to you. If you are interested in taking advantage of their service, just follow the instructions on their *Mutual Fund Computer Search Request* (Form 6–3) below.

FORM 6–3: MUTUAL FUND COMPUTER SEARCH REQUEST

MUTUAL FUND COMPUTER SEARCH REQUEST
Name
Address
City   State   ZIP
Phone Number:
FAX # (if return Fax wanted):
SEARCH CRITERIA (Check or Circle One Per Section):
FUND TYPE: ☐ Aggressive Growth   ☐ Municipal Bond ☐ Balanced   ☐ Precious Metals ☐ Growth   ☐ Taxable Bond ☐ Growth & Income   ☐ Tax-Free Money Market ☐ International   ☐ Taxable Money Market
LOADS(%): ☐ None   ☐2   ☐3   ☐4   ☐5   ☐7   ☐8.5
REDEMPTION FEE: None   Some
12B–1 FEES: None   Some
ANNUAL EXPENSE % below:☐0.5 ☐1 ☐1.5 ☐2 ☐3 ☐6
PERFORMANCE: ☐High-VeryHigh ☐Average-VeryHigh ☐Very High ☐High ☐Average ☐Low ☐Very Low
ASSET SIZE OF FUND (in $ Millions): ☐Under 10   ☐10–24.9   ☐25–49.9   ☐50–99.9 ☐100–249.9   ☐250–499.9   ☐500 & over
BETA COEFFICIENT: ☐Below 0   ☐Greater than 1.0 ☐0 to 0.5   ☐0.5 to 1.0   ☐1 to 1.5   ☐over 1.5
☐ I have enclosed: $ 25 for the first search plus $_____for_____additional search(es) at $10 each $ Total Payable to: BENEFITS RESOURCE GROUP
Return form to: *The Fund Exchange*™ BENEFITS RESOURCE GROUP P. O. Box 943, Malibu, CA 90265
Note: Please copy, complete & return one form for each search.

After screening the fields of funds, the ones left standing are your initial candidates for investment. The prospectus and the Statement of Additional Information for each *contender* fund along with the other rules in you *Financial Game Plan Rulebook* will help you zero-in on the best of the best funds to meet your goals.

Direct Investments

For your *Possibility Fund,* I recommend that you consider more direct investments, especially into rental real estate properties, such as apartments, condos, and single family homes. Why? Such assets produce tax-sheltered income and potential for equity growth and significant returns when using financial "leverage". Leverage is simply using a small amount of money (like a down payment) to control a large amount of money (like the property's entire value).

Real Estate Investment Caveats

When considering a real estate investment, keep these key caveats in mind (books have been written about each one):

- ❏ Educate yourself. Remember that *reading* is the first step to learning and that *doing* is the second step. See *Appendix B: Financial Growth Resources* for information on helpful real estate investment books.

- ❏ Your second step (doing) should be small. Start with small, inexpensive properties to get acquainted with real estate industry policies and procedures and to find out if you really like the field. Starting small is less threatening and if you do make a mistake, the cost for educating yourself not to repeat it is small. Once you are familiar with the principles of making money in real estate, you can move up to larger properties. The principles remain the same with any size property. All that changes is the number of zeros in front of the decimal point.

❑ Use mortgages; that is, do not buy properties for investment purposes using "all cash". Using mortgages gives you the financial leverage that can generate significant returns on your investment.

❑ Pick investments only with positive cash flow, that is, those for which the rental income covers your expenses including the mortgage payments.

❑ Keep in mind that acts of Congress more than acts of God can change the viability of any investment. At least you can buy insurance to fund your recovery from unexpected acts of God. Congress, on the other hand, has enacted and feels compelled to continuously change specific tax laws governing all aspects of real estate (and other) investments, especially in their treatment of income as "active" or "passive" and of depreciation. Learn *their* real estate rulebook and you can use their laws to your best advantage.

❑ Stay actively involved in your real estate investment. Even if you hire a property management firm to handle many of the details, you should still actively oversee their management of the property. There are not just tax reasons for remaining "active" in the management, but your watchful involvement is pure common sense. No one ever cares about your investment as much as you do.

❑   Do not buy into Limited Partnerships or "blind
    pools". Someone once told me that all I need to know
    about blind pools is what rhymes with pools: "Blind
    Pools for Blind Fools," he said. I saw the light: Buy
    and manage your own select properties directly or
    stay out of the real estate business all together.

Buying real estate is not just a good theoretical
investment. Real estate can help fund several practical goals,
if arranged properly. The best place to start is right in your
own home. See *Your Home As A Tax Shelter* in *Appendix B:
Financial Growth Resources* for details.

We already mentioned the idea of buying rental property
in a resort area that you like to frequent. For example, you
could buy a duplex in the resort area and then rent one half of
the property to others while saving the other half for your
own use. Resort area properties usually have shorter term
tenants and higher vacancy rates, but you can also charge
more rent. Again, you need to learn about the trade-off's of
the investment before you invest. However, do not get
involved in "time share" properties that you often find in
resort areas or in any "get-rich-quick" schemes. Remember,
you don't "get rich quick", if ever, as often as "you get rich
smart". To get smarter, read *Real Estate Wealthbuilding*. See
Appendix B: Financial Growth Resources for details.

As another example, you can use real estate to fund a child's
college education. One way is to accelerate the equity in your
home by making extra payments that apply to your principal.
For, example, by making one extra payment a year and applying
that entire payment to your principal you can significantly
increase your home's equity over the 18 years before your child
is ready to go to college. At college time, you can take-out a
tax-deductible home equity loan to pay for college expenses.
Another alternative is to buy a piece of rental property in the

anticipated college town. While waiting for your child to be ready for college, you receive all the rental income, tax deductions and growth potential typical of rental property. Then at college time, you can either sell the property or take out a loan against it to pay for educational expenses or your child can use the property for housing.

If you are initially uncomfortable but interested in such investments, then sit on the sidelines for a few years and pretend. Pretend that you already bought a specific piece of property, but don't in reality buy it. Instead, save the money in your *Infinite Financial Freedom Fund* and just play on paper. Watch your hypothetical investment and see if the return potential is enough to excite you to really buy into real estate. If not, stay out. There are plenty of other viable investments in the world.

Ladder of Investments

What else can you do with the funds allotted to your *Possibility Fund*? Again, anything is possible. Your goals and *Rulebook* will guide you here, but you can afford to take greater risk with this money than with that in your other two investment funds. Here are some other possible investments:

❑   Start your own small business in *What You Do Best & Enjoy Most*.

❑   Buy individual stocks in worthwhile companies that you know because of the type of work that you do or used to do. We will discuss this idea more fully in Rule #16 of your *Rulebook*.

❑   Invest in industry-specific Sector mutual funds. These funds concentrate their investments in the securities of one particular industry like health care, biotechnology, computers, pharmaceuticals, space technology, and the like. Due to the single industry exposure, these funds have greater risk, but greater potential reward than more broadly diversified mutual funds.

❑ Invest in Aggressive Growth mutual funds. As we discussed earlier, these funds seek pure growth and will take greater risk to achieve it.

❑ Speculate in gold or silver bullion and/or in rare coins, rare stamps or other collectibles about which you may know something. These collectibles could include antique cars, antique furniture, fine art, and the like.

See the accompanying Chart 6–3 and Figure 6–2: *Ladder of Investments* for these and other possible investment vehicles. To reduce the universe of investments to a manageable few, you know to investigate the investment itself. You should also investigate *you*. After all, it is not enough for an investment just to be a good investment. It must be a good investment *for you*. Knowing both your Money Personality and *risk tolerance* helps you to determine which investments are best for you. Buying "futures contracts on pork bellies" may be a great investment, but if you can't sleep at night because you're worrying about your investment going belly-up, then the investment is not good for you.

We covered how you can learn your Money Personality in *Chapter 4: What To Do Before You Win* and in Rule #6, we discuss how to determine your *risk tolerance*—next.

One of the greatest pieces of economic wisdom is to know what you do not know.
                                        John Kenneth Galbraith

CHART 6–3: LADDER OF INVESTMENTS

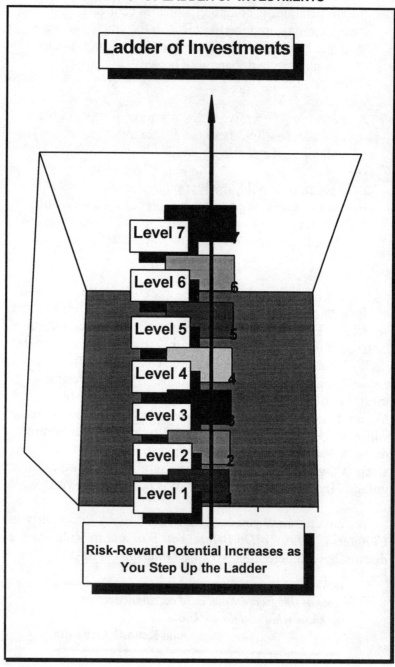

Ladder of Investments

Level 7

Level 6

Level 5

Level 4

Level 3

Level 2

Level 1

Risk-Reward Potential Increases as You Step Up the Ladder

FIGURE 6–2: LADDER OF INVESTMENTS

LADDER OF INVESTMENTS
LEVEL 7
Futures Contracts
LEVEL 6
Collectibles
Speculative Common Stocks
Speculative Bonds
Precious Metals
LEVEL 5
Put & Call Options
Limited Partnerships
Real Estate Investment Properties
Business Opportunities
LEVEL 4
"Blue Chip" Common Stocks
Growth Mutual Funds
LEVEL 3
Investment Grade Convertible Securities
Investment Grade Preferred Stock
Balanced Mutual Funds
LEVEL 2
Investment Grade Municipal Bonds
Investment Grade Corporate Bonds
Pension Plan Funds
Money Market Funds
LEVEL 1
Guaranteed Annuities
Life Insurance Cash Values
Certificates of Deposit
EE & HH Savings Bonds
U.S. Treasury Securities
Insured Checking Accounts
Insured Savings Accounts

Rule #6: Decide How Close to the Vest You Want to Play.

How "close to the vest" you play your investment cards requires that you decide how much exposure to risk you will take in return for the potential reward. You will play different hands differently. That is, you should be willing to take different risks with different investments, based on what you are trying to achieve with each investment.

For example, you should be willing to take very little or no risk at all with your *Infinite Financial Freedom Fund* (Levels 1 and 2 on the *Ladder of Investments*). For your *Possibility Fund*, however, you can climb as high as Level 7, if you are that daring. In any case, keep in mind that there are two unbreakable and related forces of the investment universe revolving around the ladder: Risk and Reward. These two investment forces produce the trade-off effects on your money shown in Figure 6–3.

FIGURE 6–3: RISK-REWARD TRADE-OFF'S

ELEVATION ON THE *LADDER OF INVESTMENTS*	THE RISK	THE REWARD
The *higher* the elevation, the greater your potential for:	The loss of your money	The growth of your money
The *lower* the elevation, the greater your potential for:	The loss of your money's buying power	The safety of your money

In both cases, you have risk *and* reward. However, you can't have both risk-free safety *and* a guaranteed high return. Life is full of trade-off's and investment life is no exception. With investments, you have to trade-off safety for return. But you must risk something. As in life, if you do nothing, you risk potentially everything. Anytime that anyone presents you with a magical investment that contradicts the undeniable interplay between the forces of risk versus reward, run away quickly and take your money with you!

Think of the risk-reward relationship this way: The higher that you venture up the ladder, the farther and quicker that you can fall (the more money that you can lose), but the air is better and the upper view is more rewarding (the more money that you can make). The lower on the ladder that you live, the less likely it is that you will fall (the less money that you can lose), but the air is thicker and the view is less rewarding (the less money that you can make). Either way, you have risk. You either risk your money (by seeking more daring returns) or you risk your money's ability to buy things (by seeking more safety).

Also, as you climb the *Ladder of Investments*, the wind increases and your return can fluctuate more than at lower levels on the ladder. In Rule #5, we found that financial people call this fluctuation *beta*. In addition, if you want your money to mean something, you have to stay ahead of wherever inflation is currently living on the ladder. Otherwise, you may safely get the return *of* your money, but not enough of a return *on* your money to be safely able to buy as much as you used to be able buy *with* your money.

Do not let the insuring of the safety of your money (like at a bank) lure you into a false feeling of security. Think of you and your investment as if you are in a boat rowing upstream. You are rowing your boat (your investment) at 5 mph (your return) against a current (inflation) traveling at 8 mph in the *opposite* direction. There is a waterfall downstream just *behind* you. Where are you going to go at *minus* 3 mph? Unless you start rowing faster, you are going over the edge of the waterfall. Too many people, who are excessively concerned with the safety of their money, believe that the solution to this problem is to insure the boat! So, they buy a bank CD that pays a rate lower than the current rate of inflation, but it's insured, so they feel safe. Meanwhile, the hidden undercurrent of inflation slowly eats away at their money's purchasing power until they finally get their money back and realize that they themselves can't eat as much with their money as they could before.

People making such uninformed financial decisions have effectively bought a losing investment and then insured the loss while assuming that the insurance somehow guarantees the investment's performance. You, of course, will not make the same mistake, because you are aware of the need to outperform inflation and your *Infinite Financial Freedom Fund* (not the FDIC or anyone else) is guaranteeing your future financial liberty. So, you can afford to take sufficient risks with your other investment funds to stay ahead of inflation and meet your other goals.

Risk Tolerance Test

Investment advisors call your ability or willingness to tolerate risk as your *risk tolerance*. You determine your risk tolerance by accepting certain trade-off's between risk and reward. To help you determine your acceptable level of risk for a particular investment, you can take the *risk tolerance test* shown in Figure 6–4.

FIGURE 6–4: RISK TOLERANCE TEST

RISK TOLERANCE TEST			
Circle the number corresponding to your answer:			
In exchange for a greater potential long-term total return, are you willing to trade:	YES	SOME	NO
A Sharp fluctuations in the value of your money over time? (Stability)	3	2	1
B Receiving the current income from you money now? (Income)	3	2	1
C Having your money always quickly available to you? (Marketability)	3	2	1
D Having your money quickly available without a penalty or any loss to the money? (Liquidity)	3	2	1
E A guaranteed, but lower return on your money? (Purchasing Power)	3	2	1
F Sum of each Column:			
G Total Score (Sum of Row F across):			

The higher your score, the greater your tolerance to risk and the higher up the ladder that you can comfortably venture. If you scored 5, you had better stay on Levels 1 and 2. If you scored 15, you will still feel comfortable even on Level 7. Re-take the test every time that you are planning to make an investment for a specific purpose. Take the test with the investment and the purpose in mind. Your test results will help you validate the suitability of the investment *for you*. See Figure 6–5 for scoring results.

FIGURE 6–5: RISK TOLERANCE TEST SCORES

RISK TOLERANCE TEST SCORES	
Your Score	Highest Acceptable Level of Risk
14–15	Level 7
12–13	Level 6
10–11	Level 5
8–9	Level 4
6–7	Level 3
5	Level 2

One of the best ways to gauge your *risk tolerance* is to simply ask yourself: "If I make this investment, will I be able to sleep soundly at night and live worry-free during the day?" If your answer is "No", then the investment is too risky for you. After all, life—despite its inherent risks—is to enjoy. Don't let any investment, regardless of its potential return, lessen your ability to enjoy life.

In dealing with risk, keep in mind these two principles:

❑ Investment is really only deferred consumption, so your eventual spending goal helps to determine the appropriate risk level to take; and

❑   You can eliminate most risk simply through sufficient diversification (see Rule #4).

So, overall, you should be willing to take increasingly more risks in trade for greater return with your four funds:

Fund #	Fund Name	Highest Acceptable Level of Risk
1	Operating Fund	1
2	Infinite Financial Freedom Fund	2
3	Balanced Fund	3
4	Possibility Fund	7

For your first three funds, the risk-reward relationship places you on Level 3 or below of the *Ladder of Investments*. For your *Possibility Fund*, you should be willing to climb to a much higher risk-reward elevation. If you are extremely risk-averse, then you could even invest *Possibility Fund* dollars at Levels 1–3. However, since you have your other three funds on the first three levels, you should and can afford to venture higher up the ladder in search of many happier returns.

Once you have selected an investment that suits your *risk tolerance*, that is, *where* you are on the ladder, you must decide *when* to climb the ladder (buy) and *when* to jump-off the ladder (sell). In Rule #7, we will discuss the investment timing of your buy and sell decisions—next.

> *To get profit without risk, experience without danger, and reward without work, is as impossible as it is to live without being born.*
>
> Gouthey

Rule #7: Know When To Hold 'Em & Know When to Fold 'Em.

This rule deals with a timeless topic: *When*. When buying and selling investments without a plan, you can panic at price changes and you may pull the buy/sell trigger prematurely (what I call *Investus Interruptus*). Impatience and such knee-jerk, reflex-investing comes *not* from the lack of discipline, but from the lack of a plan.

The plan must precede the discipline. Your self-discipline comes from your commitment to your plan. Your commitment comes from your knowledge that the plan assures your success. This assurance is extremely liberating and allows you to take the best action at the best time. So, when is the best time?

Before you buy any investment, always determine in advance at what point you will sell. How do you figure the sell point? In pursuit of your *Infinite Financial Freedom*, use these four common sense strategies to *know when to hold 'em & when to fold 'em*:

Strategy #1	Let your goal's *time horizon* guide you.
Strategy #2	Let the crowd guide you—in the *opposite* direction.
Strategy #3	Be willing to take a small, *paper* loss.
Strategy #4	Let your *insight* guide you.

Now, let's discuss the details of each of these four strategies to help you buy low and sell high.

Strategy #1:
Let Your Goal's *Time Horizon* Guide You

Although not itself a buy/sell *trading* strategy, here's how your goal's *time horizon* importantly guides your buy/sell decisions and investment selection:

❏ *Hold 'Em*:	Buy and Hold from the date of your initial investment.
❏ *Fold 'Em*:	Sell when you reach the end of your goal's built-in *time horizon*.

Since most of your *Infinite Financial Freedom* goals will be long-term, your *time horizon* for each particular goal will guide you how long to hold each investment. For your *Operating Fund*, however, your *time horizon* is "now"; that is, you need immediate access to your money for living expenses every day. This need, too, helps you to determine the best buy/sell points.

You cannot pick an investment for your *Operating Fund* that requires a long-term holding period to be profitable, such as a long-term CD or collectible fine art, and the like. You need your money today, so you must have an investment with immediate *marketability* (a market that will immediately buy or redeem your investment) and *liquidity* (immediate access to your money without any loss or penalty). So, the requirements of your goal are determining both the appropriate type of investment and your *holding period* (how long you can keep your money in it before you have to get your money back out of it). The goal of your *Operating Fund* requires that you invest in the money market, so that you can have the immediate access to your funds that you require. In this case, your *time horizon* is effectively non-existent. You need to buy and sell continuously and without high transaction fees. An investment in a money market fund meets these real-time and low-expense needs.

On the other end of your investment time continuum, your *time horizon* for investments into your *Infinite Financial Freedom Fund* is 20 years, since you have a 20-year window during which time you receive your annual lottery checks. For this investment, you can afford the longer holding period and price fluctuation inherent in long-term municipal bonds that will give you the tax-advantaged return that you require. Your biggest challenge here is to pick the best mutual fund (see Rule #5 for how). Then let the fund manager make the specific bond portfolio buy and sell decisions for you.

Still, the *time horizon* of both the investment and your goal need to match each other. Again, your goal's *time horizon* is guiding your selection of type of investment (in this case, long-term municipal bonds) as well as your holding period (in this case, at least 20 years).

Likewise, let the *time horizon* of your goals guide your investments into your *Balanced Fund* and *Possibility Fund*. For example, if saving for a child's college education is a goal, then the time between the child's current age and college age will help dictate the type of investment and its holding period. The longer your *time horizon*, the greater price fluctuation risk you can bear, as long as the long-term direction in the investment's return is up.

Strategy #2:
Let the Crowd Guide You—in the *Opposite* Direction.

So-called *contrarian* investing means making your buy and sell decisions by not following the crowd, that is, by investing *contrary* to the crowd's actions. Here's how this strategy guides you to buy low and sell high:

❑ *Hold 'Em:*	Buy and Hold fundamentally good stocks on *bad* news.
❑ *Fold 'Em:*	Sell good stocks on *good* news.

The bad news of *Tylenol* tampering temporarily tumbled its manufacturer's stock, so you could buy the stock at artificially low levels due to mass crowd hysteria. This quick depression of an otherwise fundamentally good stock creates a built-in profit, *if* the stock just returns to its initial pre-hysteria levels. In this case, the drug manufacturer's stock price moved back up *beyond* its pre-tampering levels.

On the other hand, if a pharmaceutical company announces the good news of receiving an FDA approval for a new drug that controls a prominent disease, the crowd will clamor and "buy the stock price up" (trading jargon for inflating the stock price). On this announcement of good news, be a willing seller, as the stock's price is often momentarily and artificially inflated by the crowd's over-buying hysteria. The price will soon enough correct itself (drop) to its pre-hysteria levels at which point you can buy back the stock again (for less), if you still want to maintain a position in it. If the news is permanent good news for the company, the stock will probably re-achieve and maintain at least the hysteria price levels.

Strategy #3:
Be Willing to Take a Small, *Paper* Loss.

You cannot consistently buy at the *absolute* lows and sell at the *absolute* highs. However, if you are willing to accept a small, *paper* loss, you can nearly always make a profit while limiting the downside risk, irrespective of all-time lows and highs. Here's how this strategy effects your buy/sell decisions:

❑ *Hold 'Em*:	Buy and Hold the stock as long as its price does not drop more than its historical fluctuation percentage.
❑ *Fold 'Em*:	Sell when the price drops more than its historical fluctuation percentage.

How small is a *small* loss? This amount is specific to the individual investment. You will have to do some historical homework to determine the amount of the small loss, but investigation gives you an investment edge. Most libraries carry the Standard & Poor's or similar reference manuals that contain historical price data on most publicly traded securities. Also, you can simply call the company itself and ask to speak to the person in charge of "Investor Relations" and ask for the stock's price history. Usually, they are happy to hear from prospective new investors (you represent new money to them) and they are happy to send you their stock's price history along with a current annual report.

Let's say, for example, that you buy a stock (or bond or mutual fund, etc.) currently selling at $50 a share, that you track its price movement weekly, and that historically this stock's price does not fluctuate more than 10% (on a week-to-week basis). At $50 a share, you should expect the price to fluctuate up and down by $5 to between $45 and $55 a share (10% x $50 = $5). Now, one of three things can happen:

1. The price will stay the same. If the price stays the same, continue to hold unless other than price considerations arise.

2. The price will go down. Never worry about a 10% weekly drop in price—this movement is typical. If the current price drops over 10%, sell it.

3. The price will go up. When the price goes up, the fun begins. You move with the stock. Here's how:

Keeping the sell trigger *percentage* the same (10%), move your sell trigger *price* up with the stock. Say that the stock eventually moves up to $60 a share (after some acceptable weekly fluctuations). You still sell if the stock drops by over 10%, but now the stock price has to drop below $54 ($60 - 10% or $6 = $54). If the stock either doesn't drop by over 10% or it continues to rise, then hold onto it.

Using this strategy, you will always make a profit, unless when you first buy the stock, it immediately drops below its sell trigger percentage—a risk you have to be willing to accept. In our example, you have limited your downside loss to 10% of your initial investment. However, there is no limit on the profit you can make, because you continue to hold onto the stock as long as it moves up (without any greater than 10% drops).

In Table 6–7, you can see how the sell trigger *price* moves with the stock price while the sell trigger *percentage* stays the same (10%). Notice that the stock drops by 5% down to $47.50 a share immediately after you buy it. If you didn't have the discipline of a plan and the knowledge of the stock's typical fluctuation percentage, you might panic, sell prematurely, and miss the eventual rise.

TABLE 6–7: KNOW WHEN TO HOLD 'EM AND KNOW WHEN TO FOLD 'EM

KNOW WHEN TO HOLD 'EM; KNOW WHEN TO FOLD 'EM			
Weekly Current Price	% Weekly Change from Previous Price	Advice (Hold/ Fold)	New Sell Trigger Price (-10% of Current Price)
$50.00	N/A	Hold	$45.00
$47.50	-5.00%	H	$42.75
$49.40	+4.00%	H	$44.46
$50.88	+3.00%	H	$45.79
$51.90	+2.00%	H	$46.71
$51.38	-1.00%	H	$46.24
$55.23	+7.50%	H	$49.71
$57.99	+5.00%	H	$52.19
$60.31	+4.00%	H	$54.28
$59.10	-2.00%	H	$53.19
$63.83	+8.00%	H	$57.45
$67.02	+5.00%	H	$60.32
$60.00	-10.47%	Fold	N/A

You still have a paper loss at the end of week three, but the stock is moving up, so you hold on for the ride. Even though you held the stock when the price was as high as $67.02 (in the second to last week), you sold at $60.00 because at $60.00 the stock dropped to over 10% below the $67.02 previous price. So, you took an *imaginary*, small paper loss: $7.02 per share (the difference between the $67.02 *theoretical* high and your $60.00 sell point). However, because you *know when to hold 'em and when to fold 'em*, you made a $10.00 per share *real* profit (the difference between the $50.00 original price and your $60.00 sell price)—a 20% gain.

If you use this technique to buy a stock (and some mutual funds through certain stockbrokers), you can automate the process by using a "Trailing Stop Order". In our example, you would place a "Stop Loss Order" (when you buy) at 10% below the purchase price. As the stock's price advances, so does the Stop Order. If the stock's price drops below the 10% Stop Loss Order level, the stockbroker automatically sells your position in the stock.

The above strategy is an example of what is known in investment parlance as "trading on technical analysis". In this case, you are trading based on the movement of this technical indicator: the stock's own price change within a given percentage range. There are several (too many) other technical indicators that you can follow alone or in combination, such as these principal indicators:

❑ Current price changes versus moving averages of 30, 60, 90, 120, 180 days, etc., alone or in combination;

❑ Interest Rate Curves;

❑ Payroll Employment Index;

- ❑ Advance verses Decline Lines;

- ❑ Wage Settlement Index;

- ❑ Odd-Lot Studies;

- ❑ The Dollar Index;

- ❑ Trading Volume;

- ❑ Flow of Mutual Funds Cash-to-Assets Studies;

- ❑ Inventory-to-Sales Ratio;

- ❑ S&P 500 Composite Stock Index;

- ❑ Wilshire 5000 Index;

- ❑ Dow Indices;

- ❑ Any combination of the above and more.

The list is endless. Some speculators even use the winning conference of the Super Bowl or skirt hem lines as indicators of future market movement. (By the way, the winning of the Super Bowl by the National Football Conference or rising hem lines stimulate a rise in the market.)

The above use of statistics to trade securities is known as "technical analysis" while other speculators use what is known as "fundamental analysis". Fundamental analysts study the individual characteristics of the company issuing the security to determine if the investment is viable and when to trade it. Fundamental analysts look at such factors as:

- ❑ Earnings per share;

- ❏   Unit Sales Volume;

- ❏   Pre-tax Profit Margin;

- ❏   Dividends;

- ❏   Price-Earnings Ratio;

- ❏   Debt-Equity Ratio;

- ❏   Return on Stockholder's Equity;

- ❏   And a host of other ratios developed from the manipulation of a company's financial statements.

There are many portfolio management computer programs and newsletters for both technical and fundamental analysts to help "correctly" time the purchase and sale of securities. Their goal, of course, is to help you buy low and sell high.

However, as we discussed before, beware of timing systems—computerized or otherwise—that purport to predict the perfect price points for making buy and sell decisions. The problem with such systems is *not* that they are bad. In reality, just the opposite is true—they are *too* good. The problem is that too many talented analysts are spending all their waking moments creating systems to try to outsmart every other analyst's system. This fierce competition creates an environment in which any one analyst's success is too dependent on every other analyst's mistakes.

If someone has discovered the magical market timing technique or the secret balance sheet manipulation to make zillions in the stock market, you can bet your top and bottom dollar that they are not telling you—or anyone else. For more information on the futility of known market timing techniques, see Robert Jeffrey's "The Folly of Stock Market Timing" (*Harvard Business Review*, July-August, 1984). Teaching technical or fundamental analysis is, of course, beyond the scope or even desire of this book. I am convinced that professional money managers are so adept at both approaches that they merely correct each other's moves in their continuing volley to outperform one another.

Strategy #4:
Let Your *Insight* Guide You.

Insight is more than a "gut feeling" or a "hunch", although it can include these. *Insight* is an awareness, a perception supported by knowledge and understanding. Here is how *insight* can help you make buy/sell decisions:

❑ *Hold 'Em*:	Buy and Hold a stock when you have some positive personal *insight* into the company's product or service.
❑ *Fold 'Em*:	Sell the stock when you have a new personal *insight* telling you to let it go.

Even those who spend lifetimes studying the market do not consistently outperform it (or, if they do, they're not saying and they quietly own numbered accounts in secret Swiss banks). There are, as in all things, a few notable exceptions. Peter Lynch, infamous former portfolio manager of Fidelity's Magellan Fund, likes to tell the story of a group of seventh graders in a Boston suburban school who in 1990 picked their own portfolio of stocks. Over the next two years, the portfolio of these pre-teens outperformed the S&P 500

Composite Index by over 43 percentage points and outperformed all but 1% of the professional portfolio managers directing equity mutual funds in the country. The total return on the youngsters' portfolio was just under 70%.

So, don't get caught-up in the noise of analysis. Your common sense can give you the investment edge you need to make money in the market while analysts are endlessly chasing increasingly infinitesimal data in different directions. The seventh graders were able to succeed because they picked stocks from companies who made products that the kids *knew* were good and worth having, such as Walt Disney, Nike, PepsiCo, Topps (baseball card company), and the like. They followed the *What You Do Best & Enjoy Most* principle and won, because following their passion gave them that one enviable edge that endless analysis and inexhaustible money can't buy: *insight*.

The over-riding, common sense principle of this Rule #7 of your *Rulebook* is: Make a deliberate sell decision *before* you buy—anything. To make a good sell decision, you must first clearly define your purpose for making the investment (the *vision* of your goal) and you must know the characteristics and estimate the inherent value of the investment itself (the *insight* of your common sense). Know the potential resale value of a car or a house or a stock *before* you buy any one of them. The best way to know when to *fold 'em* is to make that sell decision *before* you ever *hold 'em*. Otherwise, you might just be making investments like the blind drunk gambler who bets on his hand without ever looking at his cards.

Take all savings and buy some good stock and hold it till it goes up, then sell it. If it don't go up, don't buy it.

Will Rogers

Rule #8: Give a Cold Shoulder to Hot Tips.

Investing in a "hot" investment tip is like pumping all your quarters into the "hot" slot machine that a whispering passer-by just told you hides at the end of aisle three of the main floor at *Bally's*. If you invest in this *hot tip* you had better use the cold cash that you can afford to lose.

Such rumor-based investing may pay-off *eventually*, but you'll lose a lot of investment quarters before you hit the jackpot. If you become addicted to rumor-investing, you will inevitably give back anything that you may have ever gained, just as most people do with the one-armed bandits at *Bally's* and elsewhere.

Besides, by the time you hear of a supposed new, hot "inside tip" about a pending merger or acquisition, or a company winning a huge government contract, or a new invention or product release, etc., the news is likely to be stale, even if true. Moreover, trading on true inside information is illegal and, if caught, you could end up in prison—not exactly the best place for those seeking *Infinite Financial Freedom*.

How do you avoid this investment trap? You safely step through the mine field of investment gossip by following your *Financial Game Plan*, of course. Without the backbone of a plan, you become a financial jellyfish swaying in no particular direction with the cross-current of Wall Street's latest *hot tip* casting you out with the rumor tide to drown in the depths of misinformation. Fortunately, your *Game Plan* keeps you on course and indifferent to the tugs of the rumor mill. Remain anchored in the knowledge that you will achieve *Infinite Financial Freedom* because you have based your success on the solid ground of *Personal Growth* and a commitment to a proven, winning *Game Plan.*

Rumors ruin more lives than lies do.
                                    Anon, the Unknown Quoter

Rule # 9: Don't Chase Last Year's Return.

By the time you read the "Top Ten Mutual Funds of the Year" list, it's already too late to invest in any of them and realistically expect the same return. Such return-chasing is like first throwing a dart at a blank wall and then running over and trying to hang up the target before the dart hits. People know that they can't win at darts this way, yet they, too often, use the same method to make their investments.

Even the best historical investments can change with business cycles and other forces (new laws, natural disasters, bankruptcies, etc.). So, last year's winner could wind up as this year's dead horse. By taking such investment selection short-cuts, you can end up inadvertently cutting your own investment throat.

Instead of playing catch-up ball with investment returns, follow your plan for:

❏   Selecting the best mutual funds to use for your
     Operating Fund and your three investment funds (as
     outlined in your Rule #5); and

❑ Determining appropriate buy and sell points (as outlined in your Rule #7).

Realize that one or more of the funds that you finally select by going through your profile screening process (per Rule #5), may coincidentally be funds that you find on various "Top Ten", "Best of" or other lists. Such notoriety should not stop you from choosing these funds either. The point is: Do not pick or avoid a fund just *because* it appears on such a list. Let your own screening criteria for picking the best funds *for you* guide your selections.

Since the best funds emulate the fund profile from your Rule #5, you should not be surprised to discover your picks *among* those on the "Best of" lists. However, these lists can also contain "one-calendar-quarter-wonder-funds" that may or may not be able to sustain their performance. Even worse, some funds appearing on these lists, despite a favorable return, may have certain characteristics that make them inappropriate for you (they don't match your goals, *risk tolerance*, diversification targets, *time horizon*, etc.). As you know from developing the Nine Mutual Fund Profile Standards in Rule #5, historical performance is just 11% (one out of nine) of the reasons for picking a mutual fund. The "Best of" lists typically do not give you enough information to make the best decision.

If you can find an advisor or newsletter that mirrors your fund selection strategy, then you can reduce some the research that you must do directly. *The Hulbert Guide To Financial Newsletters* can be very helpful in finding such a newsletter (see *Appendix B: Financial Growth Resources* for details). Or you can simply use *The Fund Exchange*™ for the latest fund screening (see Rule #5) when needed.

However, even if you do invest in such outside assistance, *you* must continue to make the final decisions yourself—it's still *your* money at stake. You can delegate the research, but not the decisions. Use any purchased information as guidance, not gospel. Don't let a "Best of" list get the best of you. Always make the investment decisions yourself.

> *Neither believe nor reject anything because any other persons…rejected or believed it. Your own reason is the only oracle given you by heaven.*
> Thomas Jefferson

Rule #10: Don't Fall In Love With Your Investment.

Investment sentimentalism will cloud your financial vision every time that you look at an investment through romantic eyes. If you inherit and hold an asset or buy a mutual fund, stock or other investment only *because* of its sentimental value, then you are likely *not* to remain rational about your sell decision. You can catch yourself by listening to your *self-talk*. If you are reluctant to sell an asset *only* because "Daddy owned it" or "Mommy used to work there" or "Uncle Willie willed it to me" or "my former Siamese twin was attached to it", etc., then you are guilty of investment sentimentalism.

If you wish to hold on to an asset because of its sentimental value, then do so. Admit to yourself that you want to hold on to such an investment for other than financial reasons and accept the cost of holding on. But don't torment yourself and continue to agonize over the sell versus hold decision. Understanding your Money Personality (see

Chapter 4: What To Do Before You Win) will help you to be honest with yourself about this issue.

However, investing is not the best arena for nostalgia. If you want your good, new and future days to become "the good old days", then the best way to make this happen is to follow the rules in your *Financial Game Plan Rulebook*. The investment doesn't care how long you hold it or if you even buy it in the first place. Besides, you are not likely to hurt anyone's deep feelings by selling an investment to become more successful and better able to share some of your rewards with others.

Investment sentimentalism will likely make you hold on to an asset too long until the investment is worth less or even worthless. As far as investing is concerned, nostalgia is never what it used to be. Fall in love with your *plan* and success will be your offspring!

Remember that money is of a prolific generating nature. Money can beget money, and its offspring can beget more.

Ben Franklin

Rule #11: Don't Pay-off All Your Debts!

Don't blindly pay-off your debts—follow your plan instead. Then, pay-off only those debts that make sense to retire. It may pay you *not* to pay-off your debts.

If you are behind on any debt payments, then, of course, pay the past-due amounts that you owe to bring any accounts back to "current" status. Also, pay-off your personal interest debts (such as, credit card or auto loan balances), as personal interest is no longer federal income tax deductible (under current tax laws).

However, if you have (or buy) a home mortgage, investment property or other real estate, then do not automatically pay-off this debt, as you will probably need the interest deduction to help offset your new, presumably higher income. Additionally, you may have better use for your funds, besides paying-off the debt. So, before paying-off any debt, double-check the current tax treatment of that particular type of debt to help you choose your most beneficial move. If the tax benefits and other better uses of the funds warrant, then keep the debt, write-off the interest payments, and invest the money elsewhere for greater returns.

How do you know if the benefits warrant holding the debt? Look at the numbers.

Scenario A: You continue to pay $10,000 in
                      interest on a real estate investment,
                      assuming:

$100,000   debt (mortgage)

10%   interest rate on debt

$10,000   annual interest payment

36%   Federal income tax bracket

Given the above scenario and assuming that the interest on the debt is fully income tax deductible, then the annual cost of your debt ($10,000) is reduced by your tax bracket (36%):

$10,000	Annual interest payment
-$3,600	36% of $10,000
$6,400	Net Cost of Debt

So, your net annual cost of debt after taxes is only $6,400 (instead of $10,000) or an interest rate of only 6.4% (instead of 10%). Uncle Sam is effectively subsidizing your loan (by 3.6%) by allowing you to deduct the interest payments from your other income (plus you receive other tax deductions).

If you had paid-off the loan instead, then Uncle Sam would want 36% of the $10,000 that you no longer invest in the loan payments on the property.

Scenario B: You want to save $10,000.

Given this scenario, the amount of your savings is reduced by your tax bracket:

$10,000	Cash *not* paid on the loan
-$3,600	Federal income taxes of 36% goes to Uncle Sam
$6,400	Net cash that you keep

In both cases, you start with $10,000 cash, but what you get after taxes is far different:

Scenario A

Spend:	$10,000	in interest payments
Get:	$ 3,600	in government subsidy on interest payment plus an appreciating asset & other tax deductions

Bottom Line:	It costs you only $6,400 (after taxes) to make $10,000 in interest payments in a real asset plus you receive other tax deductions (that we discuss later).

Scenario B

Save:	$10,000	
Get:	$ 6,400	net cash after paying taxes of $3,600
Bottom Line:	It costs you $3,600 in taxes to save $6,400.	

Knowing the above tax consequences and net costs, you can now better decide whether or not to retire the debt, considering your other goals and objectives. *Caution*: There are three basic rules of tax law:

1. Tax laws change.

2. The changes change.

3. The changed changes change.

So, you have to know the *current* tax treatments when penciling-out the wisdom of paying-off a debt. The whole concept of playing and winning the tax game leads us into your Rule #12—next.

A good loan is better than a bad tax.
                                          Robert Wagner

Rule #12: Pay the Taxes That You *Truly* Love.

The way to win the tax game is to pay the type of taxes that you truly love. Accept the inescapable fact that you have to pay taxes (even *after* you die—see Rule #14). So, choose which taxes you feel best—or least bad—about paying.

For example, if you don't like paying income taxes, then just pay property taxes instead. If you like real estate, buy a piece of rental property. At least you will have a piece of real property to show for your spent dollars instead of merely a canceled check made payable to the IRS. Technically, you are shifting the income tax dollars (that you would otherwise have to send to the IRS) to those assets (in this case, rental property) that give you income tax benefits plus the ownership of a real asset.

Let's take an example to illustrate this *principle*. Say that you have $75,000 to invest. Let's look at two different ways that you could invest this chunk of change and how each method changes your rate of return due to the IRS rulebook:

Scenario A: Invest $75,000 in a 5-year CD paying a generous 6.95% *before* taxes.

Scenario B: Invest $75,000 in rental property.

Five years later—after the CD matures and the property is sold—the comparative returns are quite different as shown in Table 6–8. Later in this Rule are the assumptions and supporting financials that, although technically interesting, are not necessary for you to understand in order to appreciate the *principle*: You can use the money better than Uncle Sam can.

TABLE 6–8: TAX EFFECTS ON CD VS. RENTAL PROPERTY

SUMMARY RESULTS	Scenario A	Scenario B
Initial Investment	$75,000	$75,000
Investment Vehicle	5-year bank CD	Rental property
Total Before-Tax Cash Flow	$28,779	$25,712
Total Tax Savings (Loss)	($8,059)	$5,679
Net After-Tax Cash Proceeds From Sale	+$95,721	+$113,319
Total Benefits	$95,721	$144,710
Effective Rate of Return	**5%**	**15.4%**

Of course, in **Scenario B** you are assuming all the normal risks of owning real estate, such as fluctuations in property values and rental incomes, unforeseen physical loss to the property, competition, operating expense increases, and the like. However, real estate values historically appreciate over time, so that if you can afford to hold on to the property long enough, then you should realize significant returns. Further, if you "buy right", you can assure your profit *before* making your investment. You "buy right" by making your profit upon the *purchase* of the property, even though you don't realize the profit until you sell. For details on how to use this and other real estate investment techniques, see *Real Estate Wealthbuilding: How to Really Make Money in Real Estate* (listed in *Appendix B: Financial Growth Resources*).

In **Scenario A**, you are risking the loss of purchasing power by investing in the CD. That is, if inflation exceeds your effective rate of return, then the dollars that the bank returns to you at the end of five years will not buy as much as the dollars that you gave to the bank for safekeeping five years ago. Remember, you can't absolutely eliminate risk *or* taxes. You just have to decide which kind of each to accept and then arrange your affairs accordingly.

In addition, in **Scenario A** you will be sending income tax dollars to the IRS for Uncle Sam to use as he pleases. The federal government then may use your dollars to fund some oblique or questionable (to you) foreign program or some weird (again to you) endowment or entitlement program. In **Scenario B**, at least you know where your dollars are going: You are investing directly into an income-producing, tax-advantaged appreciating asset that you can typically sell for a profit someday in the future.

This profit will then be taxed as a "capital gain" and *could* receive even more favorable tax treatment (lower taxes) than shown above. If we had applied a lower capital gains tax rate, then the return would be even greater for the real estate investment. Capital gains tax rates fall on and off the IRS code books. So, try to hold on to the capital gain (don't sell) until reduced capital gains tax rates are back on the books.

You can even "roll" the gain and postpone the taxes completely by reinvesting the gain in "like-kind" property (such as other real estate, etc., per IRS rules). This way you can "pyramid-up" a gain into increasingly larger assets while deferring the tax hit on your profits.

For the analytically inclined, here are the assumptions, CD financials, and rental property financials, respectively, that produce the bottom-line results summarized in Table 6–8:

ASSUMPTIONS

$350,000	Original purchase price of 10-unit apartment building
$300,000	Building value (land valued @ $50K)
$75,000	Down payment
$275,000	30-year mortgage fixed @ 11% with annual payments
$266,393	Loan payoff @ end of year 5
27.5 yrs.	Depreciation period (straight line)
28%	Federal marginal tax bracket
Jan. 1	Building bought Jan. 1 to get full first year depreciation
$425,000	Sale price of property after 5 years
$12,500	Selling costs
4%	Gross Potential Income (GPI) annual increase
7% GPI	Vacancy & collection losses
35% GPI	Operating expenses, incl. property taxes
$22,125	Operating expenses in year 1
$58,500	Gross rental income in year 1 (10 units @ $487.50/mo. each)
$500	Other income
12%	Rental property historical rate of return
6.95%	Interest rate on CD (before-taxes)
5 years	Holding period for each investment

CD FINANCIALS

	Yr.-1	Yr.-2	Yr.-3	Yr.-4	Yr.-5	Total
Taxable Income	$5,208	$5,469	$5,742	$6,029	$6,331	$28,779
minus Taxes	$1,458	$1,531	$1,608	$1,688	$1,773	$8,059
=After-Tax Income	$3,750	$3,938	$4,134	$4,341	$4,558	$20,721

Net Asset Value after-tax at end of year 5:   **$95,721**

RENTAL PROPERTY FINANCIALS (all figures in dollars)

	Yr.-1	Yr.-2	Yr.-3	Yr.-4	Yr.-5
Gross Potential Income	59,000	61,360	63,815	66,367	69,022
minus Vacancy & Collection	4,130	4,295	4,467	4,646	4,832
=Effective Gross Income	54,870	57,065	59,348	61,721	64,190
minus Operating Expenses	22,125	21,476	22,335	23,228	24,158
=Net Operating Income	32,745	35,589	37,013	38,493	40,032
minus Depreciation	10,920	10,920	10,920	10,920	10,920
minus Paid Loan Interest	30,250	30,098	29,930	29,742	29,534
=Taxable Loss	-8,425	-5,429	-3,837	-2,169	-422
plus Depreciation	10,920	10,920	10,920	10,920	10,920
minus Principal repaid	1,382	1,534	1,703	1,890	2,098
=Before-tax Cash Flow	1,113	3,957	5,380	6,861	8,400
plus Tax savings	2,359	1,520	1,075	608	118
=After-tax Equity Cash Flow	**3,472**	**5,477**	**6,455**	**7,469**	**8,518**

SALE OF PROPERTY (AFTER 5 YEARS)	
Selling Price	$425,000
minus Selling Expenses	-$12,500
=Amount Realized on Sale	$412,500
minus Adjusted Basis for depreciation	-$295,400
=Realized Taxable Gain	$117,100
times tax rate	x 28 %
=Tax on Gain	$32,788
Amount Realized on Sale	$412,500
minus Tax on Sale	-$32,788
minus Loan pay-off	-$266,393
=Net Cash proceeds from Sale	**$113,319**

Keep in mind that the tax code is a moving target and that the laws (and numbers) are ever-changing. The key is to know the rules of the tax game—or hire someone who does—and then play the tax game to win by paying the taxes most favorable to you.

> *If Congress insists on making stupid mistakes and passing foolish tax laws, millionaires should not be condemned if they take advantage of them.*
>
> J. P. Morgan

Deeper in the Heart of Taxes

Despite the ever-changing details of the tax laws, there are four fundamental ways that the IRS treats all investments. The tax rate percentages may change, but the "treatments" are constant. So, be sure that you know the tax treatment of each investment that you make. Here are the four tax treatments in the order of priority for wealth acquisition (that is, for getting the *right* amount of money):

- ❑   Tax-sheltered;

- ❑   Tax-deferred;

- ❑   Taxable;

- ❑   Tax-free or Tax-exempt.

Tax-Sheltered

Tax-sheltered investments are good for building wealth, because both the income and growth of these investments are protected from taxes. That is, little or no tax is due on these investments, because tax incentives (such as tax credits, waivers, etc.) directly offset the growth and income. You are effectively creating wealth with pre-tax dollars—the biggest dollars of all.

Examples of tax-sheltered investments are getting harder to find because they are so lucrative for the investor. Still, you can find tax credits for certain investments into Research and Development, Low-income Housing, and Certified Historical Structures. Some astute investors locate Certified Historical Structures (as certified by the Secretary of the Interior) and "rehabilitate" the buildings for use as Low-income Housing, thereby taking advantage of multiple tax credits. You should know something about construction (or reconstruction) as well as the pertinent tax laws before getting involved in these "rehab" investments.

One often-overlooked place where you can always find a tax-sheltered investment is staring at you in the mirror: *You.* Starting a business in *What You Do Best & Enjoy Most* is one of the best shelters you can devise, because you can exercise all the control over the outcome to assure success while reaping the tax benefits of operating a business. Another tax shelter often overlooked is attached to your mirror: your own home, and by extension, other investment real estate as well. See the good books listed in *Appendix B: Financial Growth Resources* for the tools and techniques of successful real estate investing, starting with your own home. You would, of course, use funds earmarked for your *Possibility Fund* for investments into these tax-sheltered vehicles.

Tax-Deferred

As we saw with the Tax-Deferred Annuity in Rule #4, the benefit of tax-deferred treatment is that your investment grows without being continually depleted by taxes. That is, no tax is due now, but taxes will be due sometime in the future when you either sell the investment or begin drawing income from the investment.

The popular IRA (Individual Retirement Account) made many people aware of the benefits of tax-deferment when all taxpayers could deduct up to $2,000 every year from their income and invest these dollars on a tax-deferred basis. The IRS entirely protected this $2,000 from *current* taxes as if you had never earned the $2,000. Taxes are due on the $2,000 as well as the growth and income on the $2,000 only when you withdraw the cash. Of course, these IRA laws have changed and are more restrictive now, limiting the value of IRA's for most Americans. However, existing IRA's, even if currently invested in underperforming vehicles like CD's, can be "rolled over" without penalty into the more attractive Tax-Deferred Annuities.

Tax-deferred treatment is still readily available to *all* investors without the investment and withdrawal restrictions, penalties and limitations of the IRA. Investments into Tax-Deferred Annuities, either *fixed* or *variable*, still benefit from tax-deferral. Remember from your Rule #4 that you use a guaranteed Tax-Deferred Annuity as part of your *Infinite Financial Freedom Fund* to give you the advantage of tax-deferred growth of earning interest on your interest.

Taxable

Taxable investments are good normally for dollars that you must currently consume. Such investment vehicles would include taxable money market accounts and checking accounts, which I suggest that you do not use.

Taxable investments are not as good for wealth building as tax-sheltered and tax-deferred investments, because the more taxable wealth that you build, the higher your tax bracket and the more that the IRS confiscates from you in taxes. However, if the after-tax return on a taxable investment is significantly high, then these investments can be suitable to wealth building, though they will probably carry greater risk. Aggressive Growth plus Growth and Income mutual funds can be acceptable taxable investments if their potential after-tax returns are high enough.

Remember that you use a taxable Growth and Income mutual fund for your *Balanced Fund* to round out and diversify your portfolio. Think of your *Balanced Fund* as a hedge against unlikely, but possible, violent market swings, thus giving your portfolio market equilibrium. Your *Balanced Fund* is the defensive part of your portfolio. Your cost for this defense is giving-up some growth and income in taxes. However, you are reinvesting all income into additional fund shares to increase the ultimate growth in the investment. Remember that you reinvest the income because your *Operating Fund* takes care of all your consumption needs.

Tax-Free or Tax-Exempt

Tax-free or tax-exempt investments (two words for the same treatment) are normally best for the *distribution* or *preservation* of existing wealth, rather than the *accumulation* of wealth. Once you have accumulated the *right* amount of money, you may consider tax-free investments for the regular distribution of income to you, as you are presumably now in a higher income tax bracket. Such investment vehicles would include tax-free money market mutual funds, municipal bonds, and municipal bond funds. Buy the bonds (either directly or through your mutual fund) from your state and your yield is double tax-free: free of both state and federal income taxes.

Note that you are using a double tax-free money market mutual fund for your *Operating Fund* to distribute your annual wealth to you. Note also that you are using a double tax-free municipal bond fund for part of your *Infinite Financial Freedom Fund* because you are receiving tax-sheltered growth of double tax-free income by reinvesting the dividends into additional shares of the fund. Remember, you can afford not to consume these dividends because your *Operating Fund* provides for your daily consumption needs.

Tax Tricks: Avoidance versus Evasion

The true and legitimate trick with income taxes is to make your *gross income* as large as possible (the *right* amount of money) while arranging your affairs so that your *taxable income* is as small as possible. How do you do this—legally?

You perform this magic by taking advantage of government-encouraged social and economic policy. The U.S. Government encourages certain investments into the economy by providing certain tax incentives, that is, by giving special *treatment* (as we saw above) to certain investments.

The government gives you the incentive, so that Uncle Sam does not have to support (and tax for) these programs directly or on as grand a scale as would otherwise be required. As we saw above, you could *avoid* income taxes on the income and growth of certain investments, such as income-producing property, Certified Historical Structures, Low-income Housing, starting a business, Research and Development programs, and the like.

Caution: Although tax *avoidance* is thoroughly legal and encouraged through government incentives, tax *evasion* is unquestionably illegal. *Avoid* all the taxes that you legally can by learning the rules and playing the tax game legitimately. Never *evade* taxes or have anything to do with anyone who suggests "investments" that *evade* taxes. No amount of money is the *right* amount of money if you are locked-up in the wrong place—prison. Spending your jackpot in jail just to stay alive and unviolated is not anyone's idea of *Infinite Financial Freedom*. Financial freedom without personal freedom is nothing.

So, stay on the right side of the tax laws and pay your share of taxes—just pay your favorite ones. Use the investments that we discussed above to give you the best mix of tax-advantaged growth at acceptable risk levels while simultaneously acquiring assets *and* meeting your tax obligations. There is another factor more important than tax *avoidance* alone that we discuss in your Rule #13—next.

The hardest thing in the world to understand is the income tax.

Albert Einstein

Rule #13: Don't Bet on Tax Breaks

Despite tax incentives, investment in *merit* always outweighs investment for tax *motive*. Always seek profit and growth over tax *avoidance* alone. You can never bank on tax breaks. The Savings & Loans tried it and they broke their own bank.

Many speculators, especially in the 1980's, bought tax losses instead of investments—and losses are what they got, although not as intended. They bought—or, more correctly, *were sold*—what were then tax "advantages", such as: accelerated depreciation; depletion allowances; multiple write-off's; intangible drilling expenses; investment tax credits; and other esoteric tax "benefits". Such "tax shelter" investors sought business activities that would generate more tax losses (on paper) than income, especially in the first few years of existence, so that these investors could then use the excess losses to protect their other income (like salary) from taxes.

The danger occurred when investors began blindly buying the tax losses without much, if any, concern about the relative *merit* of the underlying "investment". Thus you had tax "avoiders", unknowingly or otherwise, putting their dollars into programs stretching from pornographic movie deals with obscene tax write-off's coming from non-recourse financing to artificial insemination syndicates for prize bulls giving birth to seminal depreciation deductions and investment tax credits.

The logic was: "Just spend $10,000 and you'll get $40,000–$50,000–$60,000 in tax write-off's and tax credits! The tax benefits are so great, you can't lose. Besides, in the 50% tax bracket, Uncle Sam is putting in half the money for you, anyway. So, who cares about the investment?" Well, too many investors didn't care. But *you* had better care, because no one else may.

Besides, what Uncle Sam giveth, Uncle Sam can taketh away—and does. Congress, who initially allowed such tax incentives (originally under the laudable guise of "affecting positive social policy and stimulating the economy"), later disallowed or severely limited the same incentives (now under the guise of "fairness") through their 1986 tax code revisions. Investors and, worse, entrepreneurs who had committed significant dollars to long-term investments with "staged-in" yearly payments were whipsawed by Congress' change in policy. Many investors, at best, were badly hurt. Even Trump took a tiny tumble. Some were financially destroyed.

If you buy on taxes, you can die on taxes. Always consider the tax consequences, but always—first and last—make your investment decision based primarily on the *merit* of the underlying investment itself. Congress can and does change tax provisions, even retro-actively. The underlying investment is all that you may have left if Congress changes the tax laws on you (which it always does).

So, be sure that the underlying investment is viable even without the tax benefits. Remember, tax benefits can vanish like tax deductions on a tax form written in disappearing ink leaving you only with phantom income: current taxable income from a disallowed prior investment without any cash to pay the taxes that the IRS says that you now owe.

The point to remember is that what the government gives it must first take away.
John Coleman

Rule #14: Outsmart Count Taxula.

Uncle Sam has created the immortal *Count Taxula* to combine two of the worst aspects of life to haunt you beyond the grave: death and taxes. Winning and dying creates a potentially deadly and inescapable estate tax liability for your heirs. For example, if you win a $1 Million jackpot on Monday, and you receive your first of 20 payments of $100,000 on Tuesday, and you are squashed to death by a bus on Wednesday, then your heirs have an immediate estate tax liability and probably no money to pay for it. Why? The remaining $900,000 in lottery winnings that you had not yet received will be added to your estate now and taxed today, even though your heirs will not receive the winnings to pay for these taxes for another 19 years! If that's not bad enough, the tax on this phantom $900,000 could be as much as $450,000 (depending on the size of your estate otherwise).

Hopefully, federal and state tax or lottery laws will change to remove this hardship from the heirs of the lucky. The likeliest change would be for the lottery to pay the present value of the remaining jackpot to the heirs of the winner. As we saw in *Chapter 3: The Do's and Don'ts of Smart Lottery Play*, the present value of the jackpot is about 50% of the winnings that will conveniently (for the IRS) equal about your entire estate tax liability. So, your heirs could effectively walk away with nothing which is, in any case, better than the current situation of no cash and a huge estate tax bill to pay.

Unless you want your heirs to suffer because you win and die, counsel with a Certified Financial Planner who specializes in "estate planning" after you win. Then, meet with an estate planning attorney. Often the planner is or can suggest an appropriate attorney, but be careful. Seek *objective* advice, *full* disclosure, and *justification* for the suitability of any recommendations. Certified Financial Planners are especially trained in providing these levels of professionalism as part of their practice ethic. Your Rule #17 goes into more detail on how to best select advisors.

When you meet with these advisors, bring them this problem: Your lottery winnings are *not* transferable, so your jackpot must remain in your name and thus pass through your estate when you die and be taxed when your heirs have not yet received the cash to pay the tax. One way to outsmart *Count Taxula* is to buy life insurance on yourself in an amount sufficient to pay for the estate taxes due on the remaining jackpot should you die before receiving all winnings. Make sure that your spouse or an heir or a trust or someone other than yourself is the *owner* of the policy. By not owning the policy on your life, you keep the policy proceeds out of your estate, thus avoiding estate taxes on the policy death benefit and the delays of probate. This technique gives your spouse (or other beneficiary) the life insurance money immediately to pacify the cash-sucking *Count Taxula* and to pay your estate taxes due today. Then, your heirs—instead of the IRS—can continue to savor the future winnings over the remaining years of the jackpot and, if they follow your plan, beyond.

The size of your winnings, current state inheritance laws, current federal estate tax laws, and your state lottery's regulations regarding the death of a winner will suggest your smartest strategies. For now, know that *Count Taxula* will chase you down—even beyond the grave—for his bite of your jackpot. Know that no single salesperson, solicitor or *con artist* will seek and siphon more from you than the taxman. According to the Washington, D.C.-based Tax Foundation, for every $1 that the average American household spends on food to keep their family alive, they spend $3 on federal, state, and local taxes to keep the government alive. Facts like these force families to have more than one wage-earner at the expense of their family life.

So, if you do not arrange your affairs properly, you may find yourself, as other ill-prepared winners have, wishing that you had never won—imagine that! Cover this tax base or leave a living nightmare for your heirs instead of the dream of *Infinite Financial Freedom*. Refer to your Rule #2 for suggestions on selecting the best life insurance and to your Rule # 17 for suggestions on selecting your best advisors. For legal guidance, see *Warning: Dying May Be Hazardous to Your Wealth* (listed in *Appendix C: Legal Resources*). Your Rule #15 gives you a charitable way to drive a permanent stake through the heart of old *Count Taxula*—next.

Our forefathers made one mistake. What they should have fought for was representation without taxation.

Fletcher Knebel

Rule #15: Give Smart.

Here's how to *give smart*: Give the gift that keeps on giving while giving the gift that keeps Uncle Sam from taking. To illustrate this *Infinite Financial Freedom principle*, let's say that you want to give away $10,000 a year off-the-top of your winnings to someone or some worthy cause that *you* have personally identified. There are a few ways to be this charitable, some much better for you *and* the charity than other methods. See Figure 6–6: Give Smart Chart for a summary of the benefits that accrue to the charity by giving in the typical way versus giving the *smart* way. Later, we'll discuss how you can better benefit, too.

FIGURE 6–6: GIVE SMART CHART

GIVE SMART CHART		
	Typical Way	*Smart* Way
Annual Donation: Years 1–10	$10,000 from Winnings to a Charity	$10,000 from Winnings to a Charitable Trust
Total Donations from Winnings: Years 1–10	$100,000	$100,000
Annual Donation: Years 11–20	Another $10,000 from Winnings	$10,000 from the Charitable Trust's earnings only
Total Donations from Winnings: Years 11–20	Another $100,000	Absolutely Zero
Total Donations from Winnings: Years 1–20	$200,000	$100,000
Annual Donation: Yrs. 21 & after	Zero (jackpot checks stopped)	$10,000/yr. from the Charitable Trust's earnings
Total Lifetime Donations	$200,000: all from Winnings	$10,000/yr. for as long as you live: only $100,000 from Winnings
Donations after your death	Zero	$10,000/yr. for all eternity

In the typical example, a total of $200,000 comes out of your jackpot pocket to pay the charity ($10,000 a year for 20 years). In the *smart* example, only $100,000 comes out of your jackpot pocket to pay the charity ($10,000 a year for only 10 years). The difference is that with the typical way of giving, you give your $200,000 to the charity and it's gone. With the *smart* way, you put the $100,000 first into a Charitable Trust (more on this idea later). Then, assuming that the trust can earn 10% on its money, you let the trust pay the charity the 10% or $10,000 in earnings every year thereafter, beginning in year 11.

With the typical way of giving, you stop giving when your lottery checks stop coming, so your total lifetime donation stops at $200,000. With the *smart* way of giving, you never stop giving, because the Charitable Trust can keep on giving $10,000 a year to the charity for all eternity. In addition, you receive several income and estate tax benefits that we will discuss later. So, for half the dollars out of your jackpot pocket, you can give an infinitely greater donation to the charity of your choice, if you learn to *give smart*. Or you could spend all $200,000 and create another *smart* $10,000 a year donation to fund a second charity for all eternity.

You can apply your *Infinite Financial Freedom* skills to everything that you touch. In this case, by giving *smart*, you are creating *Infinite Charitable Donations*. Though you may not be able to "take it with you", you can certainly leave as much of your winnings behind as you like to do the greatest good that you can imagine for as long as humanity may exist.

This is exactly what lottery winner Sheelah Ryan has done. First, she picked the first six numbers that she found on the front page of the *Orlando Sentinel* newspaper to play the *Florida Lottery* on one fortuitous day. Then, she won $55.1 Million. She has since started the charitable *Ryan*

Foundation, Inc. for abused and battered women. The good that she has put in motion is immeasurable and will live beyond her years.

Charitable Trusts

Besides the significant social good that your donations can do, you can receive significant tax benefits for you and your heirs. The laws regarding charitable giving—like all IRS rules—are continually changing. You will need to counsel with an attorney who specializes in Estate Planning to properly set-up and administer such a trust. Additionally, many principal charities have entire institutes with Estate Planning Departments founded to help you achieve your charitable goals the *smart* way. One of the best such non-profits is The American Institute for Cancer Research in Washington, D.C. (whose toll-free phone number is 800-843-8114). These organizations can help you not only plan a trust or bequest, but also understand the exact tax consequences of any trust arrangement that you may consider. So that you can converse intelligently with these people, an outline of the general characteristics of the four most popular charitable trusts follows.

Charitable Remainder Annuity Trust (CRAT)

❑   An *irrevocable* trust (that is, you can not get the donations back once you make them to the trust);

❑   When you die, whatever money is left in the trust (the *remainder*) goes to the charity;

❏   You or other living people of your choice (and not a charity or trust) must receive the income from the trust's investment every year;

❏   The income is generated by a fixed annuity that you purchase for the trust with a single lump-sum (called the *initial principal*);

❏   You or the living people of your choice must receive at least 5% of the *initial principal* as income every year from the trust;

❏   You receive an income tax charitable deduction *today* for the calculated value of the *remainder* (that is, what IRS actuarial tables determine will be left in the trust given standard life expectancies, etc.);

❏   You *cannot* add donations to the trust later, as this trust allows a one time, lump-sum donation only.

Charitable Remainder Unit Trust (CRUT)

❏   An *irrevocable* trust (like the CRAT);

❏   The *remainder* goes to the charity (like the CRAT);

❏   You or other living people of your choice must receive the income from the trust's investment every year (like the CRAT);

❏   The income that you receive is a fixed percentage of at least 5% of the *annual* principal in the trust;

❏   You receive a current income tax charitable deduction *today* for the calculated value of the *remainder* (like the CRAT);

❏   You *can* make additional donations into the trust (*unlike* the CRAT), making the CRUT more appropriate if you want to donate a portion of your *annual* winnings into the trust every year.

Pooled Income Fund (PIF)

❏   A *public* charity creates and maintains this trust;

❏   An *irrevocable* trust (like the CRAT and CRUT);

❏   The *remainder* in the trust goes to the charity (like the CRAT and CRUT);

❏   You or other living people of your choice *must* receive 100% of the income from the trust annually;

❏   You receive a current income tax charitable deduction *today* for the calculated value of the *remainder*;

❏   You *can* make additional donations into the trust;

❏   The PIF *cannot* invest in tax-exempt securities, such as municipal bonds.

Charitable Lead Income Trust (CLIT)

❏   An *irrevocable* trust (like the CRAT, CRUT and PIF);

❏   The annual trust income goes to the charity;

❑   The calculated *remainder* goes to other "non charitable" beneficiaries of your choice;

❑   There are two types of CLIT's based on whether you establish the trust for over or under 10 years:

1.   For a term of 10 years or less, the trust is called a Grantor Lead Income Trust (GLIT) from which you receive a very large income tax charitable deduction *today*, but you are also taxed on the annual trust income;

2.   For a term of over 10 years, the trust is called the Clifford-style CLIT from which you receive *no* immediate income tax charitable deduction, but you are also not taxed on the annual trust income;

❑   You are taxed on the gift of the *remainder* in the year that you create the trust.

If you intend to give more than casual pocket pennies to the salvation army bell-ringer, then you will truly need specialized counsel from a qualified attorney who practices Estate Planning on a full-time and exclusive basis. To help "simplify" the process, in 1990 the IRS published a series of 18 various model trust forms. However, even these models require revision to meet your specific needs. So, you still need an Estate Planning Specialist.

Generous people are rarely mentally ill people.
                                        Dr. Karl Menninger

Giving Your Life Away

Simpler than the trust in both concept and administration is the charitable gift of life insurance. A gift of life insurance provides notable advantages to both you and your charity.

Here are *your* advantages:

Publicity Avoidance

Unlike some other charitable bequests (such as by will), a gift of a life insurance policy is discrete. This privacy can avoid family and other disputes. You can quietly give a life insurance policy to a charity, making the charity the owner and beneficiary of your policy. When you die, the charity does not have to deal with potential challenges from your survivors or probate delays. The charity simply presents a copy of your death certificate to the insurance company and collects the policy proceeds.

Legal Challenge Avoidance

Life insurance proceeds are generally exempt from limitations on the percentage of your estate that you can donate. These rules vary by state, so double-check these regulations with your estate planning attorney.

Simplicity

In buying a life policy, you will not incur the legal expenses involved in drafting a charitable "codicil" (amendment) to your will or in creating and administering a trust. You simply buy a life insurance policy on yourself and make the charity the owner and beneficiary.

Leverage

You can buy a large death benefit for a small investment. For example, *The Insurance Exchange*™ tells me that a 44-year old male, non-smoker can buy $300,000 worth of *term* life insurance for under $500 a year initially (although premiums will later increase). *Cash value* life policies are more expensive and thus give you less leverage (you control less insurance for the same amount of money). However, as we discussed in your Rule #2, you should not use *cash value* policies, since pure *term* insurance coupled with non-insurance investments outside the policy gives you more planning advantages (more flexibility, more effective use of funds, and better returns on investment).

Here are your *charity's* advantages when you give a gift of life insurance to your charity:

Leverage, Again

The charity is on the receiving end of the same leverage that you enjoy. The charity can receive a donation (the death benefit) significantly greater that the amount that you initially pay (the premium) to buy the policy, especially if you die prematurely. For example, if you are the 44-year old male, non-smoker who buys and donates to your charity a $300,000 life insurance policy for only $500 a year and then you die in the first year, then the charity receives $300,000 when you only donated $500 cash out-of-pocket. As time goes on and you continue to survive, the leverage decreases, of course, as you pay more into the policy. You should always have some amount of leverage in your policy or you need to shop for a better policy (See your Rule #2 for shopping advice).

Probate Avoidance

The life insurance policy does not have to go through probate and probate's attendant delays, because you don't own the policy—the charity does. Only what a decedent owns goes through probate. And since the charity didn't die, what the charity owns including your policy doesn't go through anybody's probate. The charity receives the policy proceeds immediately simply by presenting your death certificate to the insurance company.

Early Access to Cash Value

If you already bought a *cash value* policy and now donate the policy to your charity, then you should also make the charity the policyowner. The gift is now irrevocable when you make someone else the owner, because you no longer have any right to make further changes in the policy. The only action left for you to take is to die someday.

So, if you have a *cash value* policy in your financial shoebox and you give policy ownership to your charity, then the charity can surrender the policy for any *cash value* inside the policy and put the money to better use. They could even use the *cash value* to buy a *term* policy on your life with a greater death benefit than the old *cash value* policy had. Alternately, the charity could borrow against the old *cash value* policy and use the dollars more effectively while you are still living.

Possible Conversion Privileges

There may be some conversion privileges hiding in the fine print of certain policies. If the charity owns your policy, the charity can exercise any of the conversion privileges. Certain policies allow conversion to a paid-up life policy with a lower death benefit, but with no further premiums due. The charity may also under certain conversion provisions change your policy into an extended *term* policy with the same death benefit as the original policy for a specified time period without any additional premiums due.

Your arrangement with the charity could be that you will donate the policy, but that you no longer wish to pay premiums. The charity could then assume the premium payments or exercise one of the paid-up or extended conversion provisions. Either way, the charity receives a donation with very little cost to you or them.

Like with trusts, gifts of life insurance policies can potentially create gift, income, and estate tax consequences. So, you need to review such implications with your Estate Tax Attorney and/or Certified Financial Planner. After all, giving *smart* requires that you use the IRS code to your and your charity's best advantage. Also, remember that charitable giving can include gifts to family and friends as well as to organized charities.

Remember...shrouds have no pockets...so give for the good of others and know the highest pleasure wealth can give.

Tyron Edwards

You and Your Charity: Getting the Biggest Bang for Your Charitable Buck

Here is one practical example of how you can use a charitable trust as a post-lottery retirement vehicle to your and your charity's best advantage:

1. Type of Trust: Charitable Remainder "Income-Only" Unit Trust (CRUT);

2. Your age 45:   When you won the lottery;

3. Your age 55:   When you set-up the Trust;

4. Your age 65:   When lottery checks stop;

5. $200,000:   Original cost of your donations into the Trust (you had invested $20K/yr. for the 1st 10 yrs. from your winnings into a mutual fund);

6. $500,000:   Current market value of your donations at your age 55;

7. $100,000:   Your immediate charitable income tax deduction when you set-up the Trust (at your age 55);

8. Zero: Your capital gains tax liability on the $300,000 in growth of your mutual fund shares (#6-#5 above);

9. Trust investment: Trust immediately sells your donated mutual fund shares and invests the cash into zero coupon bonds that grow at an 8% rate & mature in 10–15 years;

10. Your age 65–74:   Your lottery checks stop, but you get $110,000/yr. (that's a total of $1.1 Million) from the Trust;

11. Your age 75+:   You get $65,000/yr. from the Trust for the rest of your life;

12. $1.1 Million: What the charity gets when you finally die to do whatever charitable things they do.

Here's a summary of what you put into the deal and what you get out of it:

What you put in

$200,000:   From #5 above.

What you get out

$36,000:   Tax savings on $100,000 tax deduction (#7 above), assuming a 36% federal marginal tax bracket;

$90,000:   Tax savings on the avoidance of tax on the asset's growth (#8 above), assuming a low 30% capital gains tax rate;

$1,100,000:   Income from Trust, your age 65–74
(#10 above);

$650,000:   Income from Trust, your age 75–84
(#11 above), assuming you live only
through age 84;

$1,100,000:   Lump-sum donation to the charity at
your death (#12 above);

$2,976,000:   Total benefit to you.

So, for your $200,000 donation/investment you receive total benefits of $2,976,000 plus $65,000 more for every year that you stay alive past age 84. This one technique alone could create *Infinite Financial Freedom* for you—this is *smart* giving.

On the other hand, if you just held on to your mutual fund shares yourself until age 65 (you didn't set-up the trust), then your current fund value (assuming the same historical return) would be $1.25 Million. The problem with this strategy is, first, that your account would be $386,429 short of the funds needed to pay you the same annual income as the trust would pay you. In addition, you would lose-out on all the other benefits worth over another $1.2 Million associated with the formation of the trust.

This strategy of setting-up a charitable trust demonstrates the confluence of several of the rules from your *Financial Game Plan Rulebook.* Note that your rules do not exist in isolation from one another. Your rules work together in a synergy that allows you to achieve your goals with the most effective use of your time, energy, and money.

Three of the best and most user-friendly estate planning books for the layperson are: 1) *Make Your Own Living Trust;* 2) *Winning the Wealth Game: How To Keep Your Money in Your Family;* and 3) *Everything Your Heirs Need to Know: Your Assets, Family History and Final Wishes.* This last book even contains eight different document pockets for organizing copies of key information. See *Appendix C: Legal Resources* for details on these and other guides.

As you can see from the above discussion of some basic gifting techniques, you can give away a lot of your lottery winnings, if you are so inclined. You can *give smart* to family, friends, and charities. However, make sure that you give any donations according to *your* plan. Remember the earlier cautions about people soliciting you for hand-outs and about your making charitable announcements publicly (see *Chapter 3: The Do's and Don'ts of Smart Lottery Play* for caveats). If you do give, do your own research and work your giving into your plan. Above all, *give smart*, give quietly, and let your winning strengthen not weaken others.

> *Charity is injurious unless it helps the recipient to become independent of it.*
>
> John D. Rockefeller

Rule #16: Be Your Own Investment Guru.

People often look too much outside themselves for answers to life's questions. The best answers come from within ourselves. This truth is why it is so important for you to prepare for winning as we discussed in *Chapter 4: What To Do Before You Win.* Winning without wisdom is worse than losing or not playing because, in the former case, your eventual loss is greater and more painful.

Use What You Know & Know What You Use

So, when selecting investments, do not overlook your own built-in inner expertise. If you work (or worked) in a particular industry, then you will know more about the real-world "in's and out's" of that industry than any Wall Street analyst could ever hope to know. You have *lived* that industry, not just studied it.

Even after your old job quits you, you can still tap into your own, personal first-hand knowledge of your own field of expertise. You probably know or know how to find out which companies or suppliers or vendors, etc., are likely winners and losers. Think back. You may even know of some potential mergers or acquisitions in your industry.

Here's what to do: Armed with your own inside knowledge of the industry, pick a *Sector* mutual fund that specializes in buying the stocks of companies in your area of expertise. Use the *Nine Mutual Fund Profile Standards* (from your Rule #5) to select the best *Sector* funds. If you are extremely confident, buy the individual company stocks themselves. If you do buy an individual company's stocks, make sure, along with your insight, that you understand something about the company's finances. Review at least the company's Annual Report and their "10K Report" (a required annual filing with the SEC). These documents are available directly from the company, the SEC, most full service stockbrokers, certain libraries, and independent research services (see *Appendix B: Financial Growth Resources* for details). Of course, use only dollars earmarked for your *Possibility Fund* for this type of investing due to the greater risk-reward elevation such concentrated investments have on the *Ladder of Investments* (see your Rules #5 and #6).

Time your initial and subsequent purchases based upon your knowledge of the ups and downs of your industry. For example, if the business is seasonal or cyclical in some way, then the stock prices may be artificially depressed during the off season or down cycle. If so, then you are better able to know when to buy (at a low), how long to hold (through the up cycle), and when to sell (at the high).

Also, you are probably much better equipped than most investors and analysts to understand how bad the "bad news" is and how good the "good news" is about an individual stock or industry. Knowledge is powerful when you use it pro-actively. If seemingly "bad news" about the industry artificially depresses the industry's stock prices, then you can rejoice by knowing that other investors are dumping their stocks (probably on their broker's recommendation) and depressing the prices on superficially "bad news", thereby creating a happy opportunity for you to "buy low". You know that the "bad news" is not *that* bad or is just temporary or is just the result of an otherwise "slow news day" in the media.

The "Stockbroker Trading Phenomenon"

You also have what I call the *Stockbroker Trading Phenomenon* working in your favor. "Trading" is the operative word here, as trading creates both buy and sell commissions. Every time that a stockbroker allows a customer to break one of the rules of your *Rulebook*, he unknowingly or uncaringly creates an opportunity for you.

For example, Mr. Stockbroker tells Mr. One-of-the-Herd (non pro-active) Customer to buy BRG stock in your industry due to some to "good news". Mr. Customer doesn't know your industry (violating your Rule #5), but he buys based on the broker's "hot tip" (violating your Rule #8) and/or the broker's story regarding the stock's recent "hot" performance (violating your Rule #9). The only real "heat" here is the friction generated from the trading commissions burning-up Mr. Customer's investment dollars.

Next, superficial "bad news" hits the media (or vice versa). Mr. Stockbroker calls Mr. Customer in a panic telling him that the price is dropping ("the sky is falling") and recommending that Mr. Customer sell immediately to avoid any further loss (violating your Rule #7). Mr. Customer, not knowing the industry (violating your Rule #5), doesn't know any better and agrees to sell, thereby further depressing the stock price. Mr. Stockbroker can then act as if he saved Mr. Customer from further loss in the continuing-to-drop stock while happily generating sell commissions. Mr. Stockbroker now looks for another "good news" stock to recommend that Mr. Customer buy with his left-over investment dollars that have now become conveniently available, thereby generating more buy commissions.

Simultaneously, throughout this whole process, Mr. Stockbroker is calling his Mr. Contrarian Customers to take the opposite side of Mr. One-of-the-Herd's trades, again generating more buy and sell commissions. As long as enough of these customers make enough money enough of the time, Mr. Stockbroker can keep them in his stable. However, since you are self-directed, you can take advantage of the Mr. Stockbrokers of the world who are creating the controlled stampede of the investment herd.

Isn't this stockbroker trading technique illegal? No, not if the stockbroker is careful. Some brokers, after first persuading you to make a trade, will then tape record you (with your full knowledge) giving the buy/sell orders to the broker. Isn't this practice unethical? Thoroughly!

You don't think this happens? The next time that you see daily stock market trading volume figures, just ask yourself how many of these millions of trades do you believe were truly self-directed. How many original decisions does anyone make in any one day?

A commodities broker revealed this stockbroker's trading trick to me over 10 years ago. His lesson was not cheap: "If you don't call the shots, don't curse your wounds". In other words, if you don't make your own buy and sell decisions, then you are the one to blame for putting yourself at the mercy of whoever is unofficially making these decisions for you. You must, therefore, accept the results of their "judgements"—good or bad.

Exploiting Your Own Knowledge

Exploiting your own knowledge is always sweeter than the knowledge of having been exploited by others. Even Peter Lynch, after 13 years at the helm of the infamous Fidelity Magellan Fund, says:

> Your investor's edge is not something you get from Wall Street experts. It's something you already have. You can outperform the experts if you use your edge by investing in companies or industries you already understand (*Beating the Street*, Simon & Schuster, 1993).

For example, if you worked in the airline industry for any length of time, then you probably noticed that every time that Congress even threatened a fuel tax increase or that fuel prices went up or that there was a fuel shortage, airline stock prices dropped (your buying opportunity). The stock price drop was in response to investors' anticipation of the increasing airfares decreasing air travel and depressing revenue to the airlines, thereby lowering potential dividends to stockholders. So, *enough* of the stockholders (those who are not as informed as you are and are too quick on the sell trigger or are swayed by others because they don't have their own *Financial Game Plan Rulebook*) quickly sell their holdings and artificially depress the stock's price temporarily.

However, you have seen—you have *lived* through—this "fuel cost-stock price" effect 10, 20, 30 times before. You know that the *best* airlines and their stock prices always rebound eventually. People are not going to stop flying forever. You are confident that you can now buy the *best* airline stocks "low" with a built-in profit once the airlines and their stocks do take-off again.

You also know when you hear the "good news" of "air travel is at its peak", "fares have not been this low in over two years", "fuel prices are at a 30-month low", etc., that now is the time for you to sell to all those other less informed investors who are trying to catch the tailwind of the rise in airline stock prices. However, as late comers, they are unknowingly behind the price curve—they have missed the stock price run-up. Airline stocks have already taken-off without them—but not without you. They are now scrambling to "buy at the top" and you will be there to happily trade your inflated shares to them and parachute yourself into profit land with their cash, because you *know* you are near the top now—they created it themselves.

Remember, when someone loses $1,000 on a trade in the stock market, that $1,000 does not disappear off the face of the planet. Somebody, somewhere else "wins" that $1,000. Your trading goal is to make sure that you are on the winning side of the equation much more often than you are on the losing side of the equation. One way to stack the deck in your favor is to exploit your knowledge of the uniqueness of "your" industry, so that you are often "buying low" and "selling high" with built-in profits.

For more information on investment timing, see your Rule #7. An interesting book on buying and selling "against the crowd" is *Contrary Investing* (see *Appendix B: Financial Growth Resources* for details). For seeking expertise beyond your own, see your Rule #17—next.

Don't try to be a jack of all investments. Stick to the field you know best.

Bernard Baruch

Rule #17: Get Help—But Not Too Much.

One of your new challenges is to assemble your *Infinite Financial Freedom* team of advisors. These people should have a specialized body of knowledge for you to tap to help implement the policies that you have already defined in your *Rulebook*. Their function is to bring to your advisory table the *strategies* that will help you achieve your specific goals and objectives. You will provide the driving *policies* that define the ultimate outcomes that you seek. Your advisors will provide the various optional techniques or methods or tactics of achieving your defined goals.

For example, if your lofty goal is to climb Mount Everest (which you have thoroughly studied), you hire those people who can best counsel and guide you on the equipment you need, the best route to take, the best time to go, the team to assemble, and so forth, to get you to the top. You don't hire someone who then tries to convince you that the mountain that you really should be climbing is Mount Saint Helens (about which you know nothing) because he happens to know a secret passage to the top. Your policy—your *Rulebook*—drives advisors, not the other way around.

Depending upon your goals and needs, your *Infinite Financial Freedom* team can include any combination of these professionals:

- ❑   A *money manager*;

- ❑   A practicing Certified Financial Planner;

- ❑   An investment newsletter Editor/Advisor;

- ❑   A tax accountant;

- ❑   An estate planning attorney;

- ❑   A life insurance agent.

You need to decide how "hands-on" you want to be with your investments. Ask yourself: "Do I want to handle my own transactions and portfolio management myself or delegate this responsibility to someone else?" I recommend, unless stock and bond picking and market timing is already your area of expertise, that you first delegate this function to a mutual fund manager. You will still decide which funds to use and how much money to place into each (according to your *Rulebook*), but leave the day-to-day portfolio management *operations* to an expert, the mutual fund manager. We covered picking the right fund manager in the first of your Nine Mutual Fund Profile Standards when we discussed *Consistency* in your Rule #5. Now let's look at the process of picking a personal portfolio manager, if you decide that using your own *money manager* is part of your policy *Rulebook*.

Picking an Individual Money Manager

A *money manager* is a professional who handles the portfolio administration for the personal portfolio of an individual investor. That is, instead of investing your dollars into a mutual fund that pools all investors' funds together and then manages the pool of funds, you can hire an independent *money manager* to handle your personal portfolio separately from any pooled funds. There is, of course, greater potential risk and greater potential reward in not pooling your investment dollars into a mutual fund.

If you decide that you want to use an individual *money manager* to personally handle part of your portfolio instead of or along with using a mutual fund, then you need to do some extra up-front homework to find the best *money manager* for you. To avoid any potential conflicts of interest, never use a stockbroker as a *money manager* or advisor. Although not commonly known to the consumer, stock brokerage firms are notorious for buying blocks of stocks at a discount and then encouraging their brokers (through cash bonuses, free trips, etc.) to sell the stock to you. A stockbroker profits when generating trading commissions, irrespective of your profiting from the transactions. So, the profit motives of you and your stockbroker can be mis-aligned, that is, you can lose even when he wins. Always seek win-win (mutually beneficial) relationships, including when investing.

On the other hand, an independent *money manager* profits only when you do. *Money managers* typically charge 1% to 2% of the total value of your assets that they manage. So, a *money manager* has a vested (selfish) interest in seeing your account value grow: The more money that you make, the more money that the *money manager* makes. This fee structure makes sense because it takes human nature into account by aligning the profit motive for both of you on the same side. Either you both win or you both lose, unlike in the stockbroker-customer relationship. Given such a small percentage fee structure, however, most *money managers* will not work with you unless you have a portfolio of over $500,000 or $1 Million or more.

Finding Good Help

One of the benefits of using mutual funds is that you can find sufficient objective information to help you pick the best funds for you. Locating individuals can be more challenging, but there are some techniques that you can use to limit the universe of providers to the one that is best for you.

Of course, you can start with the traditional word-of-mouth method, although there are some inherent problems with this method, not the least of which is: Whose mouth? Ask people with money or those around money. Ask your former boss, if you are impressed with his or her judgment or apparent success. Also ask any accountants or attorneys that you may know if they know of any *money managers*.

The problem with the word-of-mouth method is that you are probably not getting objective information. Testimonial-givers can have ulterior motives for recommendations that have nothing to do with you. Such hidden agendas can include an unwillingness to admit to themselves that they have, through poor judgment, picked a poor advisor or perhaps they receive cash or a referral in return for your referral or other social or monetary "kick-back". Still, word-of-mouth can lead you to the prospective advisor you want, so you can *start* here. Your search needs to continue, however, beyond the mouthful of words that you may have received as a recommendation.

Certain *practicing* Certified Financial Planners (CFP's) provide personal portfolio management services. A professional who earns the CFP designation undergoes a rigorous multi-year training and multi-examination schedule based on a nationally established curriculum in these seven areas of financial expertise:

❑   Fundamentals of Financial Planning;

❑   Insurance Planning;

❑   Investment Planning;

❑   Income Tax Planning;

❑   Retirement Planning;

❑   Employee Benefits Planning; and

❑   Estate Planning.

In addition to the above initial qualification, the professional must meet strict ongoing continuing education requirements to retain the CFP designation. Because of the breadth of the subject matter, practicing CFP's typically either act as generalists quarterbacking the activities of a team of specialists in each of the above fields or they become specialists in a particular field themselves.

There are over 28,000 CFP's today, but not all of them are actively *practicing* with individual clients. Some take positions in financial firms and work internally in an analytic capacity rather than working directly with clients. Of these 28,000 CFP's, only 8,000 pay annual fees to become active members of the Institute of Certified Financial Planners (ICFP), a national CFP trade and continuing education group. Of these 8,000 ICFP members only about 1,000 choose to participate in the ICFP's national referral program called their Direct Public Awareness (DPA) Program.

You can call the ICFP's toll-free Consumer Assistance Line at 800-282-7526 to receive free CFP referrals. The ICFP will send you the names of up to three CFP's participating in the referral program with brief information on each *based* only on your ZIP code, not on any other criteria. So, unless you have a particularly magical ZIP code, you should use this service in combination with the other search-and-find ideas here—not alone. Remember, the ICFP's referrals are pulled from just about 3.5% of existing CFP's. Unfortunately, you cannot conclude that these are the *best* CFP's, but they may be among the best and the most active—or want to be.

The National Association of Personal Financial Advisors (NAPFA) provides a referral program, but they will refer CFP's only by coincidence, since non-CFP's can join NAPFA. However, NAPFA members must be "fee-only" planners. That is, they must work only on a fee-for-service basis and must not accept commissions for product placement or recommendations. ICFP members, on the other hand, may accept fees, commissions or a combination of both. Any of these practitioners may or may not act as *money managers*. You can call NAPFA for referrals at 800-366-2732.

One of the best ways to find a *money manager* is by reviewing the newsletters of those who also provide personal portfolio management services. There are over 120 principal financial newsletters published in America. Of these 120, just under half of their publishers also act as *money managers*. There is more to say about newsletters later in this rule, but always try to find out if the company is principally a newsletter publisher that happens to also manage money or if the company is principally a money management firm that also publishes an advisory newsletter.

How *Not* to Find a Money Manager

There is one way that you do *not* find a *money manager*. Do not automatically work with people who solicit you. You are pro-active now, remember. Cordially, tell all solicitors that you work with an exclusive advisory team (whether or not you have found all the members yet) and that either you or the appropriate team member will contact the solicitor if the team believes that the solicitor has something of value to offer. Offer the solicitor your Post Office Box number and tell him to send his information for your team's review. If he is not willing to play by your rules up-front and send descriptive material to your Post Office Box, then assume that you would probably have ongoing difficulty working with him later or that he is hiding that he has nothing of exceptional value to offer you.

Yes, it's possible that you may miss a good idea or two by using this screening device. However, by so screening, you will save yourself from the dozens of bad or me-too ideas, any of which could either hurt you or you could find elsewhere easily. However, you will also find good ideas this way. Keep the good ideas on file and shred and recycle the rest.

Life insurance agents are notorious for presenting what they do using various euphemisms, since to most people the words "life insurance" are not just less than exciting, they are a real turn-off. We all know that none of us get out of here alive, but we just don't like to dwell on death while living. So, be wary of life insurance salespeople presenting themselves as *financial planners* (small "f" and small "p" and not *Certified*). Such people are using financial planning as a marketing tool "to get in the door" (and into your wallet or purse) and not as a professional practice. Requiring full disclosure of their compensation program will reveal any potential conflicts of interest between your profit motives.

Such screening is a good trade-off. Your *Financial Game Plan Rulebook* will help you always hold your ground with solicitors. So, don't be intimidated. After all, it's your money. You have the *right* as well as the *duty* to yourself to "call the shots". If a potential advisor is not sensitive to this fact, then he or she is not the advisor for you.

Narrowing the Search

Always interview a prospective *money manager* as if he or she is a prospective employee—for they are exactly this. Ask for the names of 4–6 clients and *call* these people. Even ask for the names of *former* clients, who may provide even more revealing information. Do not accept the excuse that a *money manager's* clients are confidential and, therefore, cannot be revealed to you. Additionally, the *money manager* should provide you with sample portfolios from actual clients (although the client names will be appropriately masked for privacy purposes). A *money manager* who also publishes a newsletter has significant public information available in past issues of the newsletters. Ask for copies or subscribe.

Interview both the individual who will personally handle your portfolio and any assistant(s) who might handle your routine inquiries. If the *money management* firm makes portfolio management decisions by committee, then you need to first decide if this group-think arrangement is acceptable to you and, if so, you still need to interview the individual who administers your account. The key is to talk to whoever makes the investment decisions and whoever is handling your account at the *money management* firm. Also, check them out for personality compatibility ("chemistry") to make sure that they have the *right mind set*. Don't put your money into a negative work environment where some "psychic vampire" manager is running the show, because staff turnover will be high leading to, at best, administrative problems for you.

Be leery of secret "systems" or "formulas" for magically making you money. A "secret formula" is an oxymoron. If the "secret" is for sale to anyone, then how can it be a secret? Also, find out how your *money manager* receives compensation. You are hoping to find that his or her compensation is at least partially based on the performance of your portfolio.

Such advisory firms (with few exceptions) must file required documents with the Securities and Exchange Commission (SEC). These filings are public information and are available from the SEC directly (SEC, Public Reference, 450 Fifth St. N.W., Washington, D.C. 20549). The advisory firm should also be happy to give you a copy of these documents for your review:

❑   Form ADV Part I

This SEC filing contains detailed information regarding the firm's locations, principal owners, and any securities violations, lawsuits, and the like.

❑   Form ADV Part II (including Schedules F & G)

This SEC filing discloses any potential conflicts of interest, fee structure, investment strategies, affiliations with stock brokerage houses, key employee backgrounds, and the like. Request that the firm automatically send you their annual ADV forms when issued.

❑   Audited Performance Record

Although *money management* firms are not mandated by law to provide a track record audited by an independent accountant, many do. If such statistics are available, then be sure that the historical time periods illustrated include at least the market downturns of 1973, 1981, 1982, and 1987.

Setting the Standards

Since you are calling the overall policy shots, be sure to give your portfolio manager a copy of your mutual understanding for handling your account *in writing.* You can and should extract much of your "investment policy" right from your *Rulebook* (see *Chapter 7: Model Infinite Financial Freedom Game Plan* for an example).

Additionally, you should include the criteria by which you will judge the performance of the portfolio manager. We will discuss what standards are reasonable when we review the historical performance records of various investment vehicles in your Rule #18. For your stock portfolio, use these expectations/standards:

❑ Outperform the S&P 500 Composite Stock Index by at least 2 percentage points (otherwise, why not just invest in one of the mutual funds that "buys" the S&P 500 Stocks?);

❑ Outperform inflation by at least 7 percentage points (since stocks have historically done so);

❑ Not lose more than 8%–10% of your portfolio's value in any one year (the percentage you pick here will depend upon your threshold of pain—what you feel that you can stomach and afford to lose);

❑ Not have a losing performance for more than 1 or 2 consecutive quarters or years, depending upon the type of investments.

Considering your above expectations, be sure to review the provisions for canceling the contract. Do not enter into an arrangement that requires more than a 30-day notice of termination. If the firm fails to meet your performance standards, you want to be able to move your funds relatively quickly—with no questions asked or penalties.

Read All About It: Investment Newsletters

Along with—or in place of—the use of an individual *money manager*, you can consider the advice from newsletter publishers. The marketplace prints a plethora of investment advisory newsletters speaking in a cacophony of discordant simultaneous voices. Translation: You can always find "experts" who recommend opposite investment moves simultaneously. Some will proclaim that the market is headed for an all-time high while others will swear—given the same market conditions—that the market is headed for a crash. So, whom do you believe? Answer: *You!*

To investigate newsletters, start with *The Hulbert Guide to Financial Newsletters* (see *Appendix B: Financial Growth Resources* for details). This unique book is written by Mark Hulbert, Editor of *The Hulbert Financial Digest*, itself a financial newsletter of financial newsletters. Hulbert tracks the returns of various newsletters' model portfolios and reports and ranks the investment performance of each.

In his *Guide*, he profiles over 120 of the principal financial newsletters giving all the details of their performance track records, subscription costs, and whether the advisory firm publishing the letter also acts as a *money manager*. He "splices and dices" the investment performance of these newsletters over various time periods and in relation to each other and the Wilshire 5000 Index over the past 12 years. He further rates each newsletter on an A-B-C scale for clarity and separately shows the performance records of Mutual Fund Newsletters with one another and the various Market Timing Newsletters with one another as well as with all letters.

How do you use all this good information? First, you review the profiles to see which newsletters mirror the approach you have established in your own *Rulebook*. For example, if you know absolutely nothing about emerging companies in the genetic engineering and biotechnology industry, then you can ignore the *AgBiotech Stock Letter* and the *Medical Technology Stock Letter* all together, despite their very favorable returns. If this arena is not your area of expertise, then your Rules #5, #9 and #16 will not allow you to go fishing in these waters, irrespective of the good performance history there. However, if you have a background in this specialized field, then these two letters would be among the best for you to consider, assuming their approaches otherwise align with the rest of your *Rulebook*. So, your *Rulebook* will help you to eliminate certain newsletters and gravitate towards others.

For example, if you want a newsletter from a firm that also manages money, you will cut the list of letters in half. If the newsletter must also specialize in mutual funds, the list shrinks even more. If the newsletter must track only no-load mutual funds, then the list shrinks again. If the model portfolio's performance of the newsletter must equal or exceed the Wilshire 5000 Index, then the universe of letters shrinks once more. Continue the process of elimination until you get down to just a few *contenders*.

Next, order a sample newsletter or a short-term trial subscription. Most letters will send you a sample issue at no cost. Others offer a one to six month trial subscription for a fee. Annual subscriptions can range from a low of $17 to a high of $720, but typically run between $100 and $300 per year for 12 to 24 issues.

Be skeptical, however, of some newsletters' performance claims in the marketing materials that always accompany the sample or trial issues. Pay little attention to what may be exaggerated advertising claims from over zealous marketing departments or copy editors at the newsletters. Refer to Hulbert's *Guide* for objective performance information.

Keep newsletters in perspective, however. The right investment letter can provide effective *strategies* for the implementation of your investment *policy* as defined by the rules of your *Rulebook*. Again, your policy should drive the strategies, not the other way around. The two strategic areas in which an investment newsletter can help you in the execution of your plan are:

1.   the *selection* of mutual funds or individual stocks;

2.   the *timing* of purchases into these investment vehicles.

Finding An Attorney

Although you (like most of us) probably hope that an attorney never finds you, you do need to find an attorney to occupy the estate planning chair of you *Infinite Financial Freedom* team of advisors. While I am familiar with the growth statistic that by the year 2010 there will be more attorneys than people, finding a *good* attorney today can be a challenge. Of course, a word-of-mouth recommendation is the traditional technique for attorney selection, so begin with this approach. However, we discussed earlier how there can be some inherent problems with the word-of-mouth method.

The most objective approach is to review the massive *Martindale-Hubbell* reference directory. Due to the size and expense of the directory, only the larger libraries and law libraries will carry these volumes. The set is now also available on CD-ROM computer disk, however, so accessibility is becoming easier and broader.

This directory lists attorneys nationwide, so your selection challenge becomes a process of elimination. Since most people like the sound of eliminating attorneys, the process should be fun. Although the directory does not include any fee information, it does provide a peer-review rating system of attorneys through the eyes of judges and other lawyers.

Beyond this directory, your other advisors can probably recommend an estate planning attorney with whom they already have a successful working relationship. If so fine, but double-check the referred attorney against the *Martindale-Hubbell* tome, if possible, and these criteria:

Experience

You want an Estate Planning Attorney who specializes in estate planning, not a personal injury attorney who with some research and brush-up can probably figure out what to do to help you eventually. Ask how long the attorney and his/her firm have specialized in this area of law.

Staffing

Make sure that you meet the attorney who will be working with you. Don't allow a senior partner to "shmooze" you only to later learn that you have been handed-off to a rookie associate to handle your planning needs. Also make sure that you meet your prospective attorney's support staff and that you are comfortable with them.

Fees

Discuss costs up-front. Find out if the attorney will work on a flat-fee per project basis or insists on strict hourly billing. The problem with hourly billing is that the hours can be padded with such nonsense as travel time and even with the accounting time for figuring out how much time was used. Insist that non-legal services, such as photocopying, be provided at cost or offer to perform these yourself. At some law firms, photocopying is one of the biggest profit centers in the firm.

Ask for a cost estimate for the work that you need the attorney to do. Much estate planning work is based upon model documents that need only revision for your particular situation. Most attorneys now use standard computer software for such work, thereby automating much of the work and making flat fees and estimates very feasible. For example, an estate planning law firm might typically quote you a flat fee of $500 to draft a living trust (which means that they fill in your name and other specifics in a standardized computer software program and then press the print button). You can do much the same thing with the do-it-yourself books and software now available to consumers (more on this idea later).

References

Ask for three existing client references and one former client reference. Call the references and ask if they are pleased with the attorney's services enough to recommend the attorney to another member of their own family. Find out why the former client is "former".

Rolling Your Own

Along with and/or in place of using a live attorney, you can use one of the excellent guide books or software and "do-it-yourself". You can use one of the fill-in-the-blanks form books or a software package for making your own will and living trust, for example. One of the best techniques is to begin with one of the self-help law books or software, prepare your own documents, and then present the finished documents to an attorney for final review. This last technique significantly cuts down on the time that the attorney uses (and charges for), since you have already done the bulk of the work. Further, this last technique provides you with another level of liability protection (namely the attorney's) should your documents ever be challenged. See the several user-friendly, do-it-yourself law materials listed in *Appendix C: Legal Resources* for details.

For setting-up charitable trusts, you can have most of the legal work done by the charity. Often the charity has standard documents based on the IRS approved models (as discussed in your Rule #15) ready for easy fill-in-the-blanks completion. If you need an attorney at all on your end, the cost should be minimal since you are only asking the attorney for final review of standard, model documents and not for the creation or drafting of completely new documents. Flat-fees are very appropriate in these cases.

One last word regarding an estate planning attorney: Pick one that is younger than you and likely to outlive you. It's preferable for the same attorney who initially counsels you on your estate planning matters to still be alive after you die, so that your heirs have an existing level of comfort with the attorney and the attorney has a sufficient level of familiarity with your case.

Inescapable You

Despite all the good that *money managers*, Certified Financial Planners, investment newsletter editors, attorneys, accountants and other advisors can do for you, there is one thing that they cannot and must not do: define the rules of your *Financial Game Plan Rulebook*—only you can do this. The reason that your *Rulebook* policy is so important is that over 90% of your investment success depends solely on your having a solid *Game Plan*. This 90% figure is not just an exaggerated estimate used to emphasize the importance of your investment policy.

Study after study confirms the critical effect that policy has on return. Two of the most notable studies were conducted by Gary Brinson (the first published in *Financial Analysts Journal* in 1986 and the second in 1991) showing that since 1974, at least, over 90% of the long-term performance variance of major pension funds was attributable only to investment policy, that is, to the manager's *Rulebook*! In the first case only 6.4% and in the second case only 8.5% of the variance in return was attributable to either market timing or investment vehicle selection. In both cases, policy—the rules of your *Rulebook*—accounted for over 90% of portfolio performance. Policy not only drives strategy, it drives return.

You are responsible for setting policy by making-up the rules of your *Rulebook* that account for over 90% of your financial success. Your advisory team is helping you only in the areas that represent under 10% of your financial success. Keep these relative percentages in mind when working with advisors, so that you never get bit by the advisory tail wagging the policy dog.

Still, you need to monitor the performance of both your advisors and your portfolios on a regular basis. In your Rule #18, we discuss "what and when to watch" regarding the performance of your investments and how to know a good return when you see one—next.

Experts should be on tap, but never on top.
Winston Churchill

Rule #18: Be an Investment Watchdog.

If you want to keep the *right* amount of money *right*, then, among all the other things we've covered, you have to become your own investment watchdog (or spy satellite or investigative reporter or undercover agent or whatever other metaphor you like best). No one else can do this sentry work for you, because no one will have all the information contained in your *Rulebook*. Also, no one else will care as much about your investment program as you must.

Knowing What to Watch and When

There is, as you might suspect, a right and wrong way to watch. First, you have to know what you are watching and what you hope to find. To make your investment tracking easy, effective, and worthwhile, establish *investment performance criteria* as part of your *Rulebook*. We began this discussion of establishing standards when evaluating the performance of a *money manager* in your Rule #17. Such standards must apply to all aspects of your investment program. Later in this rule you will see the historical basis for determining your own reasonable expectations.

Once you establish acceptable *investment performance criteria* (what to watch), you must also determine how often to review performance (when to watch). Often the particular investment itself dictates the appropriate time period to use for a performance check-up. For example, if a commodities broker is lucky enough for you to be speculating in soybean oil futures, then you will have to watch your money and the commodities market almost constantly in real-time. On the other hand, a long-term investment into a 15-year zero coupon municipal bond for the City of Los Angeles need only be checked as part of your annual review (save extraordinary circumstances like earthquakes, etc.). In any case, I suggest that you perform at least these two check-ups:

1. A quarterly *Reality Check* of your investment portfolio; plus

2. An *Annual Assessment* of your entire *Financial Game Plan Rulebook* and all holdings.

Your annual financial review should follow your *Personal Growth* review that you do near your birthday (see *Chapter 4: What To Do Before You Win* for details). Remember, *Financial Growth* is a by-product of *Personal Growth*. Always perform your *Annual Assessment* before receiving or investing your next lottery check.

Make your life easier and invest only in financial vehicles that require no more than quarterly reviews by you. An investment program that needs no more than quarterly check-ups allows you to take a break from your investments between quarters and spend more time enjoying life. Remember that although *you* may only be performing quarterly reviews, your mutual fund manager or *money manager* is (or better be) pushing for optimum performance on a daily basis.

Some of you will still want to check your on-line computer service and other sources daily for the fun of keeping a hand on the pulse of your investments, especially if investing reaches hobby-status for you. However, such constant attention from you is optional if you are invested in professionally managed funds. Typically, you will want to be more watchful at first until you become comfortable with the performance of your entire program. Go at your own pace. You can never get hurt by checking your returns *too* often.

The financial freedom to let your investments successfully run on auto-pilot (*assigned*-pilot, is more accurate) without your constant surveillance can only come from having a pre-determined, well-conceived plan. And, as you know by now, plan follows policy—as established in your *Rulebook*.

How to Know a Good Return When You See One

In drafting your investment tracking policy (what to watch for and when), you need to make decisions regarding these two *investment performance criteria*:

1.   Your expectations or assumptions regarding the economy and inflation plus

2.   Your own required rates of return.

To make reasonable judgements regarding the economy, inflation, and returns you need a knowledge of what's reasonable—what inflation has averaged and what various investments have returned historically. Otherwise, you have no way of knowing if a return is *good*. A return can only be *good* in relation to the performance of other investments and the relative risks required to obtain their attendant returns. Refer to Table 6–9 for the most recently published 66-year history of returns on the *Ladder of Investments*.

As you can see at the bottom of the table, the inflation rate has averaged 3.1% for the last 66 years (1926–1991, inclusive). So, you might assume for your plan's purposes that inflation will continue to average about 3% (or even 4% per year, if you want to be more conservative). The Consumer Price Index (CPI) is a good indicator of the annual inflation rate in America. The CPI is published in newspapers and magazines too numerous to list. You can always find the CPI in *The Wall Street Journal* and *Money* magazine and most local newspapers' business sections.

TABLE 6–9: INVESTMENT LADDER RATES OF RETURN

INVESTMENT LADDER RATES OF RETURN		
Historical Rates of Return (1926–1991)		
Type of Investment Vehicle	Compounded Total Return Per Year	Single Year Range of Return 70% of the Time
Small Company Stocks	12.1%	-23.2% to 47.4%
Common Stocks	10.4%	-10.4% to 31.2%
Long-Term Corporate Bonds	5.4%	-3.1% to 13.9%
Long-Term Government Bonds	4.8%	-3.8% to 13.4%
U.S. Treasury Bills	3.7%	0.3% to 7.1%
Inflation (per Consumer Price Index)	3.1%	-1.6% to 7.8%
Source: *Stocks, Bonds, Bills & Inflation 1992 Yearbook*, Ibbotson Associates and *Business One Irwin 1993 Business & Investment Almanac*, Business One Irwin		

We discussed in your earlier rules and chapters the importance of considering inflation: You need to pick investments that will outpace inflation or the dollars that you get out of your investment tomorrow will be worth less than the dollars that you put into your investment today. Remember that this danger of underperforming inflation is called an investment's *purchasing power risk*. Investment professionals call your net investment return after deducting for inflation your *real rate of return*. So, you now know the long-term track record of inflation that you need to beat to avoid *purchasing power risk* and to keep your *real rate of return* positive. Accept no investment that will do any less than protect your purchasing power and beat the rate of inflation. Otherwise, you are receiving a negative return on your investment—violating all your principles of *Infinite Financial Freedom*. Don't allow this to happen!

Use the *Investment Ladder Rates of Return* table as a guideline to determine your own reasonable rate of return and expected inflation rate. Don't expect bonds to give you a 30% return if they typically have never reached 14% over the last 66 years. Your assumptions and requirements become the standards by which you will measure performance of both your investment vehicles and any mutual fund manager, personal *money manager* or other investment advisor. Substandard performance suggests the need for change in either investment or advisor or both.

Perform your quarterly *Reality Check* and *Annual Assessment* to discover trends that might signal the need for such a change. When tracking your investments, keep in mind that, as you move up the *Investment Ladder*, the rate of return increases while the fluctuation (range) in return also increases. As we discussed in your Rule #6, the increasing rate of return is your reward for the increased fluctuation or volatility that you are willing to accept—your risk. So, do not pull the sell/change trigger more quickly than the investment suggests is appropriate.

Notice that while common stocks have a 10.4% historical return, their return has varied by 20.8 points above and below their 10.4% average (from -10.4% to +31.2%). On the other hand, Treasury Bills have only swung 3.4 points above their 3.7% average historical return (from +0.3% to +7.1%). Also, individual investments will have specific inherent track records that will suggest to you their reasonable returns (rewards) and typical price fluctuations (risk). Knowing the historical price fluctuations of an investment keeps you from selling the investment too soon or from holding on to the investment too long.

Get Smart

If you are going to be your own investment watchdog and you must be, then you will need to learn new tricks, that is, to stay informed. As we covered in your Rule #5 and *Chapter 4: What To Do Before You Win*, you need to get smart and stay sharp through a continuing program of self-education.

For more detail on buy and sell decisions relative to price, review your Rule #7. For more information and tools on tracking your investments, see *Appendix B: Financial Growth Resources*. For an example of a complete game plan for a mythical lottery winner or other person with the *right* amount of money, see *Chapter 7: Model Infinite Financial Freedom Game Plan*—next.

If a man empties his purse into his head, no one takes it from him.

Ben Franklin

7

Model *Infinite Financial Freedom* Game Plan

Let's put all the rules of your *Infinite Financial Freedom Game Plan Rulebook* together so that you can see what a finished (really, beginning) plan looks like. Of course, your own *Game Plan* will be different from this mythical model based upon:

- ❑ Your own personal goals and objectives;

- ❑ Your tolerance for risk (your relative fear of heights up the *Ladder of Investments*);

- ❑ Your tax strategies (how aggressive or conservative);

- ❑ Your assumptions;

- ❑ Your required rates of return;

- ❑ Other decisions regarding your investment policy; and

- ❑ The simple passage of time.

Keep in mind that this model is a snapshot-in-time, as yours will be. Your *Game Plan* must evolve with time's passage to respond to changes in your inner goals and objectives and the outer influences of the investment and economic climates. You will take your own snapshots-in-time of your own *Game Plan* with every quarterly *Reality Check* as you refine your plan based upon your vision and the distance that you have traveled since your last review.

Additionally, you will meet or abandon certain of your goals and objectives over time as well as formulate new ones. Like life, your *Infinite Financial Freedom Game Plan* is not to be chiseled in crystalline quartz—a pencil and paper is plenty. So, while understanding the need for flexibility, revision, and change, look at this sample *Game Plan* and see how your own might compare and evolve.

Note that the rules of your *Rulebook* create the *guidelines* of your *Game Plan* that you follow. The *guideline* numbers, therefore, do not correspond to your rule numbers, because a single rule can generate several *Game Plan guidelines*, as will become apparent to you when you review the Model. Besides, *guidelines* provide more leeway for change than your rules. Though you will re-focus your *guidelines* at each review, your underlying rules (upon which these *guidelines* are based) will change very little.

Here are the assumptions for the *Model Infinite Financial Freedom Game Plan*:

1. Your Total Lottery Jackpot = $10 Million;

2. The Jackpot is an annuity paid-out over 20 years;

3. Your Annual Net Lottery Check = $400,000 (that's $500,000 *less* 20% in federal income taxes withheld);

4. This *Model Game Plan* is written for the very first quarter of your winning year.

Model Infinite Financial Freedom Game Plan

PLAN NAME

Lottie and Lot O' Munn-Knee's
Infinite Financial Freedom Game Plan

GUIDELINE #1: GOAL SUMMARY

A. Infinite Financial Freedom

Provide $100,000 per year income (in today's dollars) for the rest of our lives beginning 21 years from today (when the lottery checks will stop coming).

B. College Education

Provide $10,000 per year (in today's dollars) for 4 years, starting in 10 years from today for our daughter's college education.

C. Charity

Give $10,000 per year (in today's dollars) into perpetuity to the American Cancer Institute beginning 21 years from today.

D. Home

Buy our principal residence with 4 bedrooms/4 baths in our favorite place 5 years from today using a $400,000 budget (in today's dollars).

GUIDELINE #2: COVERING OUR ASSETS

Review, revise, and/or buy these insurance coverages:

- ❑ Kidnap & Ransom

- ❑ Health: Medical & Dental

- ❑ Life

- ❑ Disability Income

- ❑ Homeowners

- ❑ Auto

- ❑ Long-Term Care

- ❑ Personal Umbrella Liability

GUIDELINE #3: OPERATING FUND

Research and set-up an *Operating Fund* using a cash/asset management account featuring:

- ❑ A double tax-free money market mutual fund;

- ❑ Free, unlimited check writing privileges;

- ❑ Credit/Debit Card;

- ❑ Automated bill payment service;

- ❑ Expense coding capability.

GUIDELINE #4: MUTUAL FUNDS & ANNUITIES

Research and open the following mutual fund and annuity accounts to achieve the goals that we have outlined in Guideline #1:

A. Infinite Financial Freedom Fund

Use double tax-free Municipal Bond funds and fixed Tax-Deferred Annuities for Goal A.

B. College/Possibility Fund

Use Zero coupon Municipal Bond funds for Goal B.

C. Charity/Balanced Fund

Use Growth and Income funds to eventually rollover into a Charitable Trust in year 21 for Goal C.

D. Home/Possibility Fund

Use Aggressive Growth small stock funds for Goal D.

Guideline #4 Notes:

1. In year 1, we will open at least one mutual fund/annuity account for each goal.

2. In year 2 and thereafter, we will further diversify each of our "Goal Funds" with additional investments as we identify appropriate investment candidates.

3. We will keep the eventual overall total number of mutual funds/annuities for all goals between a low of 10 and a high of 15 separate investments.

4. This level of diversification is sufficient to reduce our risk, but not so much as to dilute our returns. This number of separate accounts is also a manageable number of accounts for us to track and administer.

GUIDELINE #5: ESTATE PLANNING ATTORNEY

Find and meet with an Estate Planning Attorney to:

❑   Write/Re-write out Last Will;

❑   Write a Living Will;

❑   Consider various Trust possibilities.

Guideline #5 Notes:

1. Before meeting with an attorney we will read and complete the do-it-yourself law books listed in our Guideline #6.

2. We will double-check any prospective attorney against the *Martindale-Hubbell* directory.

GUIDELINE #6: SELF-EDUCATION

We will maintain the following book reading schedule this year (which represents reading or completing about 1.5 books, manuals or guides a month) to help us meet our goals:

Quarter 1

Personal	Financial	Legal
Think & Grow Rich Action Pack	*The Hulbert Guide to Financial Newsletters*	*How to Prepare Your Own Last Will & Testament Kit*
Self-Centering Manual: How to Align Your Outward Behavior With Your Inner Belief	*Where To Make Money: A Rating Guide To Opportunities in America's Metro Areas*	*Everything Your Heirs Need To Know: Your Assets, Family History and Final Wishes*

Quarter 2

Personal	Financial	Legal
How to Get Control of Your Time and Your Life	*Your Home As A Tax Shelter*	*Make Your Own Living Trust*
LifePlan: A Goal-Setting Workbook	*Richest Man in Babylon*	

Quarter 3

Personal	Financial	Legal
Head First: The Biology of Hope	*Real Estate Wealthbuilding: How To Really Make Money in Real Estate*	*Winning the Wealth Game: How To Keep Your Money in Your Family*
What Color Is Your Parachute? Manual for Job Hunters & Career-Changers		

Quarter 4

Personal	Financial	Legal
The Rating Guide To Life In America's Small Cities: 219 Mircopolitan Alternatives to Metropolitan Hassles	*Contrary Investing*	*Warning: Dying May Be Hazardous To Your Wealth: How To Protect Your Life Savings for Yourself & Those You Love*
50 Fabulous Places To Retire In America		

GUIDELINE #7: INFORMATION ACQUISITION

We will order the following materials, as soon as possible:

- ❑ Life Insurance quotes from *The Insurance Exchange*™ now and every 5 years;

- ❑ Money Personality *MoneyMax® Profile* from Benefits Resource Group before finalizing the major investment decisions of our *Game Plan*;

- ❑ Tax-Deferred Annuity quotes from *The Annuity Exchange*™ before buying any annuity;

- ❑ Mutual Fund Computer Search from *The Fund Exchange*™ before investing in any mutual fund and every year for all mutual funds that we hold as part of our *Annual Assessment*;

❏   Books from this year's reading list shown in Guideline #6 from the *Infinite Financial Freedom Bookshelf;*

❏   Free or trial subscriptions to the top 5 investment newsletters that we identify from *The Hulbert Guide To Financial Newsletters.* We will formally subscribe to no more than 1 of the 5 contender newsletters, if that 1 meets our criteria.

GUIDELINE #8: RESPONSIBILITY FOR INVESTMENT DECISIONS

1.   Both of us will jointly discuss all investment decisions before acting on any one.

2.   If we cannot agree on an investment action, we will review the fundamentals of our goals and *Rulebook* and see if any information there helps us to agree.

3.   If we still cannot agree, then the person who does *not* want to make the investment will choose the dollar amount to commit to the investment. In any case of disagreement, the dollar amount committed cannot be less than 10% or greater than 50% of the original amount considered.

4.   The person who wants to make the investment has the final decision as to whether or not to make the investment on a trial basis once the dollar amount to commit has been decided. The investment's performance can then help us agree at subsequent quarterly reviews whether or not to commit fully to this investment.

5.   In no case, will either of us condemn the other for our investment decisions as this negativity violates our *right mind set*, *Guiding Principles*, and *Affirmations*. We understand that our investment decisions will produce various outcomes, all of which will provide us with valuable new information in making future investment decisions.

GUIDELINE #9: SCHEDULED PLAN REVIEWS

1.   We will conduct our quarterly *Reality Checks* to review and revise our *Game Plan*, as necessary, at high noon on the second Saturday of every calendar quarter (January-April-July-October).

2.   Our *Annual Assessment* is the January check-up.

3.   We will reward ourselves for performing our check-ups by going out to dinner at a special restaurant.

GUIDELINE #10: OWNERSHIP RIGHTS

We will hold all our accounts and property in joint ownership unless we are seeking to achieve certain goals (such as charitable or estate planning goals) that suggest other more advantageous methods of ownership.

GUIDELINE #11: MUTUAL FUND SHARES

Mutual Funds will hold our shares for us, as a convenience, so we do not have to store them ourselves.

GUIDELINE #12: CASH DISBURSEMENT OF ANNUAL LOTTERY CHECKS

Our disbursement of the net $400,000 per year after-tax lottery checks will be:

Annual Amount Invested	Years	Fund Name	Goal Summary
$100,000	1–20	*Operating Fund*	Maintain current lifestyle
$145,000	1–10	*Infinite Financial Freedom*	Guarantee $100,000 per year income for the rest
$150,000	11–20	*Fund*	of our lives
$5,000	1–10	*College - Possibility Fund*	College Education for our daughter
$30,000	1	*Balanced Fund* for future Charitable	Give $10,000 per year in perpetuity to the American Cancer
$70,000	2–5	Trust;	Institute;
$70,000 to $150,000	6–20	*Balanced Fund & Possibility Fund*	May share these dollars to fund charitable & other goals
$80,000	1–5	*Home - Possibility Fund*	Buy our main residence
$40,000	1	*Fun Fund*	"Blow" just for grins (10% of 1st check only)

Guideline #12 Notes:

1.   The amount invested into our *Infinite Financial Freedom Fund* increases by $5,000 in year 11 (to $150,000), because we will have met our College Education goal by the end of year 10.

2.   The amount invested into our *Balanced Fund* increases by $40,000 in year 2 (to $70,000), because we will have met our *Fun Fund* goal by the end of year 1.

3.   The amount invested into our *Balanced Fund* and *Possibility Fund* increases by $80,000 in year 6 (to $150,000), because we will have met our *Home/Possibility Fund* goal by the end of year 5. At least $70,000 of the $150,000 will continue to be invested in our *Balanced Fund* for our future Charitable Trust. The remaining $80,000 can be used for other *Possibility Fund* investment goals or to further fund our charitable goal (to meet it sooner, increase it or add other charities).

GUIDELINE #13: INVESTMENT TIMING

1.   We will make our investments at the beginning of the year upon receipt of each lottery check.

2.   We will not, as of now, experiment with any investment timing mechanisms.

3.   If we do decide to time our investments, we will do so *primarily* based on our own judgment and not upon the "secret magic formulas" of timing marketers (sellers of market timing techniques).

GUIDELINE #14: INVESTMENT ALLOCATION TARGETS

Our allocation targets for our net $300,000 in annual investment funds (after paying $100,000 in federal income tax withholding and $100,000 to our *Operating Fund* from our original $500,000) are:

❑   50% in "debt" investments (bonds or annuities and mutual funds investing in bonds) in our:

> *Infinite Financial Freedom Fund* and
>
> *College/Possibility Fund*

❑   50% in "equity" investments (stocks or mutual funds investing in stocks) in our:

> *Charity/Balanced Fund* and
>
> *Home/Possibility Fund*

GUIDELINE #15: REAL ESTATE INVESTING

We *may* be willing to manage some income-producing property after some further education and investigation. We will start by first learning how to use our own home as a tax shelter and then transfer this knowledge to managing other real estate investments.

GUIDELINE #16: CURRENT LIFESTYLE BUDGET

1.   We will not exceed a $100,000 per year lifestyle paid for by the $100,000 that we place in our *Operating*

Fund at the beginning of each year upon receiving our annual lottery check.

2.   If we do not consume all $100,000 in a year, we can use the excess dollars to fund other goals or to consume in the following year(s) in a special way (such as on a cruise, as gifts, etc.).

3.   We must not use these excess dollars, however, to create future obligations that would increase our lifestyle budget over the annual $100,000 allowance. An example of such misuse would be using the excess dollars as a downpayment on a car (or other asset) that would produce ongoing payment and other expenses that would force us to exceed our annual $100,000 lifestyle budget. If the excess dollars were enough, however, for us to buy the car with all cash and pay for the estimated annual insurance and operating costs for the life of the car, then the purchase of the car would be allowed. Otherwise, we should save the excess dollars in a fund to achieve such a goal by a certain date.

GUIDELINE #17: OUR TAX STRATEGIES

1.   Although we will use conservative tax strategies, we will take advantage of every legitimate technique to *avoid* paying unnecessary taxes and to minimize those taxes that are necessary. Our investments into double tax-free money market and municipal bond mutual funds are two examples of our conservative tax avoidance strategies.

2.   We will strive to arrange our financial affairs so that the 20% or $100,000 in federal income tax

withholding will more than cover our annual income tax liability. We understand that limiting our taxes to 20% of our taxable income may be challenging in the current tax environment, but that certain investments, such as income-producing real estate, *may* provide some additional tax benefits.

3. We will not, however, speculate in any investment solely for its tax benefits. Each investment must stand on its own merit, irrespective of its current tax treatment by the IRS.

4. We will seek professional tax advice as we also learn, through our program of self-education, how the IRS tax system works.

GUIDELINE #18: USE OF DIVIDEND AND INTEREST INCOME

We will automatically re-invest all our dividend and interest income to achieve our goals. We will not take our dividend and interest income dollars in cash and consume them. We can afford to re-invest these dollars to achieve our goals because our *Operating Fund* provides for all our current consumption needs.

GUIDELINE #19: INVESTMENT CRITERIA FOR MUTUAL FUNDS AND ANNUITIES

All mutual funds must meet the Nine Mutual Fund Profile Standards and all annuities must meet the investment criteria as established in our *Rulebook* as follows:

1. Mutual Fund Profile:

- ❑ Consistency of fund manager and return;

- ❑ No less than 20 and no more than 50 different companies' securities in the portfolio;

- ❑ Total assets of between $10 Million and $1.5 Billion;

- ❑ Portfolio turnover rate of under 50%;

- ❑ No-loads of any kind;

- ❑ Annual expense ratio of under 2%;

- ❑ Investment objective that matches the goal of our corresponding "Goals Funds";

- ❑ A 10-year track record that meets or exceeds our required rate of return for the investment goal;

- ❑ A *beta* of under 2.00 points.

2. Tax-Deferred Annuity Profile:

- ❑ Guaranteed minimum rate greater than the current actual inflation rate (not our assumed long-term rate);

- ❑ Current fixed, guaranteed rate greater than CD's;

- ❑ Competitive "signing bonus", if possible;

- ❑ Portfolio 100% invested in government securities;

- ❑ Minimal surrender and other charges.

GUIDELINE #20: INFLATION ASSUMPTIONS

We are assuming that inflation will average 4% per year. We understand that this assumed rate is about 1 percentage point higher than historical averages, so our assumption gives us a hedge on our rates of return if inflation does not reach this average 4% level.

GUIDELINE #21: OUR RISK TOLERANCE

We will initially maintain these risk/reward levels on the *Ladder of Investments*:

Fund Name	Highest Risk/Reward Level
Operating Fund	1
Infinite Financial Freedom Fund	2
College/Possibility Fund	2
Charity/Balanced Fund	3
Home/Possibility Fund	4
Real Estate/Possibility Fund	5

Guideline #21 Notes:

1. We will take the *risk tolerance* test for each investment that we consider.

2.   We will re-take the *risk tolerance* test before we make any particular investment.

3.   We will re-take the *risk tolerance* test every year as part of our *Annual Assessment* to see how our tolerance for risk relative to our various investments may be evolving.

GUIDELINE #22: REQUIRED RATES OF RETURN

Fund Name	Return
Operating Fund	4%
Infinite Financial Freedom Fund	5%
College/Possibility Fund	5%
Charity/Balanced Fund	10%
Home/Possibility Fund	12.5%
Real Estate/Possibility Fund	15%

Guideline #22 Notes:

1.   The above percentages are our minimum required after-tax rates of return.

2.   The above percentages are based upon reasonable historical performance returns over the last 66 years.

3.   If our investments meet our minimum required rates of return, we know we will meet our goals, despite our assumed 4% annual inflation rate.

For example:

❑   By investing $80,000 per year for 5 years at 12.5% after-tax, our *Home/Possibility Fund* will grow to a total of $513,301.

❑   If we discount this figure by our assumed 4% inflation rate, then our *Home/Possibility Fund* equals $421,896 in today's dollars.

Since our goal is to have $400,000 in today's dollars in 5 years for our new home, then we will meet our goal as long as our inflation assumptions and investment return expectations hold.

4.   We understand that we must learn how to perform such basic *time value of money* calculations using a financial hand-held calculator or computer program or hire someone who can perform these calculations for us until we learn. We know that this skill is easy to learn with the new financial calculators available now.

GUIDELINE # 23: JUDGING PERFORMANCE

We will judge the performance of any investments, any advisors, any *money managers*, any advisory services or other consultants based upon their ability to be consistent not only with our required rates of return and acceptable risk levels, but also with all other criteria of our *Infinite Financial Freedom Game Plan Rulebook*. We will review and judge such performance every quarter as part of our regular *Reality Check* and *Annual Assessment*.

GUIDELINE #24: GOAL STATEMENTS

We will write specific Goal Statements for completing each *guideline* as necessary and enter start and target dates for completion into our calendars. Each Goal Statement will have MASS, that is, will be: *M*easurable; *A*ction-packed; *S*pecific; and *S*tretchingly realistic.

GUIDELINE #25: COMMITMENT

We know that by designing, committing to, and following our above *Game Plan*, we are guaranteeing our future *Infinite Financial Freedom*.

Signed and agreed,

_____   _____
Lot O'Munn-Knee   Date

_____   _____
Lottie O'Munn-Knee   Date

Next Review Date to mark on our calendars:

_____

The 90% Solution

If you hold this *Model Game Plan* up against the bright light of your *Rulebook*, you will see the plan shine. Armed with such a *Game Plan* and committing and re-committing to your plan every quarter with your word as evidenced by your signature, you cannot lose. Your goals *will* be realized, so be careful about your wishes, because this plan *will* make them come true. Remember, over 90% of your financial success comes from your plan, not from market timing, stock picking, or any other outside source.

With this *Game Plan*, you set your goals in motion while covering your back-door liabilities with insurance, so that you can go forward unencumbered. You have arranged your affairs to run as automatically as practicable, freeing-up more time for life's enjoyment. You have diversified sufficiently and allocated your funds appropriately. You have addressed how you will handle your estate tax and income tax liabilities. You are educating yourself. You have made lifestyle decisions and have budgeted for assuring a lifetime of success. You have made reasonable performance assumptions based on historical track records. You have defined acceptable and unacceptable levels of risk and established your required rates of return.

But, most importantly, you have assured your *Infinite Financial Freedom*. You have pre-made many tough decisions—and this is liberating! Now, whenever you get to a decision point, you will quickly—almost instinctively—know exactly what to do. You already know what action is best. "Hot tips", investment schemes, supposed "inside information", and other "pulls and tugs" all become meaningless to you. You already know that you will meet your goals, if you simply stay on track—stay committed.

When Inquiring Minds Want To Know

Others around you will probably not fully understand the "knowing calm" that you will now inadvertently display. Still, remain quietly successful. Remember the earlier cautions about how being too loose-lipped about your investments can quickly turn good investments into bad ones. Direct the understandably inquisitive to this and other books that you have discovered.

Suggesting that you direct others to this book is not as entirely self-serving on my part as you might at first think it appears. Your *Game Plan*, as good as it now is, will only work for you. Others must develop their own game plan based upon their own goals, objectives, assets, and decisions regarding their own *Rulebook*. You truly do both of you a favor by remaining quietly successful and directing them to formulate their own game plan. You do both them and you a disservice by giving them your game plan. One size plan does *not* fit all. Besides, even your plan changes with you and time.

You are not keeping secrets from friends by remaining silent about the details of your plan. The real secret for anyone else is not *your* game plan. Tell them the *real* secret: Drafting their own game plan and committing to it.

Tell them that the *principles* upon which you have based your plan—the rules of your *Rulebook*—work for anyone and any amount of money. More or less money simply changes the placement of the decimal point relative to the number of zeros following the first digit. So, until you win your jackpot, make a before-you-win-the-lottery *Game Plan* and commit to it. You will be revising your *Game Plan* every quarter anyway, so when you hit the lottery jackpot, just plug-in the newer, larger numbers (move the decimal point to the right) to get to where you were already going a little quicker than before. Either way, you win.

Regular Reviews

Keep your *Infinite Financial Freedom Rulebook* and *Game Plan* in your safe deposit box and make the quarterly and especially the annual reviews a ritual. Reward yourselves with special nights out at favorite restaurants, concerts or whatever activity you like, following each review.

Your reviews must be active. Do not just passively skim over your *Game Plan* and *Rulebook*. You must actively track performance returns. You may have to buy or order or read or learn certain materials or do on-line computer checking and the like. You must rip-apart your plan and re-assemble it. Your plan is a *working* plan, not a monument, so work it.

Your complete review might even take a few days to finish if you have to wait for return information or learn new information and the like. Do not take these reviews lightly—this is some of the most critical work that you will do all year. You are checking to confirm that you are still on track to achieving *Infinite Financial Freedom*.

For more information regarding setting-up your *Rulebook* and *Game Plan*, re-read *Chapter 6: What To Do After You Win* and also see the many valuable resources listed in the appendices.

Goals should be written on paper, not chiseled in stone.

Keith DeGreen

Lottery Trivia

Colorado Two-Timer Doubles His Pleasure

Don Wittman may well be one of the luckiest men alive.

In December 1989 he wins $2.0 Million in the Colorado Lottery's LOTTO game. Then in October 1991, he wins another $2.2 Million. His grand total winnings, so far, are $4.2 Million.

What are the odds of winning two jackpots of over $1 Million each? Over 17-trillion-1.

There are no known triple multi-million dollar winners to date.

What does Colorado's richest construction worker have to say about all this?

"You can only go on so many vacations a year."

8
Closing Is Opening

Now that you are in the last chapter at the end of this book, you are at the beginning of the next chapter in the book of your life. As you grow personally, your apparent outer goals and objectives must change. I call this change the "inner-outer ripple effect".

The only ripples that count are the ones that begin from within. Your inner belief is the mental stone that you drop into the ocean of your existence creating waves of changes that ripple out across the surface of your entire outer life. You will be happy to the extent that your actual outer life reflects the true beliefs that you say you hold in your inner life. Your financial life is merely a monetary reflection of this degree of alignment of your outer actions with your inner beliefs.

> *I hate quotations.*
> Ralph Waldo Emerson

If you are not pleased with the financial (or other) results of your life, then give yourself the same kind of *Reality Check* and *Annual Assessment* that you apply to your investment life. You *can* develop the fundamental power of becoming the centered and successful outer person that you already potentially are on the inside. See *The Self-Centering Manual: How to Align Your Outward Behavior With Your Inner Belief* for help on developing your own fundamental

Guiding Principles of life for yourself, just as you have developed your own *Infinite Financial Freedom Game Plan Rulebook* for your investments.

> *The wisdom of the wise and the experience of ages may be preserved by quotation.*
>
> Disraeli

The more aligned you become, the luckier you will appear. The truth is, though, that your "luck" is not by chance—it's by design. A plant grows to the shape of the pot in which it is planted. Design the shape of your future by having the *right mind set*, using *possibility* and *chase thinking*, and keeping an *abundance mentality* and you will grow into the future that you have envisioned. I look forward to meeting you wherever "there" is for you.

All the best.

> *In the light of his vision, he has found his freedom: his thoughts are peace, his words are peace, and his work is peace.*
>
> The Dhammapada

Appendix A

Personal Growth Resources

There are, of course, many books on *Personal Growth*. We found those listed here to be among the best. You can find these and other books at various libraries and bookstores. However, we have made every effort here to select the particular editions that give you the most value, so that the most books are affordable by those with any amount of money. The books listed in all the Appendices represent our *Infinite Financial Freedom Bookshelf*. All are available directly from *TitleWaves*, P. O. Box 943, Malibu, CA 90265. Please see the order blank on the last page for more information and how to get a *free* Investor's Guide from *TitleWaves* when ordering two or more books.

Self-Development

Think & Grow Rich Action Pack
Napoleon Hill

This package includes a special edition of his classic *Think & Grow Rich* plus the *Think & Grow Rich Action Manual*, a personal course for lifelong success. Napoleon Hill was born into poverty in 1883 and achieved great success as an attorney and journalist. Andrew Carnegie commissioned Napoleon Hill to study the lives of successful people to learn why and how they became successful. Hill chronicled his life's discoveries in *Think & Grow Rich*. This package gives you the action steps for achieving whatever success means to you.

Softcover, $11.00   (ISBN: 0-452-26660-2) P

How to Get Control of Your Time and Your Life
Alan Lakein

Lakein first shows you how to think of "planning as writing" rather than "planning as thinking". He then gives you several short exercises to get you into writing down (not just thinking about) your goals and the activities leading to their achievement. He also gives you time-management techniques for blocking-out time vertically and horizontally in your schedule to conserve and generate time and energy through the force of habit. Lakein shows you how to eliminate (or at least outsmart) procrastination by dividing large projects into "instant tasks" that get you started and then involved in the completion of the larger task. The book presents a number of interesting role-playing games that put you into the planning mode to increase your involvement in your work or play.

Softcover, $4.99   (ISBN: 0-451-167724) P

The Self-Centering Manual: How to Align Your Outward Behavior With Your Inner Belief
Rob Sanford

This manual shows you how to and what it means to become a truly centered being. The book includes the *Secret of Life* revealed, *The Guiding Principles of Life* completely written-out, and an *Alignment Workshop* with self-evaluations that you can take repeatedly to discover your relative congruity in each area of your life today and how that congruity evolves as you progress through this experience we call life. This book is *the* construction manual for building the solid foundation upon which you can begin your balanced ascent up the *Ladder of Success*.

Softcover, $16.95   (ISBN: 1-57077-998-8)

LifePlan: A Goal-Setting Workbook
Rob Sanford

This manual gives you all the step-by-step forms, exercises, and instructions that you need to set and prioritize goals in the 10 basic Goal Categories of your life. This book gives you the tools and techniques for making *Wishlists* and then transforming your wishes into true goals. This workbook will assure that your goals have MASS, that is, that they are *M*easurable, *A*ction-packed, *S*pecific, and *S*tretchingly realistic. Finally, the book shows you how to prioritize and organize your goals into *Daily Outcomes* through active action planning and monitoring of results. Effective goal-setting is one of the key steps to your reaching the top rung of your *Ladder of Success*. This book shows you how to do it.

Softcover, $14.95   (ISBN: 1-57077-997-X)

Family

50 Fabulous Places to Raise Your Family
Lee & Saralee Rosenberg

This heavily researched book brings you detailed information on the top 50 "family-friendly" communities in America, such as those with the best school systems, the most family-oriented leisure and recreational activities, the cleanest, safest environments, and the like. Also, co-author Lee Rosenberg is a Certified Financial Planner and gives you valuable advice on how to best prepare financially for a move.

Softcover, $17.95   (ISBN: 1-56414-034-2) C

Physical/Health

Head First: The Biology of Hope
Norman Cousins.

Norman Cousins laughed himself to life in the 1970's after he contracted "ankylosing spondylitis" (a terminal inflammation of the spinal joints) and was given a death sentence by his physician. Cousins decided to be a victor instead of a victim and embarked on a mission to heal himself by filling his days with laughter, hope, faith, love, festivity and a fierce determination to live—and it worked! By embracing *possibility thinking*, *chase thinking*, and an *abundance mentality*, his "supposedly irreversible condition was reversing". Cousins' own recovery (which he chronicled in an earlier book, *Anatomy of an Illness*) put him on the path of proving that "the human body is capable of extraordinary regeneration". Medical researchers have repeatedly documented that the negative emotions of fear, frustration, panic, depression, hate, and anxiety help create an atmosphere in the body where disease is welcome. In this book, Norman Cousins, himself a UCLA Professor of Medicine, details the therapeutic link between positive thinking and healing. In *Head First*, Cousins explores *psycho-neuro-immunology*, an emerging branch of medicine that studies the relationship between the brain, the immune system, and the endocrine system. If you ever wanted living proof of the power of positive thinking and the validity of the self-fulfilling prophecy, then Norman Cousins is surely this. Cousins' advice: don't deny the diagnosis—deny the verdict that goes with it, instead.

Softcover, $9.95   (ISBN: 0-14-013965-6) P

Career

Build Your Own Rainbow: A Workbook for Career and Life Management
Barrie Hopson and Mike Scally

All of us can reach a point when we ask ourselves, "Am I *really* doing what I want with my life?" If the answer is yes, that's great, because you are already doing *What You Do Best & Enjoy Most*. However, if you are experiencing a vague dissatisfaction undermining the quality of your daily life, then you may need to re-inventory yourself to find *What You Do Best & Enjoy Most*. This workbook, *Build Your Own Rainbow*, is packed with over 40 questionnaires, exercises, charts-to-complete, progress checks, fill-in-the-blank-forms, tests, self-surveys, quizzes, drills, diagrams, maps, polls—all to help you answer these six career and life management questions: 1) Who Am I? 2) Where Am I Now? 3) How Satisfied Am I? 4) What Changes Do I Want? 5) How Do I Make Changes Happen? and 6)What If My Plan Doesn't Work Out? I believe that books should be read with a pen, pencil or marker in hand. You can't read this book without one. *Build Your Own Rainbow* is the result of over 20 years of career and life management workshop design by Hopson and Scally. By completing the book's exercises, you will uncover what is most important to you about work, your interests, your transferable skills, your optimum career pattern—in short, *What You Do Best & Enjoy Most*. If you want to do some soul-searching, purpose-probing, and self-scrutinizing, then this book gives you the tools to do it.

Softcover, $12.95   (ISBN: 0-89384-208-7) Pf

What Color Is Your Parachute? A Practical Manual for Job Hunters & Career-Changers (Annual Edition)
Richard Nelson Bolles

This book is probably *the* classic in the career development field with over 4 million copies sold since its 1972 introduction. Now updated annually, Bolles' book is a practical resource for soul-searching as well as job-searching. If you are struggling with admitting to yourself *What You Do Best & Enjoy Most*, then this is the book for you. In his "Pink Pages" section (now almost 100 pages long itself at the end of the book), he gives much insight into finding one's mission in life. Bolles includes detailed directions for finding a new career, specific suggestions for improving one's job search, and a special section on the relationship between self and the choice of work. He also provides extensive career counseling and job-hunting resources and references throughout. Plus it has some amusing cartoons!

Softcover, $14.95   (ISBN: 0-89815-492-8) T

Take This Job & Leave It: How to Get Out of a Job You Hate and Into a Job You Love
Bill Radin

If you do not have a job that allows you to do *What You Do Best & Enjoy Most*, then this is your book. Bill Radin, an executive search firm owner and consultant, first gives you the basics: creating a job-changing strategy; the job description "makeover"; re-creating your resume (including his "resume test"); evaluating your current compensation; and the hidden costs of relocation. Then Bill gives you the edge with the strategies and information that only an insider could reveal: electronic listing services; dealing with outplacement pros; putting the deal together; dealing with restrictive covenants; and more. He includes a valuable list of job-changing resources known usually only by professionals in the executive search trade: electronic resume listing services; job listing and clipping services; retail outplacement/search firms; generalist and specialist search firms; job fair organizers; and more. If you already know *What You Do Best & Enjoy Most*, then this book will help you leave the job you hate and find the one you love as smoothly as possible.

Softcover, $12.95   (ISBN: 1-56414-057-1) C

Put Work In Its Place: How to Redesign Your Job to Fit Your Life: The Complete Guide to the Flexible Work Place
Bruce O'Hara

This book gives you the alternative to changing to a new job: change the job you already have. The old one-size-fits-all work week was designed for the lifestyle of an earlier industrial era—one that bears little resemblance to the many careers of the information era of the late 20th Century. This book helps you: evaluate the benefits of job-sharing, flextime, and other innovative work options; design a work schedule that gives you time to enjoy your life; and write a proposal to sell your employer on the idea. So, maybe you don't have to quit your job; maybe you can just re-invent the job you already have and turn it into the job you really want. So, when doing your career-questioning, don't overlook this option of staying right where you are, if you can redesign your position to better fit your career and lifestyle goals and objectives.

Softcover, $16.95   (ISBN: 0-9693286-0-5) Pf

Lifestyle

Where to Make Money: A Rating Guide to Opportunities in America's Metro Areas
G. Scott Thomas

Where you live now may be more the result of coincidence than design. If you want to pro-actively answer the *Where* question of your goals, this book can help. This book ranks the 73 largest metropolitan areas in the USA, each with populations of 500,000 or greater. Each area has been analyzed statistically—using the latest government data—and graded for performance on six tests: economic momentum; future growth potential; openness to women and minorities; employment opportunities; business opportunities; and real estate opportunities. Each area is then given a final grade, from A to F. An easy-to-read "report card" for each metro area details its overall economic health. The best metro areas showed strong increases in population and per capita income during the last decade and show trends of continuing to expand in the coming years. Such areas also have rapidly expanding job bases, affordable homes, and do not discriminate when extending economic opportunities. This guide will help you pinpoint the place where you can best ride a growing prosperity wave already in motion.

Softcover, $17.95   (ISBN: 0-87975-795-7) Pr

The Rating Guide to Life in America's Small Cities
G. Scott Thomas

Though you may want to *work* in one of the best metro areas, you may prefer to *live* in one of the nearby "micropolitan" areas where you may find a more favorable quality of life.

This book provides the most up-to-date, accurate information available on the 219 U.S. "micropolitan" areas—cities with 15,000 to 50,000 residents and their surrounding territories. Each community is graded on its performance in 10 clearly defined classifications: Climate and Environment; Diversions; Economics; Education; Sophistication; Health Care; Housing; Public Safety; Transportation; and Urban Proximity. The guide includes a descriptive profile of each of the top ten small cities, a breakdown of the leaders by region and by state, and a report card for each "micropolitan" area showing its score in each of the ten sections plus a summary of its strengths and weaknesses. In using any rating guide, be sure to "weight" the different characteristics of each city for those features that are most important to you. Along with the other rating guides listed here, this book will help you zero-in on "the place" that is best for you to enjoy your *Infinite Financial Freedom.*

Softcover, $19.95   (ISBN: 0-87975-600-4) Pr

50 Fabulous Places to Retire in America
Lee and Saralee Rosenberg

This guide looks at 50 of the most popular retirement communities in America and presents the information in a very user-friendly format. Each location is evaluated on factors that retirees consider the most important when relocating, including: cost of living; taxes; crime and safety; housing costs and availability; climate; access to health care; proximity to airports; special services for seniors; cultural activities; and recreation. Each community profile features a colorful description, a map, a climate chart, and comments from retirees who moved there plus addresses of chambers of commerce, local newspapers, and Realtors. Also included is practical advice on preparing for retirement, financial planning, and moving without headaches.

Softcover, $14.95   (ISBN: 0-934829-29-2) C

Appendix B
Financial Growth Resources

As with *Personal Growth*, there are, of course, many books and other materials on *Financial Growth*. In this Appendix, we have compiled what we feel are among the most vital and practical financial resources (stuff that you really use):

❑ Recommended Books

❑ Sources of Other Financial & Investment Information

    ❑ Published Sources of Financial Information

    ❑ Computer On-Line Services

    ❑ Other Financial Resources

        ❑ Annuities

        ❑ Charitable Giving

        ❑ Credit Card Resources

        ❑ Consumer Credit Counseling

        ❑ Financial Planners

        ❑ Life Insurance

        ❑ Mutual Funds

- ❏   Real Estate

- ❏   Stockbrokers:
  "Discount" Stockbrokers

- ❏   Stockbrokers and Securities
  Regulatory Agencies

- ❏   Taxes

- ❏   Your Money Personality

Recommended Books

We have found the books listed here to be among the best. Some are classics in their field. Although you can find these and other books at various libraries and bookstores, we have again made every effort here to select the particular editions that give you the most value, so that the most books are affordable by those with any amount of money. All the books listed are available directly from *TitleWaves*, P. O. Box 943, Malibu, CA 90265. Please see the order blank on the last page for more information on ordering and how to get a *free* Investor's Guide on mutual funds from *TitleWaves* when ordering two or more books.

Investing

Richest Man in Babylon
George S. Clason

This classic book is a series of wealth-building stories presented as parables set in ancient Babylon. In this book, the wealthiest Babylonian retells the story of how the secret to wealth was revealed to him when he was a young man inscribing clay tablets in the hall of records. Eventually, this Babylonian is asked to instruct 100 teachers in the secrets of wealth-building. In the Temple of Learning, he reveals the Seven Cures for a Lean Purse and how to attract the Goddess of Good Luck. Other stories reveal the Five Laws of Gold and the plan to become free of debt contained in the Five Clay Tablets. Though set in ancient Babylon, the wealth-building principles presented here are timeless and as valid today as in any day. Learn the 10% and other solutions to achieving and retaining life-long prosperity and the 70-20-10 plan for getting out of debt.

Softcover, $9.00   (ISBN: 0-452-26725-0) P

The Hulbert Guide to Financial Newsletters (Latest edition)
Mark Hulbert

This is *the* book for investigating investment newsletters. This unique book is written by Mark Hulbert, Editor of *The Hulbert Financial Digest*, itself a financial newsletter of financial newsletters. Hulbert tracks the returns of various newsletters' model portfolios and reports and ranks the investment performance of each. In his *Guide*, he profiles over 120 of the principal financial newsletters giving all the details of their performance track records, subscription costs, and whether the advisory firm publishing the letter also acts as a *money manager*. He "splices and dices" the investment performance of these newsletters over various time periods and in relation to each other and the Wilshire 5000 Index over the past 12 years.

He further rates each newsletter on an A-B-C scale for clarity and separately shows the performance records of Mutual Fund Newsletters with one another and the various Market Timing Newsletters with one another as well as with all letters. Using this book is the best way I know to find a newsletter that mirrors the approach that you have established in your own *Infinite Financial Freedom Game Plan Rulebook.* Check out Hulbert's *Guide* before and after you order any trial subscription from an investment newsletter.

Softcover, $27.95   (ISBN: 0-79310-619-2) D

Contrary Investing
Richard E. Band

This book presents the philosophy and techniques of *contrarian* investing for determining how to better "buy low" and "sell high". Here, you will learn the "against the crowd" strategies of buying investments (with intrinsic value) when few people want them (when prices are low) and then selling such investments when they become too popular and the majority wants to buy them (when prices are high). *Contrarian* investing seeks to exploit market conditions when the excessive fear or greed of the majority of speculators temporarily exaggerates an individual stock's price up or down. You will learn how to "buy on bad news" and "sell on good news" by identifying certain market valuation measures that indicate favorable and unfavorable times to invest. You will also learn how some contrarians take a longer-term, simplified approach by buying blue-chip stocks during recessions, holding them, and then selling them only in times of an economic expansion.

Softcover, $9.95   (ISBN: 0-14-008862-8) P

Your Home As a Tax Shelter: Cashing-in On America's Top Tax Shelter
Edith Lank and Miriam S. Geisman

Using your home as the legitimate tax shelter that it is, is the best way to save tax dollars right where you live. You must spend dollars to live somewhere, so living inside a tax shelter is a smart use of your dwelling dollars. With the help of worksheets, reprints of actual IRS publications and forms, amortization schedules and easy-to-understand explanations, these two real estate experts, with over 50 years of combined experience, show you how to take advantage of one of the few remaining tax shelters—your home.

The authors provide practical advice on: tax breaks when selling your home; deductible versus non-deductible expenses; the tax difference (and benefit) between home "improvement" and home "maintenance"; tax implications of receiving your home as a gift or inheritance; how divorce effects your tax liability; computing and reporting gain on the sale of your home; rules regarding the home office deduction; postponing your profit when you sell; and special tax benefits for homeowners age 55 or older. This book helps you manage your home as an investment telling you what records to keep, how long to keep them, and how to stay organized. If you haven't kept good records up to now, don't panic. This book explains how to reconstruct lost or missing documents that the IRS will accept.

Once you understand the principles of using your own home as a tax shelter, you can apply these principles to using other people's homes (that you own and rent to them) as additional tax shelters. The flowchart for qualifying for a home office deduction is worth the price of the book alone.

Softcover, $15.95   (ISBN: 0-79310-435-1) D

Real Estate Wealthbuilding: How to Really Make Money in Real Estate
Howard A. Zuckerman

This book gives the information you need for successfully investing in real estate beyond your own home. Zuckerman, 20-year real estate veteran and president of his own Atlanta-based property acquisition and development firm, specializes in asset creation using single-family, multi-family, and commercial properties. In this book, he shows you how to formulate a long-term real estate investment strategy for building tangible wealth. He covers all the details of structuring and negotiating the deal, inspections, financing, and closing.

This book shows you how to: establish an investment goal; tell a good deal from a bad deal; find "bargains" that can be made profitable; acquire properties from the VA, FHA and other government agencies; buy properties at auctions; assemble a team of real estate experts; rehabilitate a property; and avoid taxes on resale.

The biggest plus of this book is the inclusion of extensive references, resources, and the many useful forms for all phases of property acquisition, management, and sale. The 9-page property inspection report alone is "worth the price of admission".

Softcover, $24.95   (ISBN: 0-79310-289-8) D

Risk Management

Insurance Survival Kits for Individuals:
The Do's & Don'ts of Buying Personal Insurance
(Series)
from Benefits Resource Group

These "kits" provide the information and worksheets you need to make smart insurance buying decisions. Each manual is designed to help you buy the right kind of personal insurance in the right amounts. There is also a series on Business Insurance for corporations. These kits are available directly from *TitleWaves* only. Please see the order form on the last page.

Kit #1: Life Insurance & Annuities

Kit #2: Health Plans

Kit #3: Homeowner's & Renter's Insurance

Kit #4: Automobile & Other Vehicles Insurance

Kit #5: Disability & Other Income Replacement

Kit #6: Personal Liability Insurance

Each kit is $12.95.

Sources of Other Financial & Investment Information

A good business or university library will maintain many of these and other research and reference materials. I recommend that you first review these "hard copy" published sources at the library to see which ones provide the data that you want to track and then subscribe to the on-line service that provides this data. After your library visit, you may find that you are drowning in information and starving for knowledge. Then, you will better appreciate the personal computer's ability to access and search and sort this information through commercial on-line vendors. No written description here or anywhere else can give you the sense of the breadth of information that these published sources track.

Published Sources of Financial Information

Moody's Investor Services, Inc.
over 10 major publications

Standard & Poor's Corporation
over 20 major publications

Value Line Investment Survey
over 5 major publications

Business Periodicals Index
references over 170 business-related periodicals

Wall Street Journal Index
identifies articles appearing in the Wall Street Journal

Fortune Magazine

Business Week

Forbes Magazine
   (good annual issue devoted to mutual funds)

The Harvard Business Review

Money Magazine

The Wall Street Journal

Investor's Daily

Barron's National Business & Financial Weekly
   (good quarterly issue devoted to mutual funds)

The Wall Street Transcript

The Insider's Chronicle

Financial Analysts Journal

The Journal of Portfolio Management

Institutional Investor

Journal of Finance

Federal Reserve Bulletin
Federal Reserve Quarterly Chart Book
published by the Federal Reserve System

U.S. Financial Data
Monetary Trends
National Economic Trends
published by the St. Louis Federal Reserve Bank

Survey of Current Business
Business Conditions Digest
published by the U.S. Department of Commerce

Economic Indicators
published by the Council of Economic Advisors

Securities And Exchange Commission
for statutory corporate filings

Computer On-Line Services

For the computer on-line research services, you must, of course, have both the computer hardware (including a modem) and software. The tremendous value to using such computerized retrieval services is that you can automate your research and tracking chores. You effectively let the computer do the "grunt work" and then report the results to you.

The particular on-line vendor can charge any combination of subscription fees, connect fees, usage fees, and surcharge fees for access to various databases. Often the on-line services will offer a few different pricing packages to accommodate your typical use of their system. So, you must check with these providers or vendors directly for their current pricing structure and plans, as they can change often. The two principal vendors to explore are *CompuServe* and *Prodigy*.

CompuServe, Inc.
800-848-8990

CompuServe offers extensive financial and investment databases including: S&P On-line (Standard & Poor's database); Value Line Investment Survey; Disclosure II (SEC statutory reports); D&B's Electronic Business Directory; MMS International Financial Reports (for Federal Reserve info); TRW Business Profiles; Quick Quote (for stock & mutual fund quotes); Newspaper Library; Reference Libraries; and many others. *CompuServe* has probably the broadest available interactive database research and retrieval systems of all the commercial on-line systems available to the consumer. It is a database of databases. Charges can mount up quickly, however. In addition to the above, you can access via *CompuServe*: several stock brokerage firms; various news, weather, and sports information retrieval databases; consumer publications; computer banking; shopping; travel; hobby forums; and the like.

Prodigy
800-284-5933

Prodigy is more consumer-oriented, less interactive, and less comprehensive than *CompuServe*. However, with *Prodigy* you can still retrieve stock and mutual fund quotes, access stock brokerage firms, perform on-line banking, and obtain some public company information. The research capabilities are not as great on *Prodigy*, because you cannot directly access the extensive databases available on *CompuServe*. However, *Prodigy* is easier to use (perhaps due to its limitations). You may want to subscribe to both services: Prodigy for daily stock and/or mutual fund quotes and its consumer services; *CompuServe* for its extensive, seemingly exhaustive, research capabilities due to its access to hundreds of databases. I tend to think of *Prodigy* as a magazine and *CompuServe* as a library (though *CompuServe* also includes all the consumer-oriented services available on *Prodigy*). Each vendor offers trial subscriptions.

To explore other computer on-line services, refer to:

Computer Readable Data Bases
An annual, comprehensive directory of databases and CD-ROM vendors published by Gale Research, 835 Penobscot Building, Detroit, MI 48226.

Directory ONLINE Data Bases
An annual, comprehensive service offered through Cuadra, 655 Avenue of the Americas, New York, NY 10010.

Other Financial Resources

Just as with the above references, you must always contact these resources directly for their current information. We live in fast-changing times, so vendors and other service providers often change their offerings for competitive and other marketing reasons.

Annuities

The Annuity Exchange™
Benefits Resource Group
P. O. Box 943, Malibu, CA 90265

As a no obligation service to *Infinite Financial Freedom* readers, *The Annuity Exchange*™ will search their database for the best annuity with the most aggressive rates in the country and mail the results to you. If you choose to invest in the annuity, you can do so through *The Annuity Exchange*™. For a *free*, no obligation annuity quotation, just copy, complete, and return the *Annuity Quotation Request Form* with a self-addressed stamped envelope to *The Annuity Exchange*™ as instructed on the form at the back of this book.

Charitable Giving

National Charities Information Bureau
212-929-6300

The NCIB provides reports on charitable organizations revealing how much the charity spends on administration versus actual charitable activities. Upon your written request, the NCIB (19 Union Square West, New York, NY 10003) will send you a free report on three charities of your choice and the *Wise Giving Guide* listing over 400 national non-profits. Double-check that the free offer is still available when you are ready to order the information.

Credit Card Resources

CardTrack
800-344-7714

RAM Research (P. O. Box 1700, Frederick, MD 21702) currently publishes a monthly list of 500 budget credit cards for $5 per single copy and $50 a year. Their newsletter covers low interest rate cards and cards with no annual fee for both standard and gold cards. They also alert you to new credit card offerings. Call them for current details.

Bankcard Holders of America
800-553-8025

BHA (560 Herndon Parkway, Suite 120, Herndon, VA 22070) offers, among their other publications, "Package A", a list of over 40 nationally available bank cards with no annual fee and with low interest rates plus a descriptive brochure for only $4. Call them for details about their latest offerings.

Consumer Credit Counseling

Of course, you know that the way to *Infinite Financial Freedom* is by running your life on cash and by using credit only for productive and profitable activities. However, if you need to dig yourself out of consumer debt due to past indiscretions, then contact the:

Consumer Credit Counseling Service
800-388-2227

The CCCS is a non-profit agency that can help you calculate and negotiate an acceptable creditor repayment plan for all parties involved. When you call their toll-free National Referral Line given above, you receive an automated directory of local offices in your area. You then call your local office and they help you devise a debt management plan. They do not charge for their counseling services.

Federal Trade Commission
Bureau of Consumer Protection
202-523-3727

The FTC enforces the Truth in Lending Act (among others). They can help you—especially if a business is allegedly engaging in deceptive advertising, unfair sales practices, lack of full loan terms disclosure, and the like.

Financial Planners

Any of these practitioners may or may not also act as *money managers*:

Institute of Certified Financial Planners(ICFP)
800-282-7526

You can call the ICFP's toll-free Consumer Assistance Line above to receive free referrals for Certified Financial Planners. The ICFP will send you the names of up to three CFP's participating in the referral program with biographical information on each based *only* on your ZIP code, not on any other criteria. Remember, the ICFP's referrals are pulled from just about 3.5% of existing CFP's. Unfortunately, you cannot conclude that these are the *best* CFP's, but they may be among the best and the most active—or want to be. All CFP's must maintain a monitored continuing education program in order to retain their CFP designation.

International Association for Financial Planning(IAFP)
800-241-2148

The IAFP will send you a list of members based on your ZIP code. The IAFP also maintains a "Registry of Financial Planning Practitioners" for those IAFP members who have paid extra membership fees, passed an IAFP exam, and have met certain education and experience requirements. So, ask for Registry members when you request your referrals. IAFP members may or may not be Certified Financial Planners, and may be compensated by a fee-only, commissions only, or a combination of the two.

National Association of Personal Financial Advisors (NAPFA)
800-366-2732

NAPFA also provides a referral program, but they too will refer CFP's only by coincidence, since non-CFP's can join NAPFA. However, NAPFA members must be "fee-only" planners. That is, they must work only on a fee-for-service basis and must not accept commissions for product placement or recommendations. ICFP and IAFP members, on the other hand, may accept fees, commissions or a combination of both. NAPFA will send you a free "Financial Planner Interview" checklist to help you select a planner based upon: background and experience; services offered; compensation; and regulatory compliance. NAPFA also sends you a list of practitioners in your regional area.

Life Insurance

***The Insurance Exchange*™**
Benefits Resource Group
P. O. Box 943, Malibu, CA 90265

As a *free*, no obligation service to *Infinite Financial Freedom* readers, *The Insurance Exchange*™ will search their database for the most competitive quotes from the best-rated and most aggressively priced *term* life insurance companies in the country and mail the results to you. If you choose to buy the coverage, they hope, naturally, that you consider buying your policy through them, but you have no obligation to do so and they will respect your privacy (translation: "They won't bug you."). For *free* life insurance quotations and/or for information about obtaining a formal life insurance "Needs Analysis", just copy, complete, and return their *Life Insurance Reality Check Request Form* with a self-addressed stamped envelope to *The Insurance Exchange*™ as instructed on the form at the back of this book.

Mutual Funds

Investment Company Institute(ICI)
202-955-3534 and -3536 and 202-293-7700

The ICI is a mutual fund trade association (for both load and no-load funds) that monitors legislation affecting mutual funds, acts as liaison between the mutual fund industry and the SEC, and disseminates information to the public concerning mutual funds. They publish descriptive booklets, pamphlets, brochures, films, videos and slides about understanding mutual funds and the various ways to invest in them. They also have a mutual fund executive speaker referral service. They publish their annual *Mutual Fund Fact Book* ($15.00) which compiles current and historical facts and figures on the U.S. mutual fund industry, including statistical trends in sales, assets, and performance.

Morningstar
800-876-5005

Morningstar publishes a "hard copy" database of over 1,200 mutual funds (load and no-load) every two weeks in a three-ring binder format for $395 a year. The "problem" with their offering is that it is *too* extensive: contains over 1,300 pages; updates 120 of these pages every two weeks; gives you a 32-page summary report every two weeks; and is not cheap. Yet *Morningstar* tracks less than half of the possible funds in this offering and includes load funds. Although *Morningstar* is a database and not an advisory newsletter, *The Hulbert Guide to Financial Newsletters* created both equity and bond model portfolios using *Morningstar's* highest-rated funds (those given 5-stars) and found that neither portfolio outperformed the market in the most recent 18 months. Hulbert admits that the disappointing performance may be the result of load funds being continually added to the 5-star list, thus generating sales charges that adversely effected their model portfolios' performance records.

Morningstar also publishes (targeted to professional planners) a mutual fund database of over 3,000 funds on CD-

ROM computer disc with hefty current subscription prices of $495 for quarterly updates and $795 for monthly updates. No one has yet (publicly) created and tracked model portfolios based on funds with *Morningstar's* 5-star ratings from this database to test the performance results (though *Morningstar* itself is considering publishing its own advisory letter to do such tracking themselves).

CDA/Wiesenberger
800-232-2285

Also targeted primarily to the professional planner, *CDA/Wiesenberger* offers a mutual fund database subscription service on CD-ROM computer disc for $690 a year (currently) that tracks over 3,500 mutual funds. Their software program has the capability (as does *Morningstar's*) of producing hypothetical performance results: what your investment is worth today assuming you had invested a certain amount of money in a certain fund (or funds) at a certain time over a certain period. The software program includes quarterly updates.

CDA/Wiesenberger also publishes a hard copy version of their database in two formats. One offering is a monthly subscription service costing $295 a year that gives you a 500-page annual directory of over 3,500 funds plus 12 monthly updates of 150-pages each. Their other publication is called the *Investment Company Yearbook*, issued in April of every year, containing performance results and portfolio information on over 3,500 funds, consisting of over 1,500 pages in length, and costing $295. They also offer a $395 package that includes both the monthly hard-copy subscription service and the *Yearbook*.

***The Fund Exchange*™**
Benefits Resource Group
P. O. Box 943, Malibu, CA 90265

Reducing the universe of over 3,800 mutual funds down to one takes time and, therefore, money. You can do the analysis manually or by using one of the above computer disc subscription services. The "difficulty" with these services is not that they offer too little, but that they offer so much—you can find yourself drowning in a sea of data while gasping for a single breath of fresh knowledge.

As a single end-user (as opposed to the professional planner with several clients), you are paying for data that you will never use. If you buy data on over 3,000 mutual funds, but invest in only 10, then you are discarding over 99.6% of the data. If half of the data is on load funds, then half of the information you buy is useless to you (assuming you seek no-load funds only). However, if you like the idea of having the information at your fingertips and enjoy the process of playing with the data, then these services are for you.

Alternately, you can have a service bureau who maintains or accesses such databases perform the searches for you as-needed. As a service to *Infinite Financial Freedom* readers, *The Fund Exchange*™ will perform such computer searches at a reduced charge. *The Fund Exchange*™ normally charges $50 per search and $20 per additional search requested at the same time. However, for *Infinite Financial Freedom* readers, they charge only $25 for the first search and only $10 for each additional search requested at the same time. Results can be mailed or faxed back to you. If you are interested in taking advantage of their service, just follow the instructions on their *Mutual Fund Computer Search Request Form* at the end of this book.

Real Estate

Home Owners Warranty (HOW)
800-241-9260 Eastern Region
800-433-7657 Western Region

HOW provides builder-paid Home Warranty policies for new homes. HOW's builders agree to build homes according to certain approved quality standards and warranty their construction with a 10-year protection plan against structural defects. HOW will also handle any claims that arise as a result of alleged faulty home construction for which they provide the warranty plans.

Stockbrokers: "Discount" Stockbrokers

Here are the principal discount stockbrokers, in the order of decreasing number of offices:

Number of Offices		Toll-free Number
200	Olde Discount	800-872-6533
183	Charles Schwab	800-435-4000
83	Quick & Reilly	800-222-0437
76	Fidelity Brokerage	800-544-7272
43	Waterhouse	800-765-5185
14	Kennedy, Cabot	800-252-0090
3	Accutrade	800-228-3011
2	Bull & Bear	800-262-5800
1	T. Rowe Price	800-225-7720
1	Jack White & Co.	800-233-3411

Check these discount brokers for their current cash/asset management account offerings, commission schedules, and computer on-line services. The number of offices is not as important as the range of services and relative fees. You need only one office, especially if you will be doing most of your business over the phone or on-line.

Stockbrokers and Securities Regulatory Agencies

If you seek additional information on investment advisors, potential stocks or bonds of individual companies or if you have a problem with your stockbroker, you will need these references:

National Association of Securities Dealers (NASD)
Customer Complaint Department
202-728-8217 (Washington, D.C.)
Arbitration
212-839-6251 (New York)

All broker-dealer firms and their individual representatives must be registered with the NASD. The NASD is the industry's self-regulatory entity.

Securities and Exchange Commission (SEC)
Office of Consumer Affairs and Information Services
202-272-7440 and -7450 (Washington, D.C.)

The SEC is the entity that, among other functions, maintains the ADV Forms I and II for registered investment advisors as well as the statutory reporting forms on companies offering securities (such as each company's annual 10-K and quarterly 10-Q Reports).

Securities Investor Protection Corporation (SIPC)
202-223-8400

SIPC is the entity that insures cash and securities on deposit with member brokerage firms for up to $500,000 per account ($100,000 of which is for cash on deposit).

Taxes

Internal Revenue Service (IRS)

800-829-1040 for Taxpayer's Assistance and Information

800-829-3676 for ordering IRS Forms and Publications

Your Money Personality

MoneyMax® Profile

Unlike any other aspect of human experience, there exists a special relationship between your personality and your use of money. How you think and feel about money (your inner *belief*) determines what you will do with money (your outward *behavior*). This unique interplay between your money belief and your money behavior is known as your Money Personality. Your Money Personality represents the convergence of *Personal Growth* with *Financial Growth*.

Dr. Kathleen Gurney pioneered the Money Personality concept in the emerging field of Financial Psychology. After nearly 10 years of development, she has identified 9 distinct money personalities. Each personality type holds certain attitudes towards money and finances as manifested in the way each pursues financial goals and objectives. Knowing your Money Personality provides you with a short-cut method to developing the *Personal Growth* traits that help you achieve your goals effectively.

To help people determine their Money Personality, Dr. Gurney developed the *MoneyMax® Profile*. This profile is the product of extensive national research and testing on tens of thousands of individuals. This confidential profile begins with a self-administered one-page response questionnaire that measures your existing financial personality traits in 13 different areas. The results of your profile enable you to understand how you relate to money now and what you can do to improve the way you deal with money in the future.

After returning your completed questionnaire, you will receive these Dr. Gurney reports:

Trait Evaluation Report
This Dr. Gurney summary report shows your individual score in 13 different areas of your personality. The report also portrays how your score compares with national scores in each of the 13 personal financial traits surveyed. Dr. Gurney presents the information in both tabular and graphic formats.

Trait Description Report
This report is Dr. Gurney's narrative interpretation of your score in each of the 13 personality traits evaluated in the first report. Here, Dr. Gurney explains in words the results depicted in your Trait Evaluation Report.

Profile Overview Report
In this synopsis, Dr. Gurney provides a summary of the key distinguishing characteristics of the national profile group

into which you currently fall. This report helps you to understand your distinct money management style and financial traits.

Money Action Plan Report

In this report, Dr. Gurney provides guidance for improving your money management skills and achieving financial congruity. Here, you will find the historical investment preferences of those with your personality style, so that you are better able to make investment choices (outward *behavior*) consistent with your Money Personality (inner *belief*).

If you are interested in receiving your own Dr. Gurney *MoneyMax® Profile* so that you can learn your Money Personality, complete and return a copy of the *Questionnaire Request Form* (shown at the back of this book) to Benefits Resource Group (follow the instructions on the form). You will then receive your confidential *MoneyMax® Profile* Questionnaire to complete and return for your personalized results. The process is enlightening *and* useful, because you learn your tendencies and can redirect your thinking, as necessary, for taking the most effective and profitable action.

Appendix C
Legal Resources

As with *Personal* and *Financial Growth*, there are, of course, many *Legal* books and materials. We have compiled the books and other resources that we feel provide you cost-effective alternatives to accessing the legal system.

By using these resources, you can prevent a future legal problem entirely or, if one occurs, you can significantly reduce the cost of defending yourself and significantly increase your chances of winning. Further, when you need to work with attorneys, you will be better informed, better able to know that you are getting good legal representation, avoid intimidation, and never overpay. Think of this approach as *defensive* or *preventive* law. And remember the adage: "If it's not in writing, it's not in this world".

Recommended Books and Software

We found the books listed here to be among the best. We have again made every effort to select the particular editions that give you the most value, so that the most books are affordable by those with any amount of money. Included in our selections are many "self-help" lawbooks that allow you to create your own administrative legal documents.

However, such fill-in-the-blanks kits with tear-out sheets are not favored by libraries, since borrowers often fill-in-the-blanks and tear-out the sheets before returning the kits to the library. So, you may have difficulty finding these resources (or those with all the pages attached) at many libraries. All are available directly from *TitleWaves*, P. O. Box 943, Malibu, CA 90265. Please see the order blank on the last page for more information and how to get a *free* Investor's Guide from *TitleWaves* when ordering two or more books.

Business Formation Guides

The Complete Small Business Legal Guide
Robert Friedman, Attorney

This book contains virtually every legal issue related to establishing and running a small business. Written by a lawyer in layman's language, this manual explains what routine legal tasks that you can handle yourself and save money, and when you should consult an attorney. This guide contains over 60 ready-to-use forms with instructions on how and when to use each. Topics included are: deciding whether to form a sole proprietorship, partnership or corporation; buying a franchise or existing business; negotiating a favorable lease; hiring and firing employees; working with independent contractors; creating good contracts; and resolving business disputes.

Softcover, $19.95   (ISBN: 0-79310-548-X) D

How to Write a Business Plan
Mike McKeever

This book leads you through the process of writing the business plan and loan package necessary to finance a new or expanding business successfully. This manual includes a streamlined method for an individual to write a business plan in just *one* day. The examples and worksheets help you present a convincing financial opportunity to banks and investors in a format that they understand.

Softcover, $19.95   (ISBN: 0-87337-184-4) N

How to Form Your Own Corporation Without A Lawyer For Under $75
Ted Nicholas

This easy to understand do-it-yourself kit explains how to avoid the hassle of lawyers and how to save from $300 to $3,000 in legal fees by following the simple step-by-step instructions. A complete set of all the required forms including a Certificate of Incorporation, By-Laws, Minutes, and more is provided.

Softcover, $19.95   (ISBN: 0-79310-419-X) D

The Complete Guide to Consulting Success
Howard Shenson and Ted Nicholas

This newly-revised edition is a step-by-step handbook for building a successful consulting practice. Once you admit to yourself *What You Do Best & Enjoy Most*, you will need this book to help you turn it into a successful consulting practice. Co-written by one of the country's top consultants, this guide is complete with all the forms, agreements, and advice you need to conduct a successful consulting business.

Softcover, $29.95   (ISBN: 0-79310-492-0) D

The Complete Book of Corporate Forms: Every Document You Need to Simplify Procedures and Protect Your Corporate Status
Ted Nicholas

This book, like many of the others recommended here, provides a low-cost, proven alternative to high lawyer fees. The manual includes: everything you need to solve corporate record-keeping problems; forms covering 125 different corporate actions; plus real-world corporate resolutions; agreements and certificates. All forms are written in clear, legally correct language. Each sample form can be adapted to meet the special circumstances of almost any corporate situation. This practical workbook will also help protect your corporation in case of an audit.

Softcover, $19.95   (ISBN: 0-79310-488-2) D

How to Form a Nonprofit Corporation
Anthony Mancuso, Attorney

This book explains all the legal formalities involved in forming and operating as a tax-exempt nonprofit corporation. The kit contains all the fill-in-the-blanks tear-out forms for the Articles, Bylaws, and Minutes. This manual also has complete instructions for obtaining federal 501(c)(3) tax exemption status and for qualifying for public charity status with the IRS. The package is valid in all 50 states.

Softcover, $24.95   (ISBN: 0-87337-124-0) N

Estate Planning

Everything Your Heirs Need to Know: Your Assets, Family History, and Final Wishes
David S. Magee

Magee, as a practicing estate planning attorney for over 40 years, has helped many families untangle messy estates that have unclear, incomplete or missing records. To help you avoid a similar situation he has developed this personal recordkeeping kit that enables you to gather into one simple volume all the critical documents and data regarding your assets, family history, and final wishes. Ready-made forms for entering detailed records plus eight large document pockets make this book a thorough and convenient management system for: your personal history; insurance records; benefits and pension plans; bank accounts; securities; real estate; other assets; debts; will and trust agreements; final wishes; burial arrangements; and other personal matters. After filling out these pages, explaining its purpose to your family and showing them where you keep the book (like in your safe deposit box), you will have responsibly supplied your heirs with everything that they need to know after you go to your great beyond.

Softcover, $19.95   (ISBN: 0-79310-126-3) D

Winning The Wealth Game: How to Keep Your Money in Your Family
Andrew D. Westhem and Donald Jay Korn

These authors show you how to live like a king or queen, die like a king or queen, and leave absolutely nothing (legally) to *Count Taxula* of the IRS. This text reveals the wealth-transfer techniques used formerly only by the super rich to protect assets from the IRS—techniques that co-author Westhem uses with the over 6,000 clients of his national estate planning firm, Wealth Transfer Planning, Inc. *Winning the Wealth Game* explains tax-saving strategies that you can use today, including how to: understand the basic concepts of wills, trusts, estate taxes, and probate; preparing a wealth-transfer plan; choose from among Q-TIP trusts, charitable trusts, life insurance trusts, family limited partnerships, private annuities, and others; pass on up to $1.2 Million free of estate taxes; and more. This book will help you understand how to keep your money where it belongs—in your family, not in the IRS cash register.

Softcover, $24.95   (ISBN: 0-79310-309-6) D

How To Prepare Your Own Last Will & Testament
John F. Goodson, Attorney

This kit, prepared by an attorney, provides easy to understand step-by-step numbered instructions with blank and completed forms for you to follow. The kit includes two sets of forms and instructions for a: Last Will & Testament; Tangible Personal Property inventory list; and Statement of Wishes. Valid in all 50 states.

Softcover, $14.95   (ISBN: 0-934141-01-0) F

WillMaker, Version 5.0 (Software)
Nolo Press

Available in both PC and Macintosh formats, this software has made more wills than any attorney in the history of the world. *PC Magazine* calls *WillMaker* "the program of choice". This program is easy to use, thorough, current, and reliable. *WillMaker* leads you through a series of questions, then compiles the answers to make a valid will, fine-tuned to the specific laws of your state. On-line legal help is keyed to assist you with every decision that you make. This latest release (*WillMaker 5.0*) allows for up to 99 specific property bequests and, in addition to its Last Will capabilities, contains two new estate planning modules: a Living Will; and a Letter of Final Instructions. The software's documentation comes in the form of a 288-page clearly written and witty manual. The program is valid in all states except Louisiana which has weird French-based laws, instead of English-based laws like the rest of the USA.

System Requirements: IBM or compatible with 256K RAM; DOS 2.1 or higher; includes both 5¼" & 3½" disks. Macintosh 512K or higher with 1MB RAM, System 4.1 or higher. System 7 compatible.

PC Format   (ISBN: 0-87337-204-2) N
Macintosh Format   (ISBN: 0-87337-201-4) N

WillMaker 5.0, $69.95

Make Your Own Living Trust
Denis Clifford

This do-it-yourself book and text covers every significant aspect of estate planning and gives detailed, specific step-by-step instructions for preparing your revocable living trust. This manual explains in plain English how to prepare your trust so that your heirs can avoid the expense and delays of probate. By bypassing the probate court system, your property goes directly to the people whom you want to inherit it—quickly, easily and inexpensively. Attorney-author Clifford covers: how a living trust works and how to create one; how property is transferred to the trust; and what happens when the person who sets-up the trust dies. This kit includes information on the basic Living Trust, the Marital Life Estate (A-B Trust), and Back-Up Will. You receive the tear-out living trust forms, with all the information and instructions to create your own living trust. The trust is valid in all states except Louisiana.

Softcover, $19.95   (ISBN: 0-87337-194-1) N

Nolo's Living Trust, Version 1.0 (Software)
Attorney Mary Randolph

Available in both PC and Macintosh formats, this is an easy-to-use software package that helps you create your own living trust documents on computer. Computer-based documents make changes or revocations quick and easy at any time. This program is designed for both married and single people. *MacWorld Magazine* calls it "a polished product and a great value". The software includes a 384-page user's manual and is valid in all states except Louisiana.

System Requirements: IBM or compatible with 640K RAM; DOS 3.1 or higher; includes both 5¼" & 3½" disks. Macintosh Plus or higher, with System 6.0.1 or higher. System 7 compatible.
PC Format   (ISBN: 0-87337-188-7) N
Macintosh Format   (ISBN: 0-87337-163-1) N

Nolo's Living Trust 1.0, $79.95

Warning: Dying May Be Hazardous to Your Wealth. How to Protect Your Life Savings for Yourself and Those You Love
Adriane G. Berg, Attorney

Author-Attorney Berg says "the good news is you're going to live longer; the bad news is you can't afford to". She explains that nearly half of all seniors 75 or older would be financially ruined after just three months of nursing home expenses. Worse, upon your death, you could lose 55% of your assets to the government (from the bite of *Count Taxula*)—that's *before* you pay for the attorneys' fees and probate costs. In *Warning*, she gives you the strategies for protecting your nest egg for yourself and your loved ones for generations to come. The book is directed to all adults (single and married) with families, as well as the adult children of elderly parents. The text includes overviews of: wills, trusts, gifts and probate; estate taxes; legacy and dynasty planning with life insurance; and the effects of divorce, remarriage, illness, and incompetence on your estate plan. The book also contains sample short-form and long-form wills plus a sample living will. Berg is a former chair of the New York State Bar Association in Estate Planning, currently hosts her own talk show on WABC (New York), and is a frequent guest on FNN, PBS and other national radio and TV shows including *Oprah* and *Donahue*.

Softcover, $14.95   (ISBN: 1-56414-014-8) C

Other Agreements

How to Form Your Own Partnership Kit
John F. Goodson, Attorney

This do-it-yourself kit will help you save hundreds of dollars in legal fees. Since the law says that two or more owners working together are a partnership (unless they incorporate), you had better formalize the relationship with a written document. This easy to follow kit includes step-by-step numbered instructions for drafting your partnership agreement with provisions for buy-outs and dissolution. The kit contains both blank and completed sample forms for you to follow. The agreement that you draft will be valid in all 50 states.

Softcover, $19.95   (ISBN: 0-934141-02-9) F

Nolo's Partnership Maker, Version 1.0 (Software)
Attorney Anthony Mancuso and Mike Radtke

Winner of *Home Office Computing's* "Editor Picks " award, this software prepares a legal partnership agreement for doing business in any state. The program includes a full menu of standard partnership clauses, plus you can select customized clauses for your specific needs with the extensive, plain English on-line help. The package includes tutorial, glossary, and legal help screens with a 256-page manual that takes you through the process step-by-step.

System Requirements: IBM or compatible with 512K RAM; DOS 3.0 or higher; includes both 5¼" & 3½" disks. PC Format only. (ISBN: 0-87337-188-7) N

Nolo's Partnership Maker 1.0, $129.95

Hiring Child Care
Attorney Barbara Kate Repa and Lisa Goldoftas

In light of what's come to be known as "nannygate", it's becoming painfully clear that there are certain legal and tax requirements that must be fulfilled when hiring child care services. This manual clearly explains what those requirements are and how to stay within the letter of the law. The kit contains all the necessary fill-in-the-blank, tear-out forms including employment contracts, application forms, and the appropriate IRS forms. The booklet also provides a summary of your responsibilities and shows how to determine what duties the job will cover, how the worker will be paid, and how to deal with taxes and benefits.

Softcover, $14.95   (ISBN: 0-87337-229-8) N

How To Provide Minor Child Protection Kit
John F. Goodson, Attorney

This kit provides the necessary authorizations for enabling the child sitter, teacher, scoutmaster or other caretaker to make vital decisions when the parent is unavailable. The kit includes consent for medical attention forms and step-by-step easy to follow numbered instructions for completing the agreement. The package contains both blank and completed sample forms for you to follow and is valid in all 50 states.

Softcover, $12.95   (ISBN: 0-934141-12-6) F

How to Prepare a General Power of Attorney
John F. Goodson, Attorney

A *General Power of Attorney* form helps you to protect you and your property if you become disabled or deemed "incompetent" by the courts. If you are incapacitated, this document authorizes a family member or trusted friend of your choice to make decisions for you, such as: consent of medical treatment; payments on your behalf; hiring or dismissing attorneys or doctors; acting on your behalf in other transactions that you authorize. Like the other do-it-yourself legal kits, this one is also written in plain English and includes step-by-step easy to follow numbered instructions. The kit contains both blank and completed sample forms for you to follow. This General Power of Attorney has been tested for over 10 years and is valid in all 50 states.

Softcover, $12.95   (ISBN: 0-934141-09-6) F

How to Prepare Your Own Pre-Nuptial Agreement Kit

John F. Goodson, Attorney

Written by an attorney specializing in preventive law for over 28 years, this pre-marriage agreement kit is designed to ensure a better marriage and reduce the chances of divorce. The kit includes separate property lists for each party and step-by-step easy to follow numbered instructions for completing the agreement. The kit contains both blank and completed sample forms for you to follow and is valid in all 50 states.

Softcover, $12.95   (ISBN: 0-934141-07-X) F

How to Erase Bad Credit

Stanley R. Stern, Attorney

This kit helps you clean-up your credit while saving hundreds of dollars on legal fees and commercial credit repair clinics. The package includes easy-to-use legal forms with step-by-step instructions to repair good credit status plus a credit application for you to apply for a VISA or Mastercard. The kit is valid in all 50 states.

Softcover, $ 24.95   (ISBN: 1-879191-01-6) F

***How to Protect Your Income in Your Senior Years:
101 Letters to Answer Your Every Question***
Harvey Kule

This book answers the 101 most-asked questions from seniors, especially in dealing with the government. This book tells you about the benefits to which you are entitled and how to obtain these benefits. The package includes forms and applications that you just copy, fill-in and mail. Of course, the addresses for the government agencies are given as well as information on what you can do about age discrimination in employment. The kit is valid in all 50 states.

Softcover, $19.95   (ISBN: 1-879191-04-0) F

Dispute Settlement And Legal Services

Academy of Family Mediators
203-629-8049

This organization gives you referrals to divorce mediators in your area.

American Arbitration Association
212-484-4000

Arbitration is an alternative to going to court to resolve civil disputes. Arbitration fees are typically set on a decreasing sliding scale beginning at 3% of the claim. The AAA gives referral to arbitrators and mediators in your area.

American Bar Association
Standing Committee on Dispute Resolution
202-331-2258

The ABA gives referrals to its dispute resolution centers in your area.

American Bar Association
American Bar Center
312-988-5000

This ABA center provides consumer information on picking an attorney. For the ABA's referral service, you should contact your local bar association directly.

National Resource Center for Consumers of Legal Services
703-536-8700

This organization provides general consumer information on finding an attorney and on filing complaints on attorneys.

Appendix D
Lottery Resources

This Appendix contains the following lottery information:

- ❑ *Lottery Player's Magazine*

- ❑ Biggest Claimed U.S. State Lottery Jackpots (so far) over $50 Million

- ❑ List of Lotteries: State and Major International

- ❑ Weirdest Lottery Occurrence

- ❑ Odds of Winning *Lotto* Games & how to figure them

- ❑ Compulsive Gambling Therapy Referrals

Lottery Player's Magazine
P. O. Box 5013, Cherry Hill, NJ 08034
609-778-8900 Phone   609-273-6350 FAX
Subscription price: $23.97 per year for 12 monthly issues.
To order by phone, you can call toll-free: 800-367-9681.

Despite its name, *Lottery Player's Magazine* appears in a newspaper tabloid format, rather than a "magazine" format like *Time* or *Newsweek*. *Lottery Player's Magazine* reports on: U.S. and International general lottery news; drawing results; casino and gambling news; lottery legislation; statistical analysis of numbers; gaming operations; prize structure; lottery industry news; lottery licensing; awards; and the like.

BIGGEST CLAIMED U.S. STATE
LOTTERY JACKPOTS (SO FAR) OVER $50 MILLION

$ Million	State	Mo./Yr.
$118.8	California	4/91
$115.6	Pennsylvania	4/89
$111.2	Power Ball*	7/93
$106.5	Florida	9/90
$90.0	New York	1/91
$89.8	Florida	10/91
$86.0	Florida	3/93
$69.9	Illinois	4/89
$68.6	California	2/90
$65.0	Illinois	10/92
$63.9	Pennsylvania	7/89
$61.9	California	10/88
$55.1	Florida	9/88
$51.4	California	6/88
$50.1	Ohio	10/90

*Power Ball, a Multi-State lottery, includes: Delaware, Idaho, Indiana, Iowa, Kansas, Kentucky, Maine, Minnesota, Missouri, Montana, Oregon, Rhode Island, South Dakota, Washington, D.C., West Virginia, Wisconsin.

LIST OF STATE LOTTERIES

State	Phone Number
Arizona	602-921-4400
California	916-324-9644
Colorado	303-759-3552
Connecticut	203-667-9989
D.C., Wash.	202-433-7900
Delaware	302-739-5291
Florida	404-487-7725
Idaho	208-334-2600
Illinois	217-524-5155
Indiana	317-264-4800
Iowa	515-281-7900
Kansas	913-296-5700
Kentucky	502-473-2200
Maine	207-289-6700
Maryland	410-764-5730
Massachusetts	617-849-5555
Michigan	517-335-5640
Minnesota	612-635-8100
Missouri	314-751-4050
Montana	406-444-5825
New Hampshire	603-271-3391
New Jersey	609-599-5800
New York	518-457-0440
Ohio	216-787-3200
Oregon	503-378-3545
Pennsylvania	717-986-4699
Rhode Island	401-463-6500
South Dakota	605-773-5770
Vermont	802-828-2274
Virginia	804-367-9445
Washington	206-753-3337
West Virginia	304-348-0500
Wisconsin	608-266-7777

LIST OF MAJOR INTERNATIONAL LOTTERIES

Country	Phone Number
Australia	
South Australia	(08)212-5588
Queensland Australia	(07)896-1000
Western Australia	(09)381-7511
Victoria Australia	(03)563-5366
New Zealand	(04) 852672
Canada	
Canada National	416-488-9829
Atlantic Canada	506-853-5800
British Columbia	604-270-0649
Ontario Province	416-961-6262
Quebec Province	514-282-8000
Western Canada	204-942-8217
Mexico	(5) 535-5413
Puerto Rico	809-759-8813
Spain	(1) 262-5140
Virgin Islands	809-774-2502

Weirdest Lottery Occurrence:
A Florida Lottery *player used shredded losing lottery tickets to line his pet gerbil's cage. The gerbil ate the shredded tickets and died. The* Florida Lottery *would not replace the gerbil, explaining that, since they conducted no animal testing, they would have no way of knowing that a shredded-losing-ticket-eating gerbil might die.*

ODDS OF WINNING LOTTO GAMES

Lotto Game*	Odds of Winning the Jackpot are 1 in
6/54	25,828,265
6/51	18,009,460
6/50	15,890,700
6/49	13,983,816
6/48	12,271,512
6/47	10,737,573
6/46	9,366,832
6/44	7,059,052
6/42	5,245,786
6/40	3,838,380
6/39	3,262,623
6/36	1,947,792
6/33	1,107,568
6/30	593,775
6/25	177,100
5/42	425,334
5/40	658,008
5/39	575,757
5/38	501,942
5/37	435,897
5/35	324,632
5/34	278,256
5/32	201,376
5/26	65,780

*See next page

Lotto Game Note: In this column:

The 1st #:   # of winning numbers drawn randomly

The 2nd #:   universe of possible numbers from which the winning numbers are drawn

Thus, 6/54:   6 winning numbers drawn randomly from a universe of 54 possible numbers.

The odds of this Jackpot result occurring are 1 in 25,828,165 (from column #2 in the table above).

Figuring Your *Lotto* Odds

Mathematicians call the relationship of numbers used in calculating the odds of winning a *Lotto* game *combinational coefficients*. The following example of how to calculate your odds of winning a 6/42 *Lotto* game would, of course, apply to figuring the odds of any *Lotto* game.

Figuring the Odds of Picking 6 Out of 6 Numbers

Here is the formula for calculating the odds of picking 6 out of 6 numbers (winning the Jackpot):

$$\frac{n \times (n-1) \times (n-2) \times (n-3)...\times(n-k+1)}{k \times (k-1) \times (k-2) \times (k-3)...1}$$

Where:

n = total universe of game numbers available

k = number of numbers drawn from those available (n)

Therefore, using the above formula, the odds for picking 6 out of 6 in the 6/42 *Lotto* are:

$$\frac{42 \times 41 \times 40 \times 39 \times 38 \times 37}{6 \times 5 \times 4 \times 3 \times 2 \times 1}$$

$$\frac{3,776,965,920}{720}$$

$$= 5,245,786$$

So, the odds of picking 6 out of 6 numbers (winning the Jackpot) are 1 in 5,245,786.

Figuring the Odds of Picking 5 Out of 6 Numbers

Here is the calculation:

$$\left[\left(\frac{6 \times 5 \times 4 \times 3 \times 2}{5 \times 4 \times 3 \times 2 \times 1}\right) \times \left(\frac{36}{1}\right)\right] \div 5,245,786$$

$$(6 \times 36) \div 5,245,786$$

$$216 \div 5,245,786$$

$$\cong 24,286$$

So, the odds of picking 5 out of 6 numbers are 1 in 24,286.

Figuring the Odds of Picking 4 Out of 6 Numbers

Here is the calculation:

$$\left[\left(\frac{6\times5\times4\times3}{4\times3\times2\times1}\right)\times\left(\frac{36\times35}{2\times1}\right)\right]\div5,245,786$$

$$\left(15\times630\right)\div5,245,786$$

$$9,450\div5,245,786$$

$$\cong\underline{\underline{555}}$$

So, the odds of picking 4 out of 6 numbers are 1 in 555.

Figuring the Odds of Picking 3 Out of 6 Numbers

Here is the calculation:

$$\left[\left(\frac{6\times5\times4}{3\times2\times1}\right)\times\left(\frac{36\times35\times34}{3\times2\times1}\right)\right]\div5,245,786$$

$$\left(20\times7,140\right)\div5,245,786$$

$$142,800\div5,245,786$$

$$\cong\underline{\underline{37}}$$

So, the odds of picking 3 out of 6 numbers are 1 in 37.

Figuring the Odds of Matching Each Tier

Summarizing the above, the odds of matching each tier are 1 in:

5,245,786   for picking 6 out of 6 numbers

24,286   for picking 5 out of 6 numbers

555   for picking 4 out of 6 numbers

37   for picking 3 out of 6 numbers

Figuring the Overall Odds

Here is the calculation:

$$\frac{5,245,786}{1+6+216+9,450+142,800}$$

$$\frac{5,245,786}{152,473}$$

$$\cong \underline{\underline{34}}$$

So, the overall odds of winning are 1 in 34.

Technical note: The key to calculating the correct odds for matching 3, 4 or 5 out of 6 numbers is to include the number of possibilities for the remaining numbers that do *not* match any of the 6 numbers drawn. This calculation is essential since the odds are based on the number of *sets* of 6 numbers out of the 5,245,786 *possible* sets that contain 3, 4, 5 or 6 numbers that match the *winning* 6 numbers drawn.

Compulsive Gambling Therapy Referrals

National Council on Problem Gambling, Inc.
800-522-4700
212-765-3833

This organization provides general information about gambling problems and gives referrals to various mental health services that specialize in gambling treatment. Their national headquarters is located at 445 West 59th Street, New York, New York 10019.

Gamblers Anonymous
213-386-8789 International Headquarters (Los Angeles)

This organization provides help with gambling problems through a program modeled after AA's 12-step program for alcoholics. There are no dues or fees and meetings are held every day in most cities. Local chapters provide 24-hour help. Call Directory Assistance or check your phone book for your local chapter's phone number. Most local chapters have a 24-hour recorded phone directory listing of whom you can call at anytime of the day or night including weekends and holidays for help. The mailing address for their headquarters is P. O. Box 17173, Los Angeles, CA 90017.

Index

Order Forms

LIFE INSURANCE REALITY CHECK REQUEST FORM

Name

Address

City   State   ZIP

Phone Number:

Date of Birth (month/day/year):

Gender (circle one):   Male   Female

Are you a smoker or tobacco user? Yes   No

Amount of Insurance you want: $

☐ Please send my *free*, no obligation, personalized report showing the best Term Life Insurance quotes from the most competitive companies in America.

I am also interested in:
☐ Health Insurance
☐ Disability Income Replacement
☐ Life Insurance Needs Analysis

Mail your completed form with an S.A.S.E. to:
The Insurance Exchange™
Benefits Resource Group
P. O. Box 943, Malibu, CA 90265.

Note: Please copy, complete & return one form with a Self-Addressed Stamped Envelope (S.A.S.E.) for each person that wants a quotation.

ANNUITY QUOTATION REQUEST FORM

Name

Address

City   State   ZIP

Phone Number:

Date of Birth (month/day/year):

Gender (circle one):   Male   Female

I anticipate making a single initial investment, a
monthly investment or both as shown below:
☐ Anticipated initial investment: $

☐ Anticipated monthly investment: $

☐ My Federal Income Tax Bracket:

☐ Please send my *free*, no obligation,
personalized report showing the best Annuity for
me from the most competitive companies in
America.

I am also interested in:
☐ Health Insurance
☐ Disability Income Replacement
☐ Life Insurance

Mail your completed form with an S.A.S.E. to:
The Annuity Exchange™
Benefits Resource Group
P. O. Box 943, Malibu, CA 90265.

Note: Please copy, complete & return one form
with a Self-Addressed Stamped Envelope
(S.A.S.E.) for each person that wants a quotation.

MUTUAL FUND COMPUTER SEARCH REQUEST
Name
Address
City   State   ZIP
Phone Number:
FAX # (if return Fax wanted):
SEARCH CRITERIA (Check or Circle One Per Section):
FUND TYPE: ☐ Aggressive Growth   ☐ Municipal Bond ☐ Balanced   ☐ Precious Metals ☐ Growth   ☐ Taxable Bond ☐ Growth & Income   ☐ Tax-Free Money Market ☐ International   ☐ Taxable Money Market
LOADS(%): ☐ None   ☐2 ☐3 ☐4 ☐5 ☐7 ☐8.5
REDEMPTION FEE: None   Some
12B–1 FEES: None   Some
ANNUAL EXPENSE % below:☐0.5 ☐1 ☐1.5 ☐2 ☐3 ☐6
PERFORMANCE: ☐High-VeryHigh ☐Average-VeryHigh ☐Very High ☐High ☐Average ☐Low ☐Very Low
ASSET SIZE OF FUND (in $ Millions): ☐Under 10   ☐10–24.9   ☐25–49.9   ☐50–99.9 ☐100–249.9   ☐250–499.9   ☐500 & over
BETA COEFFICIENT: ☐Below 0   ☐Greater than 1.0 ☐0 to 0.5   ☐0.5 to 1.0   ☐1 to 1.5   ☐over 1.5
☐ I have enclosed: $ 25 for the first search plus $_____for_____additional search(es) at $10 each $ Total Payable to: BENEFITS RESOURCE GROUP
Return form to: *The Fund Exchange*™ BENEFITS RESOURCE GROUP P. O. Box 943, Malibu, CA 90265
Note: Please copy, complete & return one form for each search.

DR. GURNEY'S *MONEYMAX®* PROFILE
QUESTIONNAIRE REQUEST FORM

Please send my Dr. Gurney's Money Personality
MoneyMax® Profile Questionnaire to:

Name

Address

City   State   ZIP

Phone Number:

I understand that, after completing and returning my confidential questionnaire, I will receive my personalized Dr. Gurney Money Personality *MoneyMax® Profile* that includes these 4 reports:

1. Trait Evaluation Report
2. Trait Description Report
3. Profile Overview Report
4. Money Action Plan Report

☐ For each *MoneyMax® Profile*, I have enclosed my $49.00 check with a completed copy of this form to:

BENEFITS RESOURCE GROUP
P. O. Box 943, Malibu, CA 90265.

Please make your check(s) payable to:
"Benefits Resource Group"

Note: *MoneyMax® Profile* is a registered trademark of Kathleen Gurney, Ph.D. and Financial Psychology Corporation.

BOOK & SOFTWARE ORDER FORM

Name

Street Address

City   State   ZIP

Phone Number:

Please send me at my above address the following Books/Software:

# of Copies	Name of Item	Unit Price	Total
Investor's Guide to Reading the Mutual Fund Prospectus (30-pages) *free* when ordering 2 or more items			
	Subtotal		
Local Sales Tax (California Residents only)			
	Shipping & Handling*		
	TOTAL (Payable to: TITLEWAVES)		

*SHIPPING & HANDLING:

$4.00 per 1 item

$5.00 2-3 items

+$.50 each additional item

Allow 2-3 weeks for delivery/Prices subject to change

☐ For the above items, I have enclosed a completed copy of this form with my check for the TOTAL amount due payable to: *TITLEWAVES*

P. O. Box 943, Malibu, CA 90265.

UPDATE FOR FUTURE EDITION

Your comments are important to us, or we wouldn't be asking for them. Please copy and return this form to:
TitleWaves, P.O. Box 943, Malibu, CA 90265

I would like to see the following information, changes, or resource(s), etc., included in a future edition of *Infinite Financial Freedom*:

_____

_____

_____

_____

_____

_____

_____

_____

_____

_____

Name (optional)

Address

Thank You!